Ralph Stephenson worked for eight years for the British Film Institute and was for eleven years a director of the Paris Pullman cinema in London. Born in New Zealand, he was formerly in the Colonial Service in Hong Kong (where he was a Japanese POW), the Seychelles, Ghana and Sierra Leone. He is author of five detective novels, two books on sailing and two other books on the cinema: *Animation in the Cinema* and *The Animated Film*.

Guy Phelps writes regularly for the *International Film Guide*, *Sight And Sound* and other publications. He is the author of *Film Censorship* (1975) and co-author of *Mass Media and the Secondary School* (1973). With degrees in Sociology and Mass Communications, he has worked at various times as a media academic, television critic and, for seven years, as a manager of art-house cinemas.

RALPH STEPHENSON

·

GUY PHELPS

THE
CINEMA
AS ART

REVISED EDITION
WITH FIFTY-FIVE PLATES

'ONLY BY TASTE
CAN WE ACCOUNT FOR TASTE'
(Lope de Vega)

PENGUIN BOOKS

PENGUIN BOOKS

Published by the Penguin Group
27 Wrights Lane, London w8 5TZ, England
Viking Penguin Inc., 40 West 23rd Street, New York, New York 10010, USA
Penguin Books Australia Ltd, Ringwood, Victoria, Australia
Penguin Books Canada Ltd, 2801 John Street, Markham, Ontario, Canada L3R 1B4
Penguin Books (NZ) Ltd, 182–190 Wairau Road, Auckland 10, New Zealand

Penguin Books Ltd, Registered Offices: Harmondsworth, Middlesex, England

First published 1965
Revised edition 1969
Second edition 1976
Revised edition 1989
10 9 8 7 6 5 4 3 2 1

Filmset in 10 on 11½pt Ehrhardt

Printed and bound in Great Britain by
Cox & Wyman Ltd, Reading

CONTENTS

FOREWORD TO THE FIRST EDITION

FOR the present generation the art of the film is of pressing interest. The cinema is now over sixty years old and has its own discriminating audience, but compared with the other arts it is still little written about or seriously discussed.

The term 'film criticism' is generally applied to a weekly review of new films published in a daily or weekly paper and written by a regular contributor known as the film critic. Although it may refer to questions of aesthetics and may reflect a profound knowledge of the cinema, its main purpose is to give some idea of the story and background of the pictures and to assess them as good, bad, or indifferent entertainment. It is basically a guide to current film-going.

We accept this terminology as a matter of course, but it is not quite what obtains in other fields. In literature, for instance, the equivalent of a film critic writing a weekly review is a book reviewer, and the equivalent of film criticism, as we know it, is book-reviewing. 'Literary criticism' is a different kind of writing, more occasional, less topical, dealing with broad themes, seeking by comparison and analysis to give a fuller knowledge and understanding of literature as an artistic medium and in all its implications.

It is clear that in the literary field, book-reviewing and literary criticism are rather different things, both of value but serving different purposes. It is pertinent, therefore, to turn back to the film world and inquire what there is in this sphere corresponding to literary criticism. No doubt we should look for it in the field of film appreciation, but where are its articles, its books, its exponents?

Where indeed? Particularly in English. They are represented only by a few specialized journals such as *Sight and Sound* or *Film Quarterly*, and by a handful of books published over the past forty years.

In any case, the phrase 'film appreciation' is a somewhat underrated one with, perhaps, rather amateurish connotations. It would be better if the same terminology as is used in literature became current in the film world, if the term 'film reviewing' were reserved for current assessment and 'film criticism' came to imply the broader, thematic approach of literary criticism.

The Cinema as Art can be regarded as a material contribution towards the new concept of film criticism. It discusses in detail and in depth an indispensable preliminary: the language of the film, a language as important as that of the writer, the painter, or the musician, and different from them all. For the film appreciation or film criticism of the future, this, or books like this, will be essential reading.

SIR WILLIAM COLDSTREAM
1965

ACKNOWLEDGEMENTS

THE British Film Institute including the National Film Theatre and the Information Department, Library and Stills Collection (for all plates except those mentioned below);

The Imperial War Museum for Plate 10;

A. Conger Goodyear and the Museum of Modern Art for Plate 27.

TRIBUTE TO JEAN DEBRIX

JEAN DEBRIX, co-author of the original edition of *The Cinema as Art*, died in 1978. A substantial part of the original was based on his book, *Les Fondements de l'Art Cinématographique*, and he read and agreed the text and illustrations of the first edition and subsequent reprints. Although this edition is to some extent a new book, since it has been revised, brought up to date and much new material added, with the collaboration of Guy Phelps, nevertheless the work of Jean Debrix remains as a foundation stone. This tribute is therefore in grateful recognition of the part played by a talented and sympathetic collaborator who was an inspiration in the early stages.

R.S.

CHAPTER ONE

THE FILM AND ART

IN a book on film aesthetics it is useful to consider the relationship of film to the other arts, and to regard it first as only one member of a large family. Like most rich concepts, art has been variously defined by different authors; and this diversity of approach is welcome, for each description will illuminate a different aspect of the subject and add to our knowledge.

THE NATURE OF ART

Take first a painter, who may make of a ruined building, a pile of rubbish, a junkyard or an industrial landscape, a composition in forms and colours that is dramatic, forbidding or even beautiful; the sensitive spectator will come to see them as such. He may make of rush-hour travellers or factory workers a company of tragic spectres, and again the spectator, who may have been commuting or working in a factory for years, will see them with new eyes. This is how D. W. Griffith, the American film director, saw his work. 'The task I am trying to achieve is to make you see,' he wrote. From a slightly different viewpoint, Walter Pater regarded the artist as liberating, or realizing, the potential of his raw materials and quotes Michelangelo in support of his view:[1]

> Art does but consist in the removal of surplusage ... the finished work lies somewhere, according to Michelangelo's fancy, hidden in the rough-hewn block of stone.

1. Walter Pater, *Appreciations*, Macmillan, London, 1931.

In a biography of Robert Flaherty (*The Innocent Eye*), Arthur Calder-Marshall describes an exactly similar approach in a primitive artist: 'The Eskimo rarely sets out to carve a seal, but picks up the ivory to find its hidden form . . .'

This is akin to the view that art consists in reproducing or imitating real life; and it is a plausible explanation of the origins of graphic art and sculpture, for instance, to trace them to magical imitations of the real thing – cave-drawn bison for sticking arrows into to ensure the death of real bison, and little figures of a king's household to go into his tomb to serve him after death. The view that art is imitation has led at times to its being regarded as a second-best. Browning wrote:

> . . . that's your Venus, whence we turn
> To yonder girl that fords the burn.

But, even as imitation, art may show us the true essence of things more clearly than we could see it for ourselves. The Venus may enable us to see the girl as we otherwise never would.

Aldous Huxley once spoke of art as the imposition of order ('art springs from an urge to order') and the artist selects from and arranges the haphazard profusion of nature. As Henry James wrote: 'Life is all inclusion and confusion, while art is all discrimination and selection.' Herbert Read in *The Meaning of Art* adds another element when he talks of art as 'pattern informed by sensibility' and 'emotion cultivating good form', both leading to 'harmony', which is the satisfaction of our sense of beauty. This idea of selection and arrangement leads to the concept of art as creation. The artist takes his raw materials – clay, colours, musical sounds, photographic images, words, and so on – and, in accordance with his ideas and emotions, fashions from them artistic objects. Art may also be regarded as skill in expression; as the use of the creative imagination (Émile Zola called a work of art 'a corner of nature seen through a temperament'); or as concerned with producing the abstract quality of beauty. Keats equated beauty with truth, and art has also been thought of as a quest for truth. And so it is – provided we qualify the sort of truth we mean. For great art brings us near the true nature of things, particularly of human character and conduct. But both truth and beauty cover a wider field than art; for science, philosophy and religion are concerned with truth – and they also display a kind of beauty (e.g. a brilliant mathematical solution), as does any supreme skill, from football to brain surgery.

The American philosopher John Dewey considered art to be a kind of experience. Joyce Cary in his book *Art and Reality* follows Croce in preferring the word 'intuition', describing it as 'essentially the reaction of a person to the world outside'. Coleridge, thinking along somewhat similar lines, wrote that 'the mystery of genius in the Fine Arts' was to 'make the external internal, the internal external and make nature thought and thought nature.' This quotation neatly sums up the process of artistic creation, and describes the artist absorbing experience and expressing it in the form of art.

More recently art has been regarded as a form of communication or language. I. A. Richards called it 'the supreme form of communicative activity'. Many writers tried to elaborate on the analogy between film and written or spoken language, with sequences compared to paragraphs, cuts to commas and so on. As we shall see, this literal approach proved to be misleading – the smallest unit of film, the shot, usually contains more information than the average paragraph – but more refined theories deriving from language study have been developed.

The most important of these are two related studies – semiology (from the Greek *semeion*, a sign) and structuralism. The first deals with the relation between reality and the signs used to represent it, and therefore would apply to any system of communication, practical or artistic. The second examines the relationships between the signs themselves, how they interact and are organized to produce a meaningful whole. These theories have revolutionized the study of language, and have been applied to other communication systems including cinema. In this book we have taken their conclusions into account but without using their specialized analyses or terminology.

Finally, one should take note of the once fashionable concept of *anti-art*: what Arnold Hauser described as 'a renunciation of art altogether'. Derived from utilitarianism and connected to totalitarian ideologies which regard art as a means to an end, anti-art seeks to exterminate the aestheticism of bourgeois culture's 'art for art's sake'. The technician, worshipping efficiency, arrives at a similar position by regarding art as a by-product which arises 'in the service of an ideologically conditioned purpose'. A house becomes 'a machine to live in', and the fastest aeroplane is, by definition, the most beautiful. Modern art's 'relationship to nature is one of violation', and another facet of the same attitude is that modern art is, of set purpose, 'fundamentally "ugly", destroying pictorial values in painting, and melody and tonality in music'. There is a mania for totality and documentary realism, and art is dehumanized. Even the communication aspects of art are in a sense denied – writers invent their own language, musicians their own tonal system, and painters depict a world of their own imagination.

The variety of descriptions of, and approaches to, art mentioned here, suggest that while art is clearly different things to different people, there are some common aspects. We may bring them together, in an omnibus definition, by saying that art is a process through which the creator(s) make use of their experience and intuition to select and arrange material which may be related to 'reality' to a greater or lesser extent, and that through the artistic techniques used and the meaning that flows from them, experience is communicated to an audience.

Let us now turn from attempting to delineate the qualities of art and try to delimit the territory it covers. In general we are concerned with the fine arts, excluding useful or industrial arts, sports, hobbies, science, philosophy, government and social relations. But there are many borderline cases. Ballroom dancing counts as a recreation, ice-dancing as a sport, but there is a continuous gradation from them to ballet, one of the fine arts. In a film, skilled acting (duelling, gun-play, perfectly timed slapstick) can take on the quality of ballet. But the very similar pleasure given by a great cricketer, squash player, or footballer belongs to the world of sport, not art. There is the same difficulty in distinguishing strictly between fine arts such as poetry, painting, and music (with no function other than to convey experience or feeling), and useful arts such as architecture, pottery, cabinet-making, and dress-designing (which are functional as well as aesthetic). One difficulty in making a clear-cut distinction is that the day-before-yesterday's useful objects become today's *objets d'art* – museum pieces. Another is that fine arts may have secondary 'useful' effects – Dickens's novels helped social reform; Eisenstein's film *Alexander Nevsky* boosted the Russian war effort, just as Leni Riefenstahl's film *The*

Triumph of the Will[1] spread the Nazi cult; the music of the Marseillaise encouraged the French revolutionary soldiers; the television drama *Cathy Come Home* led to the formation of 'Shelter' and to renewed pressures for changes in attitudes towards the homeless; portraits and statues are for commemoration and for stabilizing the social order. Another factor which blurs the distinction is that useful arts (for example, Greek temples, Gothic cathedrals) may convey just as deep a sense of beauty or feeling as fine arts; and, in the film world, a documentary made to persuade or to instruct may be as fine aesthetically as a purely fictional film. Furthermore, if we define the word 'functional' widely enough, the fine arts have a function of their own, ranging from recreation to catharsis, revelation, and ennoblement. Having made these reservations, we are concerned in this book with the film as a fine art rather than as a useful art. A line, however broad, has to be drawn between the two, because the film ranges widely beyond the boundaries of fine art, and there is no field of human activity untouched by the camera: physics, chemistry, mathematics, technology, history, geography, archaeology, logistics, cartography, and many more. There are important applications in medicine, surgery, microscopy, astronomy, the control of machines (motors, propellers, turbines), and the study of high-speed movement by stroboscopic cameras taking 100,000 pictures a second. As we go on, it will be clear where our interest lies and where the line of distinction runs, but it will be a shifting, indeterminate boundary, with exceptions and reservations, and we shall not try to maintain it too rigidly.

THREE STAGES IN ART

Whichever description of the qualities of art or whichever delineation of its boundaries we fix upon, it is important that art should be understood to include the whole process, from the artist's intuition to the spectator's appreciation, and not just the object (film, statue, poem, sonata) produced.

Artistic activity can be divided into three stages:

1. Plate 1.

(a) The artist's experience or intuition;
(b) Expression of this intuition in an artistic medium; and
(c) Enjoyment by, and ideally the kindling of similar experience in, an audience.

This book is mainly concerned with the second of these three stages. At the same time, the process is a continuous and integral whole, and it is debatable how separate the various stages are, or indeed where one ends and the other begins. So far as *(a)* and *(b)* are concerned, Croce[1] considered that intuition and expression were the same thing, on the grounds that it was impossible to know what an intuition was until it had been named or expressed in some formal way. This possibly looks at the process of artistic creation too much from the outside. Cary says, and many people can confirm this from their own experience, that for the artist the intuition is quite a different thing from the work of art. Between the two there lies much hard work and possibly the conjunction of various favourable circumstances. Gray's 'mute, inglorious Miltons' really do exist: those who have inspiration but lack the opportunity or the ability to express it. So far as *(b)* and *(c)* are concerned, there is no difficulty in distinguishing between expression in a work of art and the audience's appreciation, since in these stages different people are concerned. The danger here is that the opposite might happen: that the two be considered as separate, isolated phenomena, and the doctrine of art for art's sake, combined with an ivory-tower outlook, lead to the selfish seclusion of the artist. It is worth stressing that art is a social phenomenon, and the artist's job is to make the world – meaning us – a richer place. The audience may be small and full appreciation may only come after the artist is dead, but art, in one of its aspects, is communication, and only has meaning if there are at least two people concerned. The artist may even serve sometimes as audience for his own work, especially with art forms which are not fully manifested until they are given expression in a large-scale performance – an orchestral work, an opera, a play, or a film. The finished product is, of course, no more than the physical manifestation of the artist's own dream, but its

1. *Aesthetics*, Vision Press, 1953.

embodied confirmation may have a very different impact on him, and may affect his subsequent work.

The artist will also be influenced by his audience – or lack of it. For that matter, each of the three stages mentioned will affect the others. It is generally recognized how great an influence the artist's intuition has – how his personality, born of his experience, stamps the finished work. It is not such a commonplace that the second stage, expression in an artistic medium, not only affects the way the intuition comes through, but the type of intuition which can be expressed. A story in a ballet, novel, film, play, or opera will have a different flavour and a different effect on an audience. Different techniques of representation are used, the work is made public in a different way to a different audience. The spectator will ultimately have a powerful effect on the type of intuition and the manner of its expression, and one must understand the term 'spectator' in this context to mean not only the direct audience, but also the censor, the editor, the critic and, finally, the whole of society. The complete process takes place within a specific cultural framework which both influences, and is influenced by, the work. Neither the artist, nor the critic, nor the spectator can stand outside this framework and take a dispassionate view. All are themselves a part of an ongoing process.

ART AND REALITY

We have said that this book is mainly concerned with the second stage in the artistic process. As a result, it is frequently concerned with the relation of art to reality – the sort of picture of reality which a work of art gives to the spectator. It may be necessary to make the point that art arises out of reality, though this is evident enough in the case of the cinema. Kracauer bases the whole argument of his book, *The Nature of Film*, on the extraordinary facility of the cinema in representing the real world. But even the most abstract art – an abstract painting, a mystical poem, atonal or electronic music – even these arise out of the artist's experience of reality, provided we define this in sufficiently wide terms.

Art has relation to reality at three points at least. First, the artist lives in the real world, and from his living – his experience – draws artistic inspiration or intuition. For this purpose, reality should be widely defined to comprise the whole physical, mental, and emotional world, though naturally things which do not impinge on the artist in any way are irrelevant. Reality, therefore, includes everything in the artist's experience: other works of art; other people; everything he sees, feels, hears, and knows; also his own memory, his own bodily sensations, his own mental states, thoughts, imaginings, and dreams. Thoughts, emotions, and mental states are just as much 'reality' in this context as a table or a chair. It is at this stage that, in the words of Coleridge already quoted, the artist 'makes the external internal' or 'makes nature thought'.

Second, art is related to reality because it has to be expressed in the medium proper to it. We have already said that the artistic medium, the second stage, will affect the type of experience which can be expressed and the way this experience will be manifested. In the first stage, the artist is tied to the reality of his own experience. In the second stage, the artist is fashioning a work of art by combining two things: his own experience, and the physical medium of his art, and so he is further tied at this stage to the reality of the medium.

Finally, in the third stage, the artist – unless he is content to let his work remain unseen or unheard except by himself (in which case it hardly exists) – has to present it to a *real* audience. In some arts, if the artist is out of sympathy with the contemporary fashion ('ahead of his time', we say, though the phrase is open to challenge because it assumes that one time is ahead of another), he can execute his work and it may be acclaimed after his death. But in the case of a film the artist cannot pursue his dream in solitary splendour. Film is a group art which involves many quite difficult techniques, and the cost of even a modest film is beyond the means of a single individual. Films are unlikely to be made even by rich patrons unless some sort of immediate audience can be found for them – though this does not mean that films are not sometimes neglected by their contemporaries and better appreciated by posterity, or appreciated for other reasons or other qualities.

This then is a third limiting factor, a third relationship with reality: to be complete, a work of art must – sooner or later – reach out again into the real world from which it has sprung, and touch the feelings of at least someone somewhere.

In this book we are concerned primarily with the second point at which art touches reality, that is, with the influence the film medium will have – the way reality appears through a camera lens, the effect of framing on the image, the effect of different kinds of transitions from shot to shot, and so on – but the two other relationships will be relevant and should be borne in mind.

THE METHOD OF INVESTIGATION

It is time we looked particularly at the cinema itself and examined how this fits into the three-stage process of creation and appreciation which constitutes the complex known as art. But before doing so there is one further general point to make about the method of investigation. We have begun talking about art in the broadest general terms. This has the advantage of presenting, at the start, general principles and broad outlines, so that the particular discussion which follows can be set against a comprehensive background. But this is not the order in which conclusions are built up. All art consists of an endless number of artistic creations; and general conclusions about art – what it is, what it includes, what it should aim at, how it obtains its effects, what is good and bad practice – must in the ultimate analysis depend on what the best individual artists have done. Similarly, the rules of grammar and pronunciation are derived from the practice of good writers and good habits of speech. The definition of 'good' will always present difficulty, but this is a difficulty inherent in the subject and will not be avoided by seeking the guidance of aesthetic 'laws'. The only valid laws are generally those directly based on existing practice. However the findings are ultimately presented, investigation should proceed from the particular to the general and not from the general to the particular. The student or critic should study the material for himself with an open mind, and not start with preconceived notions or follow blindly other people's opinions.

We do not mean that general conclusions should not be aimed at. Film is arranged in a systematic way, and has a syntax. But this is a result of the way in which film is used, not a determinant of it. An analysis of film aesthetics must be derived from actual films, and this book quotes hundreds of examples in attempting to construct a coherent system.

Arguing from the particular case has another advantage: it allows for change and development. Particularly in the case of film, any comprehensive treatment has to allow for the protean nature of the medium. Indeed the great changeability of film may itself be the reason why film theory has been through so many stages in its search for the essence of the medium. In its short history the cinema has undergone endless metamorphoses in technical resources and methods of using them, most of which have affected the finished art form. Silent films, sound films, colour, wide-screen, television, video – in four generations the cinema has experienced more mutations than music or painting in a thousand years. We naturally seek not only to write about current films but also to discover principles of general validity throughout these changes. Though many of our examples are from recent films, others range widely, with references to films from many countries and periods and almost every type of film-making.

THE THREE STAGES APPLIED TO FILM

Stage One: *Intuition*

Let us go back to the three stages in artistic creation and apply them to the cinema. Like any art, the making of a film can be analysed into intuition, execution and exhibition, but the film's particular nature means that as early as the first stage – the intuition arising out of the artist's experience – we discover a more complex process than in most other artistic media. Commonly, this intuitive stage is a personal, internal affair, but film is a group art. The original idea may derive from a screenwriter but his work is rarely more than a blueprint from which the director and his team of technicians construct the film itself. Very often, in fact, the writer may simply be adapting a work from another medium – film has a particular ability to regenerate old material into a new form – or elaborating someone else's basic groundplan. But whatever the basis upon which a film-maker builds – an original script, an adapted story or play, an idea of his own – he has to translate it into film terms; and this may be just as difficult if he starts with another work, as if the film grows direct out of an actual experience, situation, or milieu. Not only has he got to put the material into film terms, he has also to discard the literary or theatrical form which already exists. It may be easier if he can approach the visual medium direct. Some of the strength of Flaherty's films lies in their stemming from a source – Flaherty's excitement about, and sympathy with, a human way of life, through his *direct* contact with it – which is strong and pure, and without literary or dramatic trammels.[1]

Moreover, in most arts, but more particularly in film, the first stage does not usually stop short when execution begins. The intuition goes on growing and developing right through the process of execution until the work is completed. In practice, the two processes of intuition and execution are usually inextricably commingled, one affecting the other, and it is only in theory that we can separate them. There are certain exceptional cases in which the intuition and the execution are clearly separate, when an artist is possessed of an intuition so powerful, so vivid, so complete in his mind, that he can express it without a single correction. This happens occasionally with a great genius and a master of his craft: we read of a long novel, a symphony, or an opera written feverishly in a few weeks, days, or hours, in an explosion of prodigious activity, and achieved *in a perfect form, without revision*. But this is less likely to happen in the case of a film. For although the intuition may be a personal thing, the second stage, the creation of a film, depends on many people. Film production, with its thousands of cinemas all over the world, its film-stock factories, its processing laboratories, its acres of studios, its army of technicians and workers of all kinds, is an industrial process, and the making of a film is normally a group activity.[2]

Artistic creation in a group has certain difficulties, but also certain advantages, and it by no means rules out the possibility of great art. The transfer of the idea to the medium may be more difficult, because for the best results the artistic intuition has to be shared, other people have to be won over and infused with something of the original inspiration. Because of this, and also because it entails intricate physical apparatus which has to be controlled and complex technical processes, film is a 'tougher'

1. Plate 2.

2. Plate 3.

medium than writing or painting. On the other hand an idea may catch fire from the contact of other minds, and an enthusiasm be generated in a group which an individual working alone would lack. Medieval cathedrals, a clear example of group art, are among man's greatest artistic achievements. Nor have the greatest artists been recluses: Shakespeare was at the centre of the activity of the commercial theatre of his day; some of the greatest painting has been produced by 'schools' or 'movements'; music has often run in families – the effect of group environment, as well as of heredity.

If the cinema has frequently produced inferior art, it is not because it is executed by a group (although it has been suggested that group working offers difficulties in an age of individualism in art) but for other reasons. In the creative stage the best art cannot be automatically produced in endless quantity, or on demand, even for big financial rewards. It cannot be forced or guaranteed by machine methods, or blueprinted by technicians, accountants or planners. In a thousand years of history only a few cathedrals have been built, needing perhaps a century to complete, the work of many hands who unhurriedly lived their craft, working with devotion, faith and profound belief in what they were doing. Cathedrals were not built to make money. Commercial cinema in its first ninety years has produced innumerable movies, programmed to be turned out week after week almost like factory goods. It has sought to attract the best talent by the biggest rewards of money and fame, and in the level of technical quality and professional performance has succeeded pretty well. The level is as high as the average novel, the average play or the average painting. Nor does it rule out the occasional masterpiece, though no 'system' can command them.

This is not to say that art and morality are the same thing, though perhaps they have, or should have, more in common than is often thought, and the artist can be seen as prophet and reformer as well as entertainer. Clive Bell has pointed out[1] that the most exquisite art has been associated with the decadence of the Greek and Roman empires, of Renaissance Italy, of the French Court before the Revolution. But, quite apart from the point that social background is a complex of influences and that any answer to the

1. *Civilisation*, Penguin Books, 1938.

questions 'What is morality? What is decadence?' may not by any means be a simple one, it has to be remembered that the rich patron and the artists who produced the things we admire were not the same people. But at least in such a society, decadent or not, art was cultivated and admired. In a puritan society or a nation dedicated to war, money-making or domination may become the principal aim, with art largely excluded.

Presumably in any society the best patrons will be those with the best taste, but they may still be insensitive, indifferent – what you will – without affecting the work, provided they give the artist (who is none of these) a free hand. However, the cinema with its massive financial infrastructure – the average Hollywood movie cost around $20 million in 1989 – is particularly open to interference by economic interests. The whole edifice of commercial film-making is designed to ensure that he who pays the piper controls the tune. The ways in which studio interests keep a watchful eye on their investments and step in when they consider it necessary are well documented in Lillian Ross's book *Picture*,[1] which describes the making (and, in many respects, unmaking) of John Huston's *The Red Badge of Courage*, and in John Gregory Dunne's *The Studio*,[2] which took a look inside the portals of Twentieth Century Fox during a period of 1967. John Boorman's *Money Into Light*[3] records his experiences trying to make his film *The Emerald Forest* and is particularly revealing about the ways in which the problems of his backers affected his work. Stephen Bach's *Final Cut*,[4] by contrast, illustrates a rare phenomenon, a film, *Heaven's Gate*, that managed to evade the grasp of its financiers, United Artists, to the eventual ruin of the latter. Whether studio interference is damaging or beneficial (and Joseph Losey has remarked that he made many of his poorer films after he had won complete artistic control) the point remains that film financiers are not patrons commissioning work for their own enjoyment, but businessmen making an investment – and one with a high degree of risk.

1. Gollancz, 1953: Penguin reissue, 1963.

2. W. H. Allen, 1970.

3. Faber and Faber, 1986.

4. Jonathan Cape, 1985.

Fortunately there are many cases in which the artist is left as free to express himself in film as in many other media, and sometimes, because the technique of film-making is such a comparative mystery, the patron will interfere less. A commercial firm will very likely give a freer hand to a film director making a prestige film for them than to an architect who is designing their board-room or the façade of their new building. It also seems that the artist is likely to be freer in the mixed economy of a democracy than subject to the bureaucratic supervision of a controlled economy, as the historic example of Russia and other communist states shows.

Stage Two: *Execution*

The second stage, the carrying through of the artist's intuition and the resultant work of art, is the most obvious and prominent feature of artistic activity. It is what the world sees. Because of this it may unfortunately be true that of two artists, one with deep inspiration but less facility of expression and another with little to say but a fine technique, the latter is more likely to be successful. The execution is also what clearly distinguishes one art from another. A film is very different from a play or a painting or a symphony; but the emotional inspiration which engenders each and the states of mind which each arouses in its audience are more alike.

In the case of film this second stage is particularly prominent for one reason: because the film medium is tremendously powerful in its impact. A film is such a large piece of work compared with, say, a painting, and it is easy for an audience to accept a film, as one may accept a building, without thinking of the people who made it. Further, it reaches its audience on a scale which is larger than life, and the mere size of its images and volume of its sound can have a stunning effect. It is still more powerful because it is pictorial, and still more so again because it is photographic and brings us face to face with reality, or with something that looks like reality, in a compulsive, actual way. It is far more vivid, and so can be far more shocking, than an abstract art which depends on written or spoken words. Finally, the cinema is a collective form of artistic communication, and only television reaches a wider audience.

Yet, although the film medium is so widely known and so powerful, it has aroused less expert discussion than other arts. The main reason is probably this. Most people, when they listen to music, read a novel, or look at a painting, understand the work that lies behind it. They may not understand the growth of the artist's intuition, for this is a mystery of creation in the mind which we do not fully understand. But the process of writing it down on paper, of putting the paint on a surface – these are simple (though not simple to do) hand operations as old as mankind and as uncomplex as an axe chopping wood or a wheelbarrow moving rubbish. By contrast, the processes of the cinema are a mechanical conjuring-trick, new, baffling, complex – like a motor-car, an electronic brain, or a Geiger counter. The *results* are startling in their effect and so simple to understand that they reach an unsophisticated audience more easily than most arts; but the *means* by which they are obtained are another matter entirely.

It is the purpose of this book to investigate this mystery. That is not to say that this is a book about film technique – a practical guide to making films. We are interested in the film as an artistic medium, and propose to examine the factors at work as they contribute to the final aesthetic effect. We do not attempt to describe how to frame a shot, what exposure or what aperture to use, how to cut a sequence and so on. But we shall be concerned with what aesthetic effects can be obtained by framing, by exposure, by different depths of focus and by cutting. And we shall try to deduce if any aesthetic principles lie behind these techniques, and, if so, what they are. There will be such reference to technical processes as is necessary for clarity, but the stress is on film appreciation, not on practical know-how.

The medium of the cinema is little understood for reasons other than those of its mechanical nature, its technical complexity and its newness. For most of its history, until quite recently, it was a transient medium. A book can be read and read again, music replayed on records, a picture enjoyed repeatedly in a gallery or in reproduction. Until the advent of video technology, film (and television to an even greater extent) enjoyed none of these advantages. After a short run, films generally disappeared, re-emerging infrequently, if at all, years later on television. Nor could the viewer re-see a scene or effect without watching the whole work again. Video-recording has overcome this problem, though video presentation can never match the circumstances of cinema projection.

Seen on a large screen in a darkened auditorium, film can

achieve an enormous impact, and this very power is inimical to analysis. If the viewer is emotionally absorbed in the film he may very well miss finer points of expression. Not only are many technical effects in a film extremely subtle, despite their contribution to the total impact, but part of a director's job is to ensure that they do not beg for attention, but affect the spectator even though he remains unconscious of their presence. In most cases technique is, and should be, invisible. A film can be appreciated without any knowledge of how the effects are achieved. But the 'uneducated' viewer remains more at the mercy of the film-maker, a more passive recipient of the message the film conveys. By understanding something of how a film is made, the techniques involved in. constructing images for the screen, the spectator will not only appreciate more fully what is before him, but will be able to take a more active role in interpretation.

A further reason for the art of the film not being understood lies in the long tradition in Britain and the USA that denied film the status of art. Dewey referred to things 'the average person does not take to be arts; the movie, jazzed music, the comic strip ... and newspaper accounts of lovenests and murders'. I. A. Richards lumped together 'bad literature, bad art, the cinema', and said that the latter was 'a medium that lends itself to crude rather than sensitive handling.' In Britain for many years few people wrote seriously about the cinema or, if they did, treated it as a sociological, an economic, or even an anthropological phenomenon, rather than an aesthetic one. It may be significant that the cinema has been least valued in those countries where the commercial industry's grip of mass entertainment was for a long time strongest. It was different on the Continent where the cinema has been a focus for intellectual ferment: where people like Eisenstein, René Clair, Abel Gance, Jean Cocteau, Pasolini, Godard, Truffaut and Tarkovsky, have not only made films but written articles and books and propounded theories. Until relatively recently such writing was ignored in Britain and America, dismissed as pretentious and arcane. Indeed it rarely makes easy reading – perhaps because, as the French theoretician Christian Metz put it: 'A film is difficult to explain because it is easy to understand.'

It remains true that Anglo-Saxon film-makers are still less eager to discuss their work in terms of aesthetics and theory than are their European counterparts. Equally a city like Paris offers a far wider variety of cinema to audiences than do either London or New York. But in most other ways recent years have seen a dramatic change in attitudes to the cinema. Coincidentally or not, just at the moment when it has lost its mass audience, film is starting to be taken seriously. The study of film has become established not only at college level but in schools. Books on film theory proliferate in English as well as French and whole new approaches to the understanding and interpreting of film have appeared and been widely discussed. One effect has been that the past has been seen in a new light, elevating the critical status of many commercial Hollywood products and blurring the previously clear distinction between art and entertainment. The advent of television and video has allowed the viewer both greater accessibility and greater control over what can be seen (films now gain around 97 per cent of their audience in Britain through some form of home-viewing). As moving images are being made available through an ever-increasing variety of channels, interest in how the medium of film works has grown in proportion.

Stage Three: *Presentation*

So much for a preliminary survey of the second stage in the artistic process of film-making – realization. The third stage, the viewing of the film by an audience, represents the fulfilment of the artistic process. As we discuss the various techniques by which the film-maker presents his work we will always have the final viewing in mind. Throughout the book this aspect is implicit, frequently explicit, and the last chapter discusses in more detail how audiences interpret and react to the 'reality' of film images.

The audience and its expectations are at this stage important factors – factors beyond the control of the artist, beyond the work of art itself, inasmuch as it exists at all without an audience. The nature of the audience, their knowledge of the medium, their social and cultural expectations, can all affect their impressions. Work of depth or subtlety may demand more of an audience. Wide experience of the medium and informed criticism will help an audience to see more clearly and more deeply. Publicity may be useful in telling the audience what to expect, or may be harmful in presenting a false or exaggerated image. The publicist's skill lies in creating the conditions for bringing together a film and its audience. With the regular cinema-goer now almost extinct, the audience has fragmented from the 'mass' into a series of overlapping but separate sub-groups. Few films appeal to all: the rest must be directed at those sections of the audience that will appreciate them. Unfortunately, in a situation dominated by large conglomerate organizations, too many smaller films never do find their appropriate audience. They are not allotted suitable channels in the system of distribution and exhibition. Generally the film-maker has no part in this process: he is effectively cut off from his audience and must depend on the complex administrative procedures of the corporations. The whole topic of the ownership and control of the media is hotly debated, but is only one aspect of the social and economic structure which establishes the relationship between the film and its audience. Changing leisure habits (including a decline in cinema-going), the growth of the adolescent audience, the ways in which media images may influence attitudes or behaviour, the censorship based on assumptions about this influence – all these and other aspects are relevant to a full understanding of the role of the media in society.

But what concerns us here is what goes on in that darkened auditorium (or rather less darkened sitting-room, bedroom or kitchen) when an audience, or single viewer, confronts the film itself. As the brain interprets the shadows on the screen in terms of space, time, narrative, form and so on, it makes its own idiosyncratic judgements and connections, fitting what is seen into the world as it is known to that particular individual. Even so, the viewer's role is circumscribed, by the film-maker, by the culture that envelops both of them (and the film), and by the fact that both creator and viewer are using a shared language or series of conventions which direct interpretation along certain lines.

In Chapter 9 we turn our attention from the analysis of how films are constructed to the more dynamic field of how this construction influences perception. For the moment it is sufficient merely to note that a film is only really completed when it is shown to an audience. This confrontation between film and audience is the final and necessary part of the process, without which the work remains just so much celluloid or videotape.

FILM AND REALITY

The relationship between the real world and the cinematic representation of reality has been one of the principal themes of theoretical debate from a very early date, and it will be an important point of focus throughout this book. The first notable writer to address himself to the problematic nature of film realism was the psychologist Rudolph Arnheim, whose *Film as Art* was published in 1933. His approach consisted of a clearly developed contrast between the real world of the senses and the world we see on the cinema screen, and an analysis of the elements of difference between real and artistic experiences. Indeed Arnheim went so far as to feel that it was the very differences between screen 'reality' and the real world which make the cinema an art. The closer film approaches to the mere reproduction of what lies before it, the harder it is for the artist to impose his vision.

In the earliest days the attitude that cinema was not an art, which lingered longest perhaps in England, was generally held everywhere. Neither cinema nor photography were at first accepted as forms of art, but were regarded merely as methods of registering the appearance and movement of the real world.[1] Perhaps this was natural, since by the nature of things the first film-makers, like Lumière and Edison, were scientists rather than artists, and quite content to be so. It was only gradually, through experiment and improvisation, that the cinema developed into an art by transforming its mechanical means of reproduction into an artistic means of expression. Film-making, as contemporary aesthetics saw it, was a mechanical task which had nothing in common with artistic creation. Film apparatus with its cogs and gears and strips of celluloid was to all appearance far from being artistic, and the shadows jerking on the screen, apart from their scientific interest, were considered good for little more than to provide a few minutes' diversion in a funfair. However, there were visionaries (one of whom was the conjurer Méliès) who saw that this vulgar, showground attraction had hidden powers of magic. One of the most perceptive writers about the cinema, André Bazin,[2] in an article on its origins, describes it as an 'idealist phenomenon', by

1. Plate 4.
2. *Qu'est-ce-que le Cinéma*, Editions du Cerf, 1962.

which he means that its development was due more to the fantastic imagination and enthusiasm of dreamers like Méliès[1] than to the prosaic research of the scientists. Both were necessary, and it is right to stress the contribution of the artist and the showman as well as that of the inventor. An indication of the energy with which show-people took up the new invention is shown in the enterprise of a stall-holder in an early French fair who gave his side-show the tremendous title of *Lenti-Électro-Plasti-Chromo-Mimo-Poly-Ser-penti-graph*. But even these illusionists, these cinemaniacs, saw the new invention only as a new combination of traditional arts which would enable them to achieve a total spectacle – some grand coalescence of stage and natural effects. Nobody foresaw that there would emerge, quite independent of all the older-established arts and different from all of them, a new autonomous *art of the film*.

The mechanical nature of the cinema was important in another way. Like that of photography, the compelling realism of a film depends on the fact that there is, or seems to be, less human intervention than in other arts. We think that we can rely on a machine to be faithful in reproducing an original in a way that is not possible with human agency alone, and consequently we *believe* in the reality of a machine reproduction. In fact, contrary to common opinion, the cinema with all its technical and scientific resources is quite unable to reproduce reality without imperfection. Although it may appear to be an exact copy, the world we see on the screen is quite different from the world we live in. In particular, neither space nor time have the same characteristics. In the everyday world of our senses, everything exists in a space–time continuum constructed from real space and real time, and forming a continuous framework of reference and identification. The space–time of the cinema is completely different. Spatially the screen shows us a flat world reduced to a single plane, lacking the basic dimension of depth, and limited by the frame which surrounds it. For much of its history the screen has been without colour and (except for 3-D) without the relief of sculpture and other plastic arts. Furthermore, by montage and camera movement the cinema makes all kinds of transformations of space which would be impossible in reality. Time also is constantly subject to contrac-

1. Plate 5.

tions, extensions, breaks, and jumps which do not occur in the continuous chronology of the real world. Finally, the cinema was for a long time without sound or speech and when it does make use of these elements it does so in ways which are very different from our experience of them in everyday life.

It is clear then that, by comparison with our ordinary experience, the film world is an artificial one – albeit one which more obviously approximates physical reality than can be achieved in any other art form. This paradox stems from the two different directions in which the cinema has been pulled since its earliest days. Lumière showed how film could 'possess' the real world by capturing its appearance, an approach which led to the documentary tradition which aims to present the truth about an event with as little human intervention as technology will allow. Méliès used narrative, animation, and fantasy to demonstrate that the film image can be tailored to the creator's imagination: the film-maker can present his unique version of the world, ordered by his particular will and the wide range of manipulative techniques at his command.

From these two roots emerged the two theoretical branches which for many years dominated discussion of the medium. Expressionism derived from Méliès, with its vision of a controlled world whose creator uses his powers to emphasize differences from the real world. The essential manipulative tool was montage (cutting) which forced both time and space to dance to the film-maker's personal tune. This theory was dominant for the first half-century of cinema. It was not until the 1950s that critics laid the basis for a theory derived from Lumière. Technical developments had allowed the camera to include more detail in the individual shot, and to move within the shot. Cutting became less crucial and the newer, more 'objective' approach allowed realism to come to the centre of the stage, emphasizing content rather than form. Film could record and reveal reality; it could give the spectator the experience of reality itself.

These theories will be discussed more fully in Chapter 5 after a consideration of the techniques with which they are associated. It is sufficient here to note that modern theory denies the primacy of any one technique. Rather, the role of the artist is to achieve the appropriate balance and tension between the contrasting urges to control and to reveal. Left to its own mechanical devices, the camera is incapable of creating a meaningful world: it needs the intervention of the film-maker with all his technical and artistic skills and his own personal cinematic vision. Even so (unless he is working in animation, abstraction or pure fantasy) his raw material consists of the real world. Each single image acts both as a recording, showing us a staged or unstaged reality, and also as an element, interacting and combining with others to suggest the meaning and significance of the whole.

The film world also possesses an anthropomorphic quality common to all arts which helps to create a deliberate emotional and mental effect in the spectator simply because, in the making, the film has been charged with this quality by the artist. Scenes which exist in nature are emotionally and dramatically 'neutral', in the sense that they do not seek to move or influence us at the bidding of any exterior will. If an aurora borealis fills us with wonder, or a storm makes us afraid, the emotion comes from within ourselves; nobody has staged them with the express purpose of producing a reaction from an audience. But the images of a film reflect the film-maker's own feelings and imaginings, and they become mental images as much as physical. They are designed not only to affect the senses but also to seize the imagination. The natural scene is *there*. It stays detached. It can be enjoyed, but remains aloof, indifferent. But the film as a work of art is deliberately made to attack us, to force its way into our feelings and beliefs.

CHAPTER TWO

SPACE IN THE CINEMA:
Scale, Shooting-Angle, Depth

WE have already, in Chapter One, mentioned some of the ways in which a film differs from reality. The conditions under which a film is viewed occasion further differences. As soon as we start to analyse the situation of a spectator in the cinema it is apparent that he apprehends the objects on the screen quite differently from those of the world which surrounds him. The most important difference is that the screen is external to the spectator, who is not involved with it as he is with his normal surroundings. At the same time the spectator's normal surroundings (seats, other spectators, etc.) are obliterated by darkness. Secondly, in the cinema we can only see and hear – our visual and auditory sensations are not supplemented by touching, feeling, measuring, or weighing, and as a result we cannot estimate accurately volumes, distances, or densities. Our senses, which in nature operate as a whole, are cut down to sight and sound.

FILM VISION

Let us consider first the sense of sight. The images on the screen show us the external world in a very arbitrary fashion. The camera lens is a crude device compared with human eyes, possessing neither their stereoscopic vision nor their power of continuously refocusing, changing angle, and accommodating to light. Because of this, and because of the nature of film projection, the cinema gives us, even visually, only an approximate and incomplete account of the real world. The spectator has to accustom himself physically and mentally to the peculiarities of *film vision*.

Let us take an example. Because the cinema gives a two-dimensional picture of a three-dimensional world, objects will not necessarily be recognizable on the screen irrespective of how they are photographed. They must be taken from the right angle and with the right lighting, and this involves selection by the cameraman from the many aspects of the objects which exist in reality. This has to be borne in mind even when filming such a simple thing as a cube. In the real world, we can see it from a distance or close to, can walk round it, count its sides, compare it with its surroundings or with ourselves, localize it in space – in short we can identify it completely. It is in the same world as ourselves. In the cinema, the spectator is not only outside the spatial framework of the things he sees in the film; he is also immobile. The camera has to move for him, or the object has to move on the screen. If we film our cube from directly in front, the audience will not recognize it as a cube; it will appear on the screen as a flat surface – a square. To be recognizable the cube has to be suitably lighted, and photographed from an angle which will show three of its sides and so its three dimensions; or else it must be shown turning, or the camera must move round it to show its different faces.[1] It is so easy to misrepresent common objects by using the wrong viewpoint or lighting that such misleading photographs are often used for guessing games.

As another example, let us suppose we want to show an audience either the depth of a valley or the height of a mountain or, generally, the size of any object. To achieve satisfactory results it is not enough to set up the camera anywhere, or film the scene anyhow, even if we get far enough away from the object to include the whole of it in the picture. The spectator outside the screen lacks any system of reference or any scale of dimensions by which to judge its size. The operator must choose a suitable viewpoint or give some other artificial means to help the audience assess the object. In the case of the valley, for instance, a sense of depth will be given by choosing a time of day when the sun casts shadows on the slopes of the hills. In the case of the mountain, the director

1. This example is taken from Arnheim's *Film as Art*.

may arrange to include in the picture a house or a tree or a human figure to give a relative scale of size.[1] This is a rule which even holiday snapshots follow. There is an excellent example in Robert Flaherty's film, *Moana*. In one shot (not a particularly impressive one) he shows waves breaking over rocks and the spray filling the screen. A little later we see exactly the same scene with two Polynesians standing in the shower of spray in the foreground. These two tiny figures at the bottom of the screen show us the true size of the tremendous waves and give the second picture a far greater impact.

From these examples there grows the idea of *lighting, shooting-angle* and *scale* as forming the rudiments of an art of the film. Lighting is discussed more fully in a later chapter. Scale and shooting-angle are considered further below.

SCALE

We have seen that a film audience may fail to appreciate the size of large objects. The lack of a scale of reference also works the other way, so that models on a tiny scale, if carefully made and lit, and cut in with shots of live action, are accepted as real. The bombing scenes of the film *The Dam Busters* (director, Michael Anderson), showing the destruction of the Möhne Dam during the war, were photographed from a model no bigger than an ordinary table-top, and the same is true of innumerable film spectacles from the films of Méliès to *Star Wars*. In the cinema it is as easy to make a mountain out of a molehill as to do the opposite. In John Huston's film *The Night of the Iguana*, lizards are used to set off the credits at the beginning of the film. Actually they are about as large as small dogs but, by shooting in close-up and with no other frame of reference than the letters of the credits, they are made to look as big as prehistoric monsters. In the Hammer movie *One Million Years BC*, the monsters are sometimes models, but also real animals, a turtle for instance, shown towering over the tiny humans. In *King Kong Meets Godzilla*, an octopus is shown as large as a house. It is the combination of reality (the animal's oozing, slithery movement)

1. Plate 6.

and illusion (its immense size) that gives the sequence its shocking effect. At the other extreme *The Incredible Shrinking Man* was blessed with a six-foot leading actor and giant props were created to reduce him to smaller proportions – huge raindrops were fabricated from water-filled condoms for example. Similar solutions were found in *Brats*[1] in which Laurel and Hardy played the parts of children. Nowadays special effects are much more sophisticated and such simple procedures are rarely adequate.

Scale is still used to surprise and mislead audiences. Nicolas Roeg's *Castaway* includes a nice joke based on viewer assumptions about scale. Lucy and Gerald, on their desert island, are fishing. Lucy gets a bite and shouts, 'Shark'. As Gerald takes over her line we see shots of the giant creature, photographed from below and filling the screen as the sound-track rumbles with ferocious sounds. After a mighty struggle the fish is finally landed, and proves to be only two or three feet long! Through camera angle and a mild evocation of *Jaws*, Roeg was able to mislead his audience as thoroughly as the baby shark fighting for its life had misled its captors.

Manipulation of scale can imply a comment on what is being shown. Near the beginning of Pakula's *All the President's Men*, the two journalist heroes are seen in the Library of Congress. At first we are shown just them and the dozens of file cards in front of them. Then gradually the camera moves back and upwards to the very top of the vast dome-shaped room, leaving the two men dwarfed below, the magnitude of their task emphasized. In David Lynch's *Blue Velvet* an opening sequence of suburban tranquillity is interrupted by the sight of a man suffering a heart attack in his garden. Unexpectedly the camera leaves the stricken figure and plunges deep into the undergrowth, seeking out a colony of tiny beetles until their unceasing activity fills the screen. This eerie shot is the first indication that all is not what it seems beneath the smooth surface of small-town life.

Properly used, scale by itself can give an emotional tone to a film. Close shots will give a scene an oppressive or intimate feeling; medium or long shots, an effect of formality or coldness. We use this language in ordinary life and speak of 'being close to someone'

1. Plate 7.

or 'a distant manner'. In some of the love scenes in Bertolucci's *Last Tango in Paris*, the camera, by never leaving the couple, expresses a brooding atmosphere of obscene sexual obsession. The same close shooting in Bergman's *Cries and Whispers* expresses a more sympathetic atmosphere of family tragedy and courage in facing sickness and death. In George Roy Hill's *The Sting*, close shooting gives atmosphere to a tense poker game in the compartment of a train. There are many examples of a director using insistent close shots with emotional effect. At the same time, if used insensitively or overdone they will defeat their purpose. Medium and long shots can have other qualities: formal beauty, richness of detail, peaceful detachment. Scenes on a small scale, skilfully handled, can be just as menacing as close-ups. In Hill's *Butch Cassidy and the Sundance Kid* there is a chase in which the two outlaws are being followed by a posse. We never see the pursuers in close-up, only as tiny figures in the distance. But they are all the more menacing for that, since they are always there and appear every time the fugitives think they have got away, until in the end they get on our nerves.

SHOOTING-ANGLE

The example of the cube on page 36 shows the importance of shooting-angle for simple identification, but when making a film it is not only a question of recognizing an object and grasping its physical properties. In the case of more complex objects (a building, a statue, a person) shooting-angle may be used to bring out their essential nature.[1] Certain aspects will be more typical than others, or will embrace others. In Steven Spielberg's *E.T.*, the group searching for the extra-terrestrial being are usually shot from a low angle looking up at their heavy bodies, their authority symbolized by the keys dangling at their waists. The angle emphasizes their power and menace and is augmented by backlighting which keeps details hidden. The angle also reflects the fact that this is a film seen from a child's point of view – so the camera looks up from a child's height: as in the classic cartoons, adults are seen only as legs and trunks.

1. Plates 8 and 9.

The essential characteristics of a locomotive are its speed and power, and consequently newsreels generally favour upward-angle shots taken as the train rushes past. There are some striking shots of trains in the Spanish feature *Spirit of the Beehive*, in which two little girls in the foreground make an effective contrast. In Lindsay Anderson's film *This Sporting Life* the mud-covered football players taken from a low angle appear as black brutal giants. In filming a crowd of any size, the only way to show its typical feature (its numbers) is by setting up the camera in a dominating position and shooting at a downward angle.[1]

If some aspects are typical others are atypical, and abnormal camera-angles can be used to give an object or person a misleading character. Seen in a certain way, a frank expression can seem hypocritical, an inoffensive gesture threatening, a dwarf a giant. By filming a ballet dancer from below through a sheet of glass at a vertical angle, René Clair in *Entr'acte* makes her look like a flower. In Jack Clayton's *The Pumpkin Eater*, Jo's father is made into a grotesque figure on his first appearance by photography which gives a distorted perspective of his face. A similar technique is used in Sidney Lumet's *The Hill* to give a brutal appearance to the face of a sadistic sergeant-major. In Joseph Losey's *The Servant*, Dirk Bogarde is made by camera-angles into a dominating, most unservant-like figure.

The way a director shows an object will depend very much on the dramatic action or on the type of film being made or on the audience for which it is intended. An operation will be filmed in one way for an audience of medical students, and in another way for a general audience in an entertainment film. In Altman's *M.A.S.H.*, for purposes of black comedy, the bloody side of surgery is wildly exaggerated. A telephone will be treated differently in a documentary about the G.P.O. and in a feature. Besides its physical properties, every object has other properties – dramatic, psychological, poetic – which in certain circumstances are more important and should be stressed.

In appropriate cases, shooting-angles can be used to express subjectively what things are like as seen through the eyes of a character in the film. At the beginning of John Huston's spy film,

1. Plate 10.

Across the Pacific, the hero, Bogart, has just been cashiered and has changed into civilian clothes. As he stands there the camera looks down at his old uniform with its badges and buttons ripped off, the downward shooting-angle expressing what we assume to be his feelings of shame at his dishonourable discharge. In Hitchcock's *Spellbound* and in Jean Delannoy's *Aux Yeux du Souvenir* the camera shows us the world seen by a sick man coming out of a coma: an upside-down world of people seen from below; a nurse whose silhouette appears on the ceiling lowering a spoon from the skies. Many Japanese films are shot with the camera two or three feet off the ground, roughly the height of the head of a person seated on the floor, a typical Japanese posture. In Carol Reed's *The Fallen Idol* (as in *E.T.*, noted earlier) many scenes are shot from the visual angle of a young boy. Unusual angles, abnormal framing and lighting – all suggest with delicate precision a world which is familiar but is not that of grown-ups. A subjective camera-angle is used in Pier Pasolini's film *The Gospel According to St Matthew*, in a sequence showing John the Baptist by the River Jordan As Jesus comes forward to be baptized the camera draws backwards and into the clouds as we hear the words 'This is my beloved Son in whom I am well pleased.' Because the film is restrained and quiet in its general treatment, this larger camera movement is extremely effective. In Buñuel's *Tristana* almost the first downward-angle shot in the film is of Tristana and her lover meeting in a courtyard. Again, because of contrast with what has gone before it is striking and stresses a change in her feelings which influences the whole of the story.

This question of subjective and objective shots could be developed further and it is interesting to compare it to the novelist's technique of switching from the viewpoint of one character, to that of another, to that of the novelist himself. Many films (thrillers in particular) are told *through*, perhaps even *by*, one character. Hitchcock appeared to be using this convention when he made *Psycho*, which for half an hour follows the exploits of Marion (played by the film's star, Janet Leigh). It comes as a shock when this character is suddenly murdered, though study of the murder sequence reveals how Hitchcock cunningly moves the focus away from Marion and towards Norman Bates, the killer from whose point of view the rest of the film is seen.

Most films appear to be told by someone outside the plot, an unseen omniscient narrator. But even here, certain shots may be shown from the point of view of a character in the story. In the 'stalk-and-slash' type of horror film the audience is often placed in the position of the aggressor creeping up on the victim. We are asked to share the slasher's strategy (and perhaps also his emotions) whereas we simply watch the victim's fear and panic. It is clear that point of view can therefore have an ethical component in some circumstances, though it would be wrong to suggest that all such shots demand identification with the particular character. We may not even know who the character is or what their motives may be. At the start of John Carpenter's *Halloween*, there is a long sequence seen from the point of view of someone entering a house and creeping upstairs. All we know is that they are wearing a mask which frames what we see. Through the mask we approach a young woman in her bedroom. A knife is raised and she is brutally murdered. Only after all this do we discover that we have been seeing through the eyes of her small brother.

Subjective shots need not be so dramatic or even so 'realistic' as this. The classic dialogue sequence is based on a series of shots over the shoulder of first one character, then the other. We see each person more or less from the other's point of view – but not quite. We are slightly to one side and can usually see part of the back of the second character. We maintain a slight distance which enables us to be moved from one character to the other without confusion.

The camera can of course mislead us and this capacity can be used for dramatic or humorous effect. In many thrillers the camera is placed in such a way that we never quite see the face of the villain and can be kept in suspense concerning his identity. At the beginning of Dupont's *Variety*, the camera tracks into a fairground where the showgirls are posing outside a booth. At a distance they look attractive, but as the camera moves in we see they are old, ugly harridans. In Sam Fuller's *The Naked Kiss*, the director achieves a sensational opening by concentrating on a bald head which different angles reveal to be that of a woman whose head has been shaved as a punishment by a gangster. In Schaffner's *Planet of the Apes* at the climax of the movie, when the space travellers look up at a vast object half-buried in the sand, the camera first shoots it from behind. We start to wonder what it is, and only gradually realize it is the Statue of Liberty.

In an early Chaplin film, *The Immigrant*, we see Chaplin bent over the rail of a ship which is pitching violently. From the convulsive movement of his back it is obvious that the poor fellow is sea-sick like the rest of the passengers and we are full of pity for him. But when he turns round we find that in fact he is fishing, and has just landed a monster catch. Another example from a Chaplin film shows Charlie with shaking shoulders, apparently sobbing his heart out because his wife has left him. When the camera moves, it turns out that he is shaking a cocktail. In Jacques Tati's *Traffic*, there is a shot of what looks to be a well-endowed woman displaying an impressive cleavage. Only when she turns do we realize that she is actually holding a baby and that what we were admiring was the baby's bottom! There is an effective comic scene in one of Laurel and Hardy's films which shows Hardy apparently strangling Laurel to death. A shot from a different angle shows us that he is only tying Laurel's bow-tie. In all these examples the director has made artistic use of the camera's inability, when placed in a certain position, to give a correct interpretation of a scene. He has manipulated the spectator to misread the image without any form of cutting or trickery. The camera has no morals: it lies or tells the truth depending on how it is used. Louis Malle's *Pretty Baby* explicitly recognizes this fact. The story of a young girl brought up in a New Orleans bordello early in the century, it opens with a shot of young Violet (Brooke Shields). We see only her face as she listens to the apparently orgasmic noises emanating off-screen. Eventually we discover that she has been watching her mother giving birth. Another moment when Malle uses the ability of the camera to lie comes later, when a professional photographer arrives to execute a series of studies of the brothel. His first picture is of Violet's mother, sweaty and tousled after a hard night's work. His photograph tells a different story, showing her glowing and fresh as the photographer himself wished to see her. Likewise, every decision the film director makes influences how his camera will reveal the world and suggests how the audience will interpret this reality.

PERSPECTIVE

Another peculiarity of the camera which affects the cinema's interpretation of reality is its rendering of perspective. Film perspective combined[1] with an upward shooting-angle gives some of the cinema's most common effects. Mathematically, the size of objects in nature decreases in proportion to the square of their distance away from us. Thus, *as far as the image on the retina of our eye is concerned*, a man twenty feet away from us appears four times smaller than a man ten feet away, while a man forty feet away appears sixteen times smaller. But, as modern psychologists have demonstrated, we instinctively correct the message we receive from our optic nerve, so that differences in proportion registered on our retina are mentally reduced. If we accepted the immediate reaction of our eyes, natural perspective would be much more exaggerated. In practice our mind sees objects in inverse ratio to the distance (not the square of the distance), and we see a man at forty feet as a quarter (not a sixteenth) as big as the man at ten feet, and the man at twenty feet as a half (not a quarter) the size of the man at ten feet. This *mental* correction is the fruit of long experience, acquired from infancy, of the relative size of external objects. We are used to fitting what we see into an intuitive system of reference which makes everything of 'reasonable size', so that our mind 'sees' things differently from our eye. Scientists call this a 'constancy' effect,[2] and it is the same phenomenon which enables the spectator to adjust to the size of the screen in different parts of the cinema.

The camera lens registers perspective in the same proportions as the retina, that is objectively instead of subjectively, so that on the

---

1. Note the word 'combined'. The point should be made here (and borne in mind throughout the book) that to separate one aspect of technique and discuss it in isolation from others (e.g. *scale* separately from *shooting-angle*) is an artificial procedure necessary for purposes of analysis which does not correspond to the conditions of actual viewing. In the viewing of a film all the different effects – scale, perspective, lighting, etc. – operate together in combination. It follows that many of the examples quoted from films would serve to illustrate more than one point. Generally they are cited as examples of the point for which they make the best illustration, but there will often be other applications which the reader can see for himself.

2. R. H. Thouless, *General and Social Psychology*, University Tutorial Press, 1945.

screen the rule of the square of the distance operates. A man photographed with his finger pointing at the camera has a giant hand larger than his head; a skyscraper filmed from a low-flying aeroplane is like a tall pyramid standing on its apex. We see them in this way because, when we are in the cinema watching the screen, we are unable to correct this 'distortion' as we would in the real world, since the cinema presents a special world external to us and outside our ordinary experience.

Once more, film images differ materially from those we experience directly and, as a result, certain shots, certain angles are normally avoided because they give this unnatural impression – because the difference from our habitual observation is too violent. To bring the camera image into line with our customary way of seeing things, and to give the screen image verisimilitude, the director has to intervene and control the 'automatic' mechanism of the camera. In some cases this is merely a process of control aimed at presenting reality in an acceptable way. But in other cases this very defect of the camera can be deliberately used for artistic effect.

If, instead of filming a building square to the camera and far enough back to approximate normal vision, we go close and shoot from below at an upward angle, then the building will show the violent foreshortening we have described, and will appear to tower above us, larger than life. A person filmed from the same angle will give an impression of force, power, majesty, even if he is a dwarf. This was a constant device of propaganda films, and has been used again and again to add to the stature of dictators and tyrants. There are innumerable shots of Stalin, Mussolini, and Hitler addressing the faithful as if they were gods looking down from heaven. The same upward shooting-angle is used constantly in feature films to establish predominance, and a downward angle is used to suggest inferiority. An upward angle may also be used more prosaically to increase the height of a short actor. An outstanding example of changing the whole appearance of an actor is in John Ford's *Young Mr Lincoln*. The name part is played by Henry Fonda, an actor of average build. By costume, make-up, shooting-angle, posture and even setting he is transformed into the tall, lanky figure of the President-to-be. In Kurosawa's *The Hidden Fortress*, partly by scale, partly by shooting-angle, partly by actual build, the hero Mifune is made to look huge in relation to the rogues he overcomes.

Many examples of the psychological effect of shooting-angle could be given. In Jacques Feyder's *Pension Mimosas* a woman (Françoise Rosay), having discovered that her son is stealing from her, bursts into his room to punish him, full of rage and indignation, and is shown in *upward angle*. She goes straight to him, and despite herself, slaps him with all her force (*horizontal angle*); then, realizing that she has been brutal and horribly unjust, she sinks on to a couch and bursts into tears (*downward angle*). The camera angle very accurately reflects the woman's feeling of moral indignation, of getting even, then of regret at what she has done. In Hitchcock's *Frenzy* the hero has given up an uncongenial job, had an unexpected windfall, and is going to a comfortable hotel with his girl-friend. As he gets out of the car and swaggers into the building, striking upward-angle shots express his cheerful mood. But already the police suspect him of murder and in later scenes when they catch up with him and he is on the run, the camera angles are predominantly downward. In Truffaut's film, *La Peau Douce*, the ending of a tenuous love affair is expressed by a long-shot and a downward camera angle. The man has taken the girl to a half-finished block of flats, where he is planning they should live, and there asks her to marry him. The answer is no; an affair is all right but not marriage. She goes off and leaves him. From the top of the tall building he watches her tiny figure go out into the street, get into a car and drive away. By means of long-shot and downward angle the camera gives an air of finality to her departure and reinforces the mental concept of parting by the physical means of emphasizing the distance between the two.

A further advantage of the camera's unusual vision is that a film can achieve the sort of formalism we find in the work of primitive painters who were ignorant of perspective, or of modern painters, like Picasso and Braque, who reject it. It enables reality to be stylized, and allows a director to express more freely his own personal vision. A good example is Dreyer's *La Passion de Jeanne d'Arc*, in which unusual angles are constantly used. With the slight distortion of camera perspective and a non-realistic décor, the whole picture is given a formal, abstract feeling. Stanley Kubrick's *Doctor Strangelove* is another picture with a brilliant style in which an inhuman, unearthly effect is obtained by extreme angles, violent lighting contrasts and unusual aspects (for instance, of cloud-scapes). In Richard Lester's *A Hard Day's Night* camera angles and sudden variations in scale and pace are used for humorous effect in a ballet sequence of the four Beatles on a playing field – a ballet which is created not by the actors but by the camera. In *Woman of the Dunes* by Hiroshi Teshigahara, strange patterns of sand, extraordinary angles, double-exposure, huge-scale close-ups, unusual lighting – all combine to give this film also a completely individual style. Because of its ability to alter reality, film is an ideal medium for science fiction. Though special effects now dominate, one can cite movies like Godard's *Alphaville*, Kubrick's *A Clockwork Orange*, Tarkovsky's *Solaris*, Lucas's *THX 1138*, Lynch's *Eraserhead*, Bergman's *Shame* and Rudolph's *Trouble in Mind*, which use every means – acting, camerawork, setting, music, colour – to alienate the spectator from the everyday world.

TRANSFER OF DIMENSIONS

Another phenomenon, connected with perspective, stems from the fact that, in the absence of stereoscopic vision, distances away from the spectator are conveyed entirely by differences in size. In the case of tracking-shots this sometimes leads to an optical illusion. Instead of seeing objects come nearer or go farther away, we get the impression that they are staying in the same place but increasing or decreasing in size. The basis of this phenomenon is that the third dimension of depth is interchangeable with the other two dimensions. What is really a change in depth is 'transferred' and appears as a change in length and breadth. Also because of exaggerated camera perspective, the increase or decrease will itself be exaggerated. With very fast tracking-shots, and especially with the use of a zoom lens, the effect may be so strong as to make the audience feel dizzy. In Haskell Wexler's otherwise exceptional political thriller, *Medium Cool*, there is continuous use of zoom and hand-held camera which, if viewed from the front rows, produces a distinctly nauseous effect.

An early example of transferred dimensions is Méliès's film *The Indiarubber Head*, made in 1901. In it a man's head is apparently blown up with a pump. It swells and swells, talking and grimacing to prove it is a real live head, and finally bursts. In fact the man, the rest of his body concealed, is slowly getting nearer and nearer to the camera. Transferred dimensions are also strongly present in shots with long-focus and telephoto lenses which, in addition, tend to destroy relief by flattening the image. It is thus common in newsreels (horse races or cricket matches) and in nature films (close-ups of wild animals). The effect is similar whether the camera itself moves or whether an animal or human being moves in relation to the camera, although transfer of dimensions is less likely in the latter case, since the rest of the scene, which stands still, gives a standard of reference and prevents ambiguity. However, this reference is often absent in telephoto shots because the moving being occupies the whole screen.

This phenomenon is, on the one hand, a defect which needs to be controlled by the film-maker – for instance by choosing an appropriate lens, or by arranging that movement shall be transverse or at a reduced speed or, in extreme cases, avoided altogether. But, on the other hand, it can have striking artistic or dramatic uses. The effect, on an audience already aroused by suspense and vague forebodings, of a threatening figure suddenly increasing to giant proportions is a tool in the hands of a film-maker far more powerful than any exact reproduction of reality. We see this particular effect in thrillers, gangster pictures, Western, and horror films. There is an example in James Whale's *Frankenstein* and another in Michael Crichton's *Westworld* when Yul Brynner as the robot cowboy runs amok and chases one of the tourists.

The opposite effect – the exaggerated rate of diminution caused by a figure going directly away from the camera or by the camera itself tracking back – can express powerful emotional feelings of farewell, of hopeless parting, of final ending or even (if combined with a deep, plunging viewpoint) of a sort of resigned, philosophical *Weltanschauung*. Such shots are typical of hundreds of film endings but, in good hands, they can still be extremely effective; for instance, there are the endings of Stroheim's *Greed* (the two tragic figures in the desert),[1] of Clair's *À Nous la Liberté* (the couple going down the long tree-lined road), of Renoir's *Le Crime de Monsieur*

1. In this case, however, the effect is achieved by cutting and not by camera movement.

Lange (the hero and heroine crossing the wet sand and turning to wave at the camera), of Antonioni's *La Notte* (the camera going away from husband and wife lying in the grass), of Fleming's *Gone with the Wind* (with Scarlett silhouetted under the tree), of Penn's *Night Moves* (with the half-dead hero marooned on a boat steering a never-ending circular route far out at sea), of Mazursky's *An Unmarried Woman* (with the heroine merging into the background of a New York street). Not to mention innumerable Westerns in which the lone cowboy rides off into the mythic sunset.

CONTRASTS IN PERSPECTIVE

So far, we have been considering the camera's peculiar perspective in relation to single objects. But it plays just as important a part in the relationship between two objects. It means that in shots taken in any depth the contrast in size between the foreground and background is very much exaggerated.[1] In the hands of a beginner this peculiarity can give ridiculous results, but properly used it can be another artistic resource. For example, the ending of Antonioni's *Il Grido* has, in the foreground of the picture, the man about to commit suicide; he is on the top of a tall tower looking down on the tiny figure of the woman he cannot forget who gazes up from the ground below, and the shot achieves its effect partly by this contrast. The ending of Eisenstein's *Ivan the Terrible*, with a huge close-up of Ivan's profile in the foreground juxtaposed against an endless winding queue of tiny figures in the distance, is not only pictorially effective but makes the point which Eisenstein wants to bring out – the paternal relationship between the Tsar and his flock, the Russian people. This point is made symbolically – the Tsar huge and alone, the people myriad and tiny – but at the same time with the strongest realism. There is another good example of this technique in Pudovkin's *The End of St Petersburg*, in the sequence where two peasants, fleeing from the famine conditions of the country, come to the town to look for a livelihood. One shot shows us in the foreground the huge mass of an equestrian statue of the Tsar, a black metallic silhouette with the horse's and rider's limbs outstretched, and, far off in the background, the two peasants, in minute scale, tramping across the empty square.

1. Plate 12.

Although the basic method is the same in each, the last two scenes have quite different effects. In *Ivan the Terrible* the bond between the elements is emphasized, while in Pudovkin's film it is the antagonism between them which comes out. This difference partly depends on context and meaning; but in the Pudovkin film both the statue's qualities – the lack of modelling, the deep-black grotesque outline, the hard texture – and also something in the attitude of the peasants, stress the city's might and hostility, and the peasants' miserable helplessness. If the distance between the men and the statue could be assessed by the eye, as in real life, the effect would not be the same. Even when watching the film, we know mentally that the men are not really *so* much smaller than the statue, but the transformation from reality to the cinema throws our usual sense of adjustment out of action, and the men are accepted emotionally as insects crawling at the feet of a colossus which could crush them with its power. In this scene, too, the meaning is expressed through a striking visual symbolism, the sort of symbolism used by Egyptian artists who made their victorious emperors huge figures while the enemies they defeated were shown as tiny beings. But the film, unlike Egyptian art, completely retains the realistic character of the scene.

To set against these two Russian examples, there is a striking shot in a British film, *A Taste of Honey*, directed by Tony Richardson. The heroine, a slum girl neglected by her mother, has just said good-bye to the handsome Negro sailor with whom she has been having an affair. They part at a swing-bridge across a ship-canal and, with conflicting emotions, she watches him going across to the other side. At this point there is a close-up of her face, and behind it is shown, in the middle-ground, a ship going down the canal – a complicated pattern of machinery, masts, stays, etc., full of life, with the crew working round the hatches and a group on the bridge. Besides being most striking visually, the shot is more deeply expressive, as though the ship symbolized both the vitality of the girl and the confusion of her thoughts. In another of Richardson's films, *The Charge of the Light Brigade*, there is a finely composed setting in depth in which Vanessa Redgrave sits in a Pre-Raphaelite drawing-room weeping, while dimly in the garden outside, her husband and Colonel Newton (whose belligerence causes the disastrous attack) discuss the projected campaign. In

Losey's *The Servant* already mentioned, which depicts a servant corrupting, dominating, and finally destroying his weak-minded master, this particular technique is used with striking effect to reinforce the impact of the whole film. At the beginning of the picture, the servant (Dirk Bogarde) always appears in the background, an insignificant, subservient figure. Gradually as the film goes on he is brought more and more into the foreground, and he grows in stature and power while the master steadily becomes by contrast smaller and more ineffectual.

The importance of one plane as opposed to another will depend very much on the context. In Bo Widerberg's *Raven's End* a loud-mouthed, drunken father and his son are shown large-scale in the foreground, listening with great excitement to a noisy sports programme on the radio. But the important action takes place in silence in the background when the son's girl-friend comes in at the back, stands mutely until he becomes aware of her presence and slips away to her; we then see them through the open door of the next room silently talking to each other, and we know she is telling him that she is expecting his baby. In Bob Fosse's *Sweet Charity*, near the beginning there is a colourful ballet of dance-hostesses who are showing off in front of a male customer We hardly see the man in the foreground, but the smoke of his cigar drifts just in front of the camera lens, and dominates the scene. One could quote other examples from modern films. Some of Stanley Spencer's paintings have a similar emphasized contrast between foreground and background and one wonders whether, consciously or unconsciously, he was not influenced by the cinema.

Horror films continually use different planes to show the aggressor and potential victim in the same frame, but with the latter unaware of the imminent danger. Ridley Scott's *Alien* includes a typical example in the scene in which Brett, a member of the crew of the Nostromo, searches the spaceship for the missing cat. He locates it at last and is puzzled by its increasing nervousness and hostility. When the camera cuts to the cat's eye view of Brett we see the cause of its anxiety. Emerging out of the steaming architecture of the ship itself, we see the outline of a gruesome alien predator. Our horror is heightened by the realization that Brett's attention rests firmly with the now hissing cat.

We have already mentioned in passing the particular qualities of different lenses. The lens of the human eye is able to refocus continuously every time it changes its view from one object to another. The camera lens does not possess this capacity, but advances in optical technology now give the film-maker a wide variety of lenses, each of which perceives reality in a different way and introduces its own aesthetic dimension. We can distinguish three basic types of lens, covering a distinctive range of focal lengths, although these merge into each other at their extremities. The normal lens offers the least distortion and is the nearest equivalent to the human eye. At one extreme the long-focus or telephoto lens magnifies distant objects.[1] As anyone who has ever looked through binoculars will appreciate, it also 'flattens' what it sees: it cannot convey the impression of depth. In addition it only covers a small area. At the other extreme the short-focus, wide-angle lens offers an enormous field of vision but overstates depth so that objects appear far apart from each other.[2]

Modern lenses are sophisticated combinations of elements, not merely chunks of glass. The zoom lens takes advantage of this characteristic by making the elements exceptionally mobile, so that the focal length can be altered while the camera is shooting. The result is that the image can be progressively changed from long-shot to close-up (or vice versa) without any camera movement. The zoom provides an optical alternative to the tracking-shot – but there are significant differences resulting from the changing depth perception that accompanies the change of focal length. While objects in the distance will stay much the same size in a tracking-shot, in a zoom they will gradually alter from appearing small and distant, to appearing large and near.

As well as changing lens focus, the film-maker can control the amount of light entering the lens. He can do this by altering the lighting itself (see Chapter Six), by interposing filters in front of the lens, or (more relevant in this context) by adjusting the size of the aperture through which the light reaches the lens.

The size of the aperture governs how much of the picture will be in focus. A small aperture allows objects both near and far to be in focus, giving a style known as 'deep-focus'. With a large aperture the 'depth of field' will be shallow. In photography, aperture size is

1. Plate 14.

2. Plate 13.

closely connected to shutter speed, the two having a direct negative relationship. A small aperture will demand a slow shutter speed in order to allow enough light to reach the film. In cinematography, this relationship is constrained by the need to shoot 24 frames per second. This characteristic has meant that only the development of faster film-stock allowed film-makers to achieve depth of focus in low light conditions.

DEPTH IN THE FILM IMAGE

Finally, we come to perspective as it affects the whole scene. From a technical viewpoint the flatness of the image has always been considered one of the great disadvantages of the screen spectacle, and inventors have been trying since the beginning of the century to overcome it by mechanical means. Many attempts have been made to add a third dimension to the screen, but even the most recent 3-D systems give results that look unreal. While the human eye does perceive depth, it does not do so to the extent that objects jump out at the viewer as they do so alarmingly from the 3-D screen. The fact is that the ordinary cinema image more closely approximates to the perception of the human eye than any stereoscopic process yet devised. The perfectly flat surface can very successfully give the illusion of a third dimension. Unlike systems of painting which are flat and completely formalized, a photograph is more like those works of art which use chiaroscuro or perspective to suggest the third dimension, and a photograph naturally gives an effect of depth. This is partly because it so strongly recalls the real world, partly because the shading of a photograph gives strong relief to the picture. Starting from this norm the film-maker can either increase the depth of the image or reduce it by various means: for example, by using different camera lenses and different apertures; by lighting (side lighting intensifies modelling, front lighting flattens it); by camera angles (oblique angles will stress depth); by emphasizing or avoiding contrast of scale; and by using either flat settings or settings in depth. Depth can also be brought out by movement of the actors or the camera itself in the line of its axis; by movement of the camera *round* a person or thing either horizontally or vertically; by camera movement combining panning and tracking; and finally, by the use of montage to give different viewpoints of the same object.

Historically, the rendering of depth by film-makers has developed in an interesting way. Space in the theatre and the cinema are very different from each other. The cinema has the advantage that the camera is free to look out from its central point to the limits of the horizon or beyond; it can look out, over a narrow or a broad field, for millions of miles – up to the stars, and down from the clouds to the earth. When Kracauer says that the film enables us to 'penetrate reality' he is talking in a wider, partly metaphorical sense; but this is just as true in purely physical terms. We look out through a window into the whole of the world. Compared with this the theatre is completely circumscribed and contained – we are not looking *out* but *in* – into a box which holds the actors and the action. But the theatre has the advantage that, within this box, the space is real, solid, three-dimensional stuff, not the cinema's moving shadows.

If the cinema and the theatre are different – one asks – why compare them? For one reason because, in the cinema's early beginnings, film directors thought of their work as similar to that of theatrical producers and one can look on the treatment of depth, historically, as a process of emancipation from theatrical influence. In the beginning films were often handled so as to stress their disadvantages compared with the theatre; gradually film-makers learned to minimize the cinema's disadvantage and to make the most of its very real advantage. In the earliest silent films, treatment was completely static, with no movement of the camera and no attempt to build up a composite scene by cutting. The lack of relief was simply accepted or compensated for as far as possible by *trompe-l'oeil* scenery and theatre lighting. Cinematographic space was circumscribed to coincide with theatrical space, for, in the eyes of producers and audience, the one was a reproduction of the other.

But this was all changed when the camera freed itself (and the spectator with it) from the 'orchestral stalls viewpoint', and became mobile, either changing place between shots by cutting, or by moving during the filming of a single shot by panning or tracking. A new phenomenon had arisen: the combination camera-spectator, which had been outside looking on at the scene, now stepped inside the circle of dramatic action and moved about within it as in a real space. A new concept of *cinematographic* space developed which was different from natural space, but was just as different from that of the theatre stage. The way was clear to develop to the limit depth-of-field effects, and the subsequent development of the film spectacle has been along these lines.

The problem of bringing in the third dimension was partly (but only partly) a technical one. It was also very largely a question of deciding that depth was the thing to go for, and determining the best means of achieving it. In fact, almost the first film made by Lumière, *Arrivée d'un Train en Gare*, uses depth of setting, movement (of the train) in the axis of the camera, and oblique shooting-angle to achieve a strong three-dimensional effect. Nevertheless, technical progress did affect style. The earliest lenses, such as Lumière's, could be used only with a narrow aperture, so that depth was a natural feature of the image, unless it was limited (as it often was) by a flat theatrical setting. The narrow aperture demanded strong light to ensure a clear image, so the early roof-top film-makers headed for the clear skies of the south of France and California. As movie production moved indoors, better lenses allowed wider apertures, leading to the era of short depth of field (shallow-focus) with one part of the picture in sharp-focus, the rest in blurry soft-focus. This style naturally allowed the director to lead the viewer's eye towards that part of the image he considered important – and this period saw the dominance of expressionist film theory, which stressed the role of the creator and his moulding of the material.

The director was also more likely to operate by brief shots, with frequent changes of camera set-up, and to move between foreground and background by cutting rather than by letting the action proceed naturally within a setting in depth. The German expressionist school compensated for the flatter settings by careful composition of the image and by using strong chiaroscuro, and there is great solidity about, for example, Fritz Lang's early films, despite shallow-focus and a comparatively static camera. For instance, in *Dr Mabuse* setting in depth is used in several scenes for dramatic purposes.

Then, in the thirties, faster film-stock and stronger studio lighting made the use of small apertures possible under the most difficult conditions, and enabled all parts of the scene at whatever distance from the camera to be kept in sharp-focus. Although in earlier films we find occasional examples of setting in depth, such as the opening of Renoir's *La Chienne* (a shot through a serving-hatch into the room beyond), or the shot of the statue and peasants from *The End of St Petersburg* already mentioned, it was not until Renoir's *La Règle du Jeu*, Orson Welles's *The Magnificent Ambersons*, and William Wyler's *The Best Years of Our Lives* that the style was fully developed.

Welles's *Citizen Kane* was the first film which really used the possibilities offered by improved technology, though the relationship between science and art always works both ways. Welles insisted that cinematographer Gregg Toland find technical answers to the artistic problems Welles set him. Unlike most directors of photography who were (and still are) assigned to a film a few days before the start of shooting, Toland was working on *Kane* for a full six months. The result was a film in which scene after scene uses a setting in depth,[1] with contrasts in dramatic action between background and foreground: there is the death-bed scene, Kane enthroned in bed, the nurse at the door in the background; there is the reporter's first interview with Kane's second wife, Susan Alexander, the reporter in the telephone booth, the drunk woman at a table in the background; there is the shot with Kane's parents in their house and the boy outside in the snow; a counter-shot from outside, the reverse of the previous one; there is the *Chronicle* party taken from behind Bernstein's shoulder; the shot over the shoulders of the *Chronicle* staff looking out of the window at Kane and his fiancée in a cab, just back from Europe; there is the political meeting, Geddes looking down from the gallery at Kane on the platform; opera scenes with Susan Alexander singing; the much-quoted scene of her attempted suicide, with the poison bottle on a bedside table in the foreground; Susan and Kane talking across the vast hall of Xanadu; the scene where she walks through door after door to leave him; and there are many others.

In Tati's *Jour de Fête* there is a scene where contrast between background and foreground is deliberately used for humorous effect. We see a reaper in a field on a hill waving his arms about

1. Plate 15.

frantically to ward off a wasp, while the postman on the road below is cycling peacefully along. Then the reaper, in the foreground, calms down while the postman on his bicycle, in the background, starts waving his arms. And so it goes on, the invisible (and improbable) wasp attacking each of them in turn. The effect is irresistibly comic.

Different visual planes can be created by using windows and mirrors. In Robert Altman's *The Long Goodbye*, Marlowe (Elliott Gould) leaves the house of a couple whom he suspects of some involvement in the case he is investigating. He goes out through glass doors and stands on the beach while they quarrel inside. As they argue, Marlowe's back is reflected on the glass. In one shot we look both into the house and (through the reflection) away from it, and Marlowe's pose emphasizes his limitations as a private eye. He is outside the action, looking the wrong way and cut off from the suspects by the glass. The same director used a mirror in his film *Come Back to the Five and Dime, Jimmy Dean, Jimmy Dean*. The whole story takes place in a café. The wall-mirror behind the counter not only gives depth and variety to this single set, it is also used to extend the action into the past. In the mirror we see the same group of characters on a crucial day several years before: the mirror doubles both space and time. At the climax of Wim Wenders's *Paris, Texas* the hero finally traces his missing wife to a seedy peep-show where he can talk to her only through a two-way mirror. At first he can see her but not she him. Later they adjust the lighting so that each can dimly see the other. The mirror is not only a metaphor for their restricted communication and a very real barrier between them, it also increases the variety of shots of the two faces during a very long scene.

A mirror is used again and again in Fassbinder's *Martha*, in a scene between mother and daughter, and in scenes between Martha and her sadistic husband. As Fassbinder uses it here, the dominant figure is viewed directly, facing the camera and beside a mirror in which the other actor, also full face but smaller and diminished in stature, is reflected. The effect is inclined to be artificial, but it suits Fassbinder's picture of a rich girl terrorized by her husband, with its frequent shots of the heroine obscured by luxuriant indoor foliage, iron grilles, heavy furniture, and with its décor of massive wealth that overpowers and stifles humanity. A more common arrangement is to show the back of an actor or actress looking into a mirror and beside it to show what they see – either their own face, the face of another, or (in the case of vampires!) nothing at all.

CAMERA MOVEMENT AND DEPTH

Camera movements are discussed in the next chapter, but should be briefly noted here as a means of giving a scene solidity. Almost the earliest known use of a moving camera was to achieve this result. The story is that Pastrone had had huge pyramids, palaces, and statues constructed for *Cabiria* (1914), but found with dismay that, when they were filmed from in front with a static camera, they looked quite unimpressive, the relief being so flattened on the screen that they resembled the painted backcloths of a cheap film serial. Then he had the idea of mounting the camera on a cart and wheeling it about the set while filming. The result was a complete success and the sets came alive with startling realism. But, no doubt because of the difficulty of moving heavy apparatus with precision, it was not until much later that camera movements became universal. *Citizen Kane* uses camera movements as freely as setting in depth. It opens with a series of forward tracking-shots, each dissolving into the other and penetrating layer after layer of Kane's physical environment. This physical penetration of space in a way epitomizes the whole film, which is a psychological penetration of Kane's character and private life. Nowadays, as we shall see, the camera is so mobile that it can move round or under or over, even into and through, objects at will. The real depth of locations or sets can be demonstrated to the audience by a camera physically penetrating it. Many films open with complex scenes designed to establish the milieu in which the action is to take place. Alan Rudolph's *Choose Me* starts with the camera prowling up and down the street outside 'Eve's Bar' (a vast neon-lit set) and revealing to us a series of night-life incidents. The camera, and so the viewer, reflects (and reflects on) the activity of the prostitutes who are also patrolling the pavements, 'looking' for action, an appropriately ironic introduction to a story of sexual and emotional entanglements.

Kubrick probed the claustrophobic confines of the army barracks from which there is no escape in *Full Metal Jacket*, while in his earlier film, *Paths of Glory*, he used rapid travelling shots through the comfortless trenches of World War One to contrast with the elegant but cold compositions of the scenes inside the generals' chateau.

Camera movement lies behind the styles of directors as diverse as Murnau, Ophuls, Welles, Bertolucci, Tarkovsky and many lesser talents. Brian de Palma has a predilection for circling shots. His exhilarating hand-held movements round and round the reunited father and daughter at the climax of *Obsession* (harking back to the gentler scene of the two dancing together many years earlier at the film's opening) achieves a delirious emotional impact, lifting the characters free of the sordid airport corridor and their various traumas. Scorsese looks for the opposite effect in *The Color of Money*, in which his circling camera pins his pool players to their tables. Herzog keeps his distance when, at the end of *Aguirre, Wrath of God*, he isolates his doomed conquistador, trapped on his drifting raft with his monkeys and his madness.

Unmotivated, unnecessary camera movement can be distracting and self-regarding, calling attention to itself rather than the material it is showing us. In Stanley Kramer's *Judgment at Nuremberg*, movement is overdone and the camera is constantly prowling round the witnesses until we are giddy. The technique can become tedious, but (like Doctor Johnson's banging his hand on the table) it can almost prove the solidity of a setting.

MONTAGE AND DEPTH

Montage is discussed more fully later, but requires brief mention here in relation to depth. It can be regarded as doing the same thing as a moving camera, but episodically rather than continuously. We look from different *angles* at a scene: we look round a thing through a number of different *shots*. In its way this is equally effective, and we take away just as solid an impression of the space occupied by the Odessa Steps, which are composed from various shots in *Battleship Potemkin*, as we do of Stanley Kramer's Nuremberg court room. There is an interesting shot in Polanski's early film *Knife in the Water*. One of the characters on a yacht holds his finger up and, by a jump cut, the director imitates the effect we get when we look at our finger first through one eye and then the other. When we do this we are seeing *consecutively* what we see *concurrently* in stereoscopic vision, and it is interesting that the cinema can imitate this.

The fundamental difference between montage techniques and setting in depth combined with mobile camera work, is not so much that the newer techniques make space more solid, but that they allow longer shots, longer periods of continuous action, and thus avoid the extreme chopping up of space and time which is the result of concentrated cutting. In doing this they bring the spectator closer to reality by allowing freedom of choice in the focus of his attention; they reintroduce the possibility of ambiguity. With a montage style the viewer's attention is much more firmly directed by the film-maker. Another difference can be illustrated by an example. When a revolver is lying on a table, and someone comes into the room without seeing it, instead of playing on the tension created by the distance between the person and the object, it may be found more convenient in a montage style to show first the person, then the revolver, in separate shots. If the story gains in clarity however, the drama loses in force. The danger is that directors and audience lose the 'sense of the interplay of objects in space' as well as the dramatic values of their physical relationships. The single shots may be made up of very fine pictures but they are often only 'abstract extracts from reality, whereas the architectural view of the world is founded on perception of volumes, constituting, according to *Gestalt* psychologists, meaningful wholes'.[1] Because of the extreme fragmentation due to montage, certain sequences of Eisenstein's *Strike*, as we see them today, are downright incomprehensible. Also montage can lend itself to faking which may be convincing up to a point, but becomes suspect in the end. The familiar scene of hero or heroine threatened by a marauding wild beast is less convincing to the viewer than if he sees (or appears to see) man and animal in the same shot. Numerous underbudgeted films have made use of stock library footage, notably of war scenes, that do not always fit smoothly into the surrounding fiction. The

1. From lectures given by Louis Raitière at the Institut des Hauts Études Cinématographiques, Paris (1945-8).

use of documentary material at the start of a film to set the scene and give veracity is common and often successful, but in Clint Eastwood's *Heartbreak Ridge*, the black and white credit sequence of Vietnam war footage serves only to point up the theatricality of the fiction that follows.

Films adopt a wide variety of means to suggest depth, which ensures using to the full the cinema's power to make us kings of infinite space. This is one reason for the popularity of Westerns, for they allow the eye to travel with more freedom than most films. But it would be wrong to think that depth cannot be created in filming a drawing-room or a prison cell. Much depends on contrast, and the contrast between one foot and ten feet can be as striking as that between half a mile and two miles.

Although it is the norm now to use deep-focus photography, there are always moments when other styles are preferable. Towards the end of Olivier's *Henry V*, for the king's courtship of Katherine, gay, box-like sets give a deliberately theatrical air to the scene. In Godard's *Weekend*, the camera moves along an interminable traffic jam, a procession of accidents, quarrels, breakdowns, an endless ribbon of frustration. The horizontal track is matched by the vertical plane trees that line the road, breaking up the long sequence into something resembling a cartoon strip and ensuring that two dimensions are strongly present in the relative absence of the third. We have already seen how the camera lens can change depth perception. In Altman's *Buffalo Bill and the Indians*, the eponymous hero (Paul Newman) and his entourage are seen approaching on horseback. Using a long-focus lens and shooting from half a mile away, the director flattens the group. They are moving but getting no nearer, emphasizing the lack of vitality in a character already reduced to living a myth, his present a pale and fraudulent reflection of an imaginary past.[1]

All the features of the cinema considered in this chapter – scale, perspective and depth – have demonstrated that the camera's view of the world differs from the eye's. Distortions of perspective, ambiguities of scale, the lack of a third dimension, all can be used by the film-maker to help achieve his aims. They increase the choices available to him both to create a world and to comment upon it. Like every art, the cinema has its special characteristics and techniques, its special way of communicating, through which the artist interprets reality in terms of his unique vision.

CHAPTER THREE

SPACE IN THE CINEMA:
Cutting, Camera Movement, Framing

IN everyday life we are able to focus our whole vision on an object by concentrating our attention on it. This is something we can do consciously at will, but also, just as a matter of everyday habit, we tend to see only what interests us. It is partly the result of moving the head and eyes unconsciously, to direct them and focus them, partly the result of ignoring mentally what is not at the centre of our attention. Our optical system is controlled by the mind, and in the real world the isolation of the object of our attention is achieved subjectively. Part of an artist's training is to unlearn this habitual visual accommodation and educate himself to see the whole scene objectively as the camera does. For camera vision is unlike ordinary human vision in that the camera reproduces the whole of a scene without discrimination and the cinema can imitate the selective capacity of human vision only in a very inferior and clumsy fashion.

In filming, an important method of isolating a particular object is to set up the camera close to it, so that it fills the whole frame and to take a 'close-up' view. Another common method is gradually to move the camera towards an object so as to draw attention to it. Less common methods are to use masks, or to focus sharply on the important part of a scene and leave the rest in soft-focus. Finally, in a film our attention may be caught by a moving figure in an otherwise still landscape, or may be riveted on a particular character or object in the scene because of its position in the setting or the significance it possesses in the development of the plot.

The last three instances are similar to selection in the real world, that is selection exercised by the spectator. The others are dependent on the mechanics of filming and projection, and imply a greater intervention by the film-maker. The presentation of changing viewpoints, which began as an expedient to enable film vision to give the same effect as ordinary vision, soon became a major means of artistic expression. The development of film from a fixed continuous spectacle into a series of points of view enormously increased the scope for film-makers to choose and select their material – fundamental requirements of all artistic creation. How this should be done to make best use of the cinema's essential character has been the subject of much debate. An important theme in the history of film theory has been whether cutting (montage) or framing plus camera movement (*mise-en-scène*) is the fundamental cinematic technique. Both of course depend on the decisions of the film-maker, influenced by the conventions he shares with the audience about film images and ways of presenting them. Since virtually all films incorporate both techniques (which are in any case interrelated) we may assume that both are important.

CUTTING

The technique of cutting determines the nature of cinematographic space and differentiates it from space as we know it in the real world. In the real world, space and the things it contains present themselves to us as an unlimited continuity. We isolate different parts of space by an effort of attention, but the adjoining parts are present peripherally. Our total field of vision is of course limited and changes as we walk, or drive, or move round a corner or into another room. But the change is continuous, its nature is predictable both as regards what appears and what disappears. We know by experience that space and objects in the real world exist before we see them and continue to exist after we have lost sight of them.

In the cinema, by means of shot-change, we are continually jumping from one view to another. There is a parallel in the real world. Watch someone moving their eyes from one side of the room to another: almost invariably you will see them blink as if to eliminate some of the unnecessary visual information passing in front of them. Certainly nothing looks less 'real' than a fast pan from one object to another. The brain simply does not bother to interpret all that is set before it: irrelevant material is just not 'seen'. But in the cinema we can be transported not just across a room or landscape, but from the house to the street, from the town to the country, and from the present to the past. Different parts of space appear before our eyes discontinuously, and objects on the screen appear and disappear without any predetermined spatial relationship. In the cinema we accept this as a matter of course. It is an artistic convention to which we are so accustomed that we are hardly conscious of it. But it is unlike the real world and it may prevent unsophisticated spectators properly understanding a film. Bela Balazs's *Theory of the Film* quotes the case of a well-educated girl visiting Moscow from Siberia who thought the first film she had seen in her life (a comedy) was horrible, because 'human beings were torn to pieces, the heads thrown one way and the bodies the other'. When Griffith showed early close-ups, and a huge severed head smiled at the audience, it caused a sensation. A short Cuban film, *For the First Time* by Octavio Cortazar, shows the amazement, uncontrollable hilarity, even horror, of remote peasants seeing their very first movie, Chaplin's *Modern Times*.

In changing scenes by cutting, the method most commonly used is a straight cut, that is, a shot of one scene is joined directly to a shot of another and when projected the film simply flicks from one scene to the other. For most of the time the spectators watching a film are not consciouly aware of these switches, particularly as the director normally takes care to make his cuts unobtrusive. He may do this by 'cutting on movement', that is, waiting until an actor moves before switching the scene. Or cuts may be to an adjacent part of the same set or to another character and following, or motivated by, the action or the dialogue. The camera follows a glance, a word; there is an underlying musical theme; sight follows sound; a letter sent in one shot is received in the next; and so on. Even if they are to an entirely different scene the audience will not notice them if there is a sufficiently strong motivation in the story. This is what André Bazin calls 'invisible cutting' and it is the normal practice within a single sequence or scene of a film. Although the scene-changes of the cinema are many times more numerous than those of the theatre they are not so obtrusive – mostly we are quite unaware of them.

Transitions

However, when the film-maker wishes to change the action, to carry the plot a stage further or to move to a different place, he will normally wish to stress the change more, so as to give the audience time to adjust themselves and enable them to follow the structure of the story more easily. It is like the break a writer makes by starting a new paragraph, a new section or a new chapter. In this case the director will frequently use, not a straight cut, but a slower transition such as a fade, a dissolve, or a wipe, or he may use various other means of emphasizing the change.

In the case of a fade the old image gradually fades out and there may be a brief period of darkness on the screen. Then the new scene will gradually become visible. A slow fade is particularly suited to indicate the passing of a night or a longer period, or to show a change to another place, perhaps by a journey.

In a dissolve, also called a mix, the new image appears on the screen before the old image fades away and for a moment the two images appear together. A dissolve is a special case of double-exposure and is further discussed under the section on double-exposure in Chapter Six. It is mostly used for transitions from the present to the past or the past to the present, to introduce a memory sequence, to connect two characters who may be physically separated but emotionally linked together or to introduce the thought of a deceased character or a ghost.

A striking transition depending on a dissolve occurs in Peter Medak's *The Ruling Class* when, late at night in the castle, Lady Claire is saying a seductive 'good night' to Jack, Earl of Gurney, who by now sees himself as Jack the Ripper. As they stand embracing the screen grows darker and changes round them until we realize they are in a London street and the scene is set for him to stab her to death.

Again there are devices, such as wipe, iris-out and iris-in, and turn-over, which are more obtrusive and have been criticized for this reason. At one time wipes became a wearisome cliché and lines moved over the screen in every possible direction, wiping out the old image and establishing the new. They can, however, if well handled, be effective. In one of Franju's short films about pollution, *Poussière*, a wipe is used to follow the jaws of a mechanical digger clearing rubbish.

Turn-overs, in which the whole screen seems to turn over, are another artificial form of transition. They are used in Tony Richardson's *Tom Jones*, together with wipes, to make the violent transitions from one sequence to another which suit the hectic pace and jocular tone of the film. George Roy Hill's *The Sting* uses turn-overs in the credits and to separate sequences. The film is constantly turning things inside out, whole incidents prove to be faked or staged, right up to the last episode with its pretended killings. Thus the turn-overs are an appropriate symbol of the main theme. Nowadays such obtrusive devices are rare in the cinema and have found a home in television, where video technology allows an almost infinite variety of bizarre transitions.

Iris-out and iris-in, with its shadow invading from the edges of the screen, is allied to the masking of the German expressionist school of the twenties. It was used by them and also earlier in sentimental silent films but is little seen nowadays. It has been used by 'new wave' directors, for example by Truffaut in *Shoot the Pianist*, but if not as a parody, at least with the self-consciousness of a 'literary reference'.

References to and borrowings from earlier movies 'have occurred right through film history; favourite subjects like *Ben Hur* are repeated again and again, and Hollywood frequently remakes continental pictures. *Dr Mabuse*, to take but one example, has echoes in at least three later films. The police attack on the criminals' hideout in *The Man Who Knew Too Much* owed something to Lang as well as the Sidney Street siege; the shower of banknotes in Clair's *À Nous la Liberté* is remarkably like the shower of banknotes in Mabuse's forgers' den; and Antonioni's stock-exchange scene in *L'Eclisse* presents a realistic version of a similar scene in *Mabuse*. However, the conscious use of film allusions is a modern fashion, stemming largely from the French 'new wave' when Jean-Paul Belmondo seemed almost continually to be re-enacting old American films. Undoubtedly the sequence most subject to plagiarism, parody or 'homage' (it is not always clear which) is Hitchcock's famous shower murder in *Psycho* which has reappeared in countless movies from all parts of the world.

If the early films of Godard probably still contain the most frequent conscious allusions to other films, the new movie-conscious film school graduates, who now figure large in Hollywood circles, are not far behind. A film like Joe Dante's *Gremlins* virtually consists of film references with settings, plot devices, characters and (to a lesser extent) style, recalling movies as diverse as *It's a Wonderful World*, *The Searchers*, *The Thing*, *Snow White and the Seven Dwarfs*, *The Birds*, *The Texas Chainsaw Massacre* and others – one critic counted fifteen titles. Steven Spielberg is another director who consciously refers back to old films: his *Indiana Jones and the Temple of Doom* contained allusions to at least twenty films, all from the period 1934–49, very roughly the setting of the film itself.

One finds cinema allusions not only in style and content but in sets and background. Movie posters figure frequently in the decoration of flats and houses, characters often go to see a film or pass a cinema at some point. Television sets are shown switched on to some well-known and relevant film, most often a science fiction movie or, if it's a Spielberg film, probably a cartoon. In Godard's *Le Mépris*, Fritz Lang played the part of a film director, and commented at various points on his own earlier work. Since then the sight of film-makers playing small roles has been a common one. In *The American Friend*, Wim Wenders cast Nicholas Ray in the part, significantly, of a faker, an artist producing 'original' works by a dead painter. Sam Fuller has appeared in a number of films. Wenders, in *The State of Things* (another film rich in movie allusions), had Fuller in the role of a veteran movie photographer in the 'film within a film'. Fuller actually played a film director in both Dennis Hopper's *The Last Movie* and Godard's *Pierrot Le Fou*. John Landis's comedy-thriller, *Into the Night*, included brief appearances by Don Siegel, Roger Vadim, David Cronenberg, Lawrence Kasdan, Paul Mazursky, Jack Arnold and others with Landis himself playing an incompetent gangster. As we shall see later, many films have taken film-making itself as their theme.

Returning to transitions, the move from one sequence to another may be emphasized by a variety of other methods. There may be for instance, a recurrent *leitmotif* – visual or musical. In Griffith's *Intolerance*, there is a repeated shot of a woman (Lillian Gish) rocking a cradle, a symbol of time, of eternity, of rebirth, taken from a poem by Walt Whitman ('out of the cradle endlessly rocking') – this shot is used as a link between the different episodes of the film. In Max Ophuls's *La Ronde*, there is a hurdy-gurdy tune as well as the image of the roundabout which connect episode to episode. In Godard's *Vivre Sa Vie*, each part of the film is introduced by fully-worded, numbered chapter headings written as sub-titles on the film. James Ivory used the actual chapter headings written by E. M. Forster to introduce each section of his film *A Room With a View*. In Bob Fosse's *Cabaret*, the progress of the story is punctuated by cabaret turns, each referring to incidents – money troubles, Nazi brutality, love betrayed – in the life of the characters. There is a similar interaction in Richard Attenborough's *Oh! What a Lovely War*, though in that case the music-hall atmosphere flavours the whole film.

A transition from sequence to sequence may be stressed by a sort of visual or sound pun – in Hitchcock's *The Thirty-Nine Steps* we switch from a woman shrieking to a train whistling. In Karel Reisz's *Saturday Night and Sunday Morning* one sequence ends with Albert Finney banging down the dustbin lid because his girl-friend's mother has sent him off home; the noise then changes to the clang of the factory where he works, and introduces us to the next sequence. In Bo Widerberg's *Raven's End*, there is a series of transitions depending on football jerseys. First we see them taken off the washing line, then ironed by the hero's mother, then in the dressing room, then on the football field: the camera follows the jerseys.

The link between two sequences may be one of similarity or opposition. Sometimes there is a similarity of shape, as when the picture changes from the angular limbs of a cricket to those of a reaping machine in Eisenstein's *The General Line*, or in Kubrick's dramatic transition in *2001* from the bone thrown by the pre-historic ape to the bone-shaped spaceship drifting through the heavens four million years later. In Losey's *King and Country*, there is a grim transition, by similarity of shape, from a corpse huddled in the mud to the doomed hero, Hamp, lying asleep in the mud of his dug-out prison. In Buñuel's *Tristana* there is a cut from a round stove in the room, over which Don Carlos, old and forlorn, is crouching, to the round top of a gay lottery machine in the park with people crowding round. In this case there is similarity of shape and opposition of mood. In Faraldo's *BOF* the camera moves from the bare feet of the easy-going wife lying in bed to the bare feet of the negro street-sweeper as he lolls in the husband's lorry, his feet against the windscreen. In Alan Sekers's *Arp Statue*, the camera goes from the tangle of a girl's hair to a tangle of barbed wire in a Belfast street. In Bert Haanstra's film, *The Human Dutch*, there is a sequence in which he shows live-action shots of streets in Amsterdam completely still and deserted during the two minutes' silence of Armistice Day; in each case these dissolve into a photo of exactly the same street, this time with civilian prisoners being marched away or with Nazis ill-treating the inhabitants. As he has chosen exactly the same places with the same outlines of houses one shot dissolves exactly into the other and forms a most effective bridge connecting the present to the past. On the other hand there is a clashing contrast in a transition at the start of Sam Peckinpah's *The Getaway*. The movie opens with a rural, park-like scene of deer grazing, then we move to a prison set in these open grounds and to its violence and brutality. In Fugard's *Boesman and Lena*, there is a striking sequence in which the camera cuts from the derelict African couple floundering in the mud to a flock of seagulls circling overhead.

There may also be a connection through identity of shooting-angle. Following an aerial sequence, for example, the director may introduce the next scene with a shot from above, to bring us down from air to ground. The camera may move quickly through one or more intermediate shots. In *Devi* (*The Goddess*), directed by Satyajit Ray, one sequence ends with a young wife thinking of her husband who is away studying at a university. Her face dissolves into a shot of water, the camera pans upwards over the water to a shot of a sailing boat in the distance, then there is a cut to a shot of the husband sitting in the boat coming to visit his wife.

Transition may be by means of an unadorned straight cut. But unlike the invisible cutting of narrative, the director will want to make it startling rather than unobtrusive – for instance, by going straight into a close-up. It used to be normal practice to use a close-up only after an audience was used to a scene by seeing it in long or medium 'establishing' shots. But for scene-changing purposes (and not uncommonly nowadays) the director will cut directly to a close-up of some completely new object or person. For a second the viewers may not even be able to identify it. Then the camera will pull back or turn and the new scene become clear. In Bertolucci's *La Commare Secca* the story is cast in the form of a police inquiry, each part of the film is connected with a different witness, and is introduced by a close-up of the person concerned. Another straight cut (though not to a close-up and with affinities to previous categories) is in Coward and Lean's *In Which We Serve*. Celia Johnson is reading her children *The Walrus and the Carpenter* and as she gets to the lines: 'He did his very best to make The billows smooth and bright', there is a sudden cut to a great explosion in the sea as her husband's ship, the *Torrin*, is bombed by enemy planes.

Finally, the scene may be changed not by editing at all, but by camera movement – movement into the future, into the past or through space to another place. This comes up again in the section on camera movement, but an example from James Ivory's *Savages* may be given here. The movie shows two worlds – an elegant, cultured society, and the primitive 'mud' people who gradually invade the decadent culture. We move from one world to the other when the camera follows a croquet ball which has been struck too hard and rolls off the lawn through more and more tangled undergrowth and forest until it reaches the 'mud' people who pick it up wonderingly.

Uses of Cutting

Having discussed the different means of cutting from one scene to another, we consider now the purpose for which cutting can be used by the film-maker. In the first place it enables him to change the scene as the story requires, to further the action and to provide variety. It corresponds more or less to changes of setting or scenery in the theatre although in the cinema the changes can be far more frequent. This is the most important and obvious use of cutting.

A second function of cutting – exercised in practice at the same time as the first – is to eliminate unwanted material. All the narrative arts generally condense the events of real life. It is only exceptionally that they either retain everything within a restricted space and time, or expand and dwell on it. Normally a film will cut from a shot of a man catching a train to one of him having lunch in the dining-car, arriving with bags at a house, answering the question 'Did you have a good trip?', keeping a prearranged appointment abroad, or simply strolling in a strange town – in every case omitting much that would be there in reality but is not significant for the story. How much can be left out is a matter of style and convention.

Over the years convention can become fossilized into 'rules' that directors feel compelled to obey. The French 'new wave' was, in part, a reaction against such long accepted conventions. In *À Bout de Souffle* (*Breathless*), Godard broke the rules of cutting, making his characters jump from one place to another in a way that ignored the established practice.

Besides the new wave, the influence of television has been important. In fact a wide variety of styles caters for the more fragmented audiences of the present. While the smoother cutting of convention continues in films made for generally more conservative audiences, a violent jump-cut style with fast action, garish lighting and sudden time change, is seen in many films, stemming from a number of influences, among them animated cartoons and the video-films which accompany pop music programmes.

Much of the elimination of unnecessary action takes place in the script, but there is further paring down during the making of the picture. For every shot a little more than the minimum will be photographed and the exact length determined when the film is edited. Many scenes shot will be excluded from the final print, other scenes will be shot from a variety of angles, and the best selected during editing. Most shots will be repeated and only the best of the takes will appear in the film itself. Thus more film will be exposed than is ultimately used. The proportion of film shot to film projected is known as the 'cutting ratio' and varies from director to director and from film to film. It may be higher than 20 to 1 (Elaine May is reputed to have gone as high as 140 to 1 when making *Mikey and Nicky*, Fritz Lang's *Metropolis* had a ratio of 150 to 1 and the extravagant Howard Hughes with *Hell's Angels* a baffling 250 to 1) or as low as 4 to 1 or less. All depends on the film-maker's personal approach which varies as it does in all the arts. Cecil Beaton took many photographs of a subject, Cartier-Bresson only a few. One painter will do dozens of sketches for a painting, another will paint it without a single draft. Robert Louis Stevenson was said to have written almost without correction, Honoré de Balzac wrote draft after draft, each a mass of alterations. A high cutting ratio may imply perfectionism as in the cases of Chaplin, von Stroheim, Kubrick or David Lean, who will carry on shooting until their precise vision has been transferred to film; or it may reflect the style of a director 'shooting on the wing', using improvisation and waiting for a magical moment. It may mean that the director doesn't know what he is looking for – just as a low ratio may reflect either a high degree of preparation and rehearsal, or a greater concern for spontaneity and the broad picture than for the precision of individual images, or simply a low budget and short schedule. Whichever way, it is the final result that matters.

Thirdly, cutting can be used to build up a picture of an object, an action, or a person, by taking them from different aspects. By doing this it can give a very full picture with great economy, perhaps bringing out various traits which can be contrasted, or combined, with emphasis on particular features. For instance in *Last Tango in Paris* the camera introducing us to Marlon Brando shows his rather flamboyant coat, peers at his wrinkles, at the bags under his eyes, at his morose expression. Again in the tango dance scene, the camera cuts from shot to shot of legs at odd angles, of couples frozen in grotesque stances making them both beautiful and ridiculous. In Pollack's *Out of Africa*, when the heroine (Meryl Streep) is going from Mombasa to Nairobi, shots from different angles, close-ups and long-shots, build up a picture in the round of the old-fashioned train in which she is travelling.

Because of cutting, the cinema can show actors' faces large enough to let us see their expression in every detail.[1] It can show contrasting expressions, turn and turn about, in the shot and countershot of conversations. Cutting also enables the camera to follow a glance or a gesture and reveal its meaning; or it may be used to follow a person moving. Thus, like camera movement, it allows action over a wider field to be shown in the closest detail.

Cutting may make space seem larger. Half-a-dozen shots of a prison-cell from half-a-dozen different points of view, seen in succession, will give a mental impression of much greater amplitude than looking round the actual cell from inside it. The camera can give a powerful impression of a crowded party, of a jostling crowd, of packed traffic through cutting together shots which by themselves would be unimpressive.

Again, cutting can create space affinities which do not really exist. We see the hero of a film struggling in a river that is racing faster and faster, then we cut to a shot of a huge waterfall with a

1. Plate 17.

body going over the falls. The racing stream and the waterfall may be entirely different rivers, the shots may be taken at entirely different times and the body going over the falls may be a dummy – but the audience accepts the relationships of place and time which the director has suggested by cutting them together. When we see two men struggling on a parapet and then a shot looking fifty storeys down to the street, we are convinced that the two men are on top of the building. Horror films are interesting in this respect as they play upon the spectator's desire for pattern and meaning. Time and again in such pictures we are led to believe in a particular spatial relationship between the victim with whom we are encouraged to identify and the assailant, creature or nameless horror that lies in wait. Once we have been led to expect an attack from one direction we are confounded when it suddenly erupts from another, or 'we' run desperately *away* from the menace, only to dash straight into its arms. On other occasions we are led, through intercutting of killer and victim, to expect an imminent confrontation. As we stare transfixed, the door handle turns, the door opens – and a friendly face greets us. This surge of relief is often followed almost immediately by the now unexpected appearance of the aggressor. John Carpenter is one director particularly adept at manipulating an audience in this way.

This associative cutting, whereby meaning is carried over from one shot or series of shots to another, will be discussed further under montage. It can be used quite mundanely to reduce the cost of a movie by, say, taking a few shots of a real castle in Germany, then combining them with shots of studio-built walls or less authentic locations nearer home. It can be used for contrast humorously, dramatically or with bitterness as for example in Solanas's *The Hour of the Furnaces*, which intercuts shots of cattle being slaughtered with women's glossy advertisements. Another brutal contrast is in *The Godfather*, when scenes of an infant being baptized in church are intercut with the bloody murder of the Corleone family's enemies. Here the visual contrast is matched by a thematic parallel between the two apparently different scenes: they are linked by the single concern of the family's retention of power. Both are crucial for the continuation of the Corleone influence into the next generation. In Harry Watt's war documentary *Squadron 992*, one sequence opens with poachers setting a terrier on to catch a hare. The sound of the planes is heard and we see a Spitfire chasing a German bomber. The parallel action is intercut until the terrier catches the hare and the bomber is shot down.

It should be noted that, in the real world, vision is controlled by attention, but in the cinema it is the other way round: attention is controlled by vision. In everyday life we see what we attend to; in the cinema we attend to what we see – that is, what the film director chooses to show us. In fact in a dozen different ways (not only by cutting, but by camera movement, by setting, by lighting, by movement of actors, by composition, by colour, and so on) it is part of the film-maker's art to determine what the viewer will see. If he so wishes, the director has a wide array of techniques at his disposal through which he can attempt to dominate and manipulate his audience. We cannot escape the insistent close-ups[1] of the cinema: the hands of Lillian Gish in *Intolerance*; the shattered glasses and face streaming with blood of the woman in the Odessa Steps sequence of *Battleship Potemkin*; the ragged feet of the prisoners-of-war in Lean's *The Bridge on the River Kwai*; the fingers of the dying Harry Lime in *The Third Man* as they gradually slip from the grating of the sewer; the explosive world of *Rambo* with its rippling muscles and glamorized weaponry. Cutting is one of the most powerful techniques through which the film-maker can guide the viewer and, as we shall see, has been the subject of much speculation as to its aesthetic dimension.

CAMERA MOVEMENT

Russian directors in the great era of montage avoided camera movements because, it was said, they tended to remind the spectator of the presence of the camera. It must be supposed that they did so largely because camera movements were something out of the ordinary. Nowadays when they are used so freely in almost every film, the audience takes them for granted and is most likely to get an artificial impression from films like Ozu's *Early Autumn* or *Tokyo Story*, in which camera movements are entirely avoided. It

1. Plate 48.

is an impression which Ozu deliberately cultivated, as does Shengayala in *Pirosmani* where the static style suits the subject – a primitive Georgian painter. From an objective point of view, cutting is just as arificial as camera movement, and in some ways camera movement is closer to our experience of real space than constant cutting from one shot to another. Certainly camera movement can give an emotional effect very different from shot-change. When the camera at the end of *Black Orpheus* (directed by Marcel Camus) pans upward from the sad mortality of the lovers, dead upon the rocks, to finish on the eternal loveliness of Rio's hills and sky and seas – when, in the first part of Antonioni's *L'Avventura*, the camera lifts from the scurrying human ants searching the island for the missing girl to brood on the majesty of the approaching storm – when, at the end of *L'Avventura*, we lift our eyes from the unfaithful lover and the betrayed girl, from the contemplation of human limitation and weakness to the massive strength of a distant, snow-covered mountain – in each of these three cases it would not have been possible to get exactly the same effect by cutting from one image to the other. Because it is continuous, the panning is able to say: here is this, there is that – so different, yet they belong to the same world.

It is the same with a tracking-shot, which starts off with a general scene and steadily moves so as to concentrate on a particular person or thing of dramatic importance. While cutting to a close-up works suddenly and dramatically surprises us, the tracking-shot takes us by the hand and leads us to the heart of the drama. There is a gradual selective process, progressive elimination of unnecessary elements, until finally only the essential central element remains. Cutting may be regarded as the spatial equivalent of a sudden leap of thought or feeling: tracking as the spatial expression of a gradual growth of ideas or emotion. Tracking can work up to a focus of attention and slowly and fully emphasize the key point of a drama. In *The General Line* when the moujiks are gathered round the separator, Eisentein uses a slow forward tracking-shot to express their wonder at the magic of the thing, its gradual invasion of their consciousness, a physical projection of their curiosity and expectation.

But camera movement, although it is more natural than cutting, is still very far from reality. When we turn our head there is not the same finality, not the same evenness of pace, as when we turn the camera. In nature our attention bounds, stops, goes on, goes back – it is more flexible, more spontaneous; above all, it is unconscious. Also, in reality both what is to come and what has just been left are *there* simultaneously; there is no edge to our attention. In a panning-shot what is to come is unknown, what is left behind is decisively gone. As with cutting, so with camera movements – in the cinema there is constant 'material creation and annihilation of space and what it contains'.

Again, camera movement gives rise to transference effects. We have already discussed these in connection with tracking-shots. They can be present just as strongly in panning-shots. To someone watching a vertical panning-shot of a building from the ground floor to the roof, it may seem as if the building is sinking into the earth, while a lateral panning-shot may make it seem as if the landscape for some mysterious reason is moving in the opposite direction. In everyday life when we turn our head so that the landscape moves, the muscular and the visual sensations form a habitual total experience to which we are accustomed, and we know by experience what is happening. In the cinema we miss the feeling of muscular movement – we know we have *not* turned our head and, therefore, the movement must be elsewhere. By going repeatedly to the cinema, viewers become accustomed to making an automatic distinction between the space world which the characters of the film inhabit (the screen) and the space world they are sitting in (the auditorium), but an unsophisticated spectator has the feeling that he is in the same world as that which appears on the screen.

To illustrate the strength of visual habits it is worth mentioning a fairground illusion called 'The Crazy Cottage' which depends on transference. It consists of a small lightly-constructed room, fixed to revolve round a pole which runs horizontally through it. There is a bench fixed along the pole on which a dozen people can sit. To all appearances the room is furnished normally but everything (carpet, table, vase, flowers, plates, cup, books, pictures, etc.) is invisibly fastened or stuck down. When the people have been seated on the bench and, to complete the illusion, strapped in, the box of a room is rocked by machinery. For the people on the bench, habituated all their life to the stability of the rooms they live in, there is complete transference of movement. It is they on the bench who seem to move, and they lean this way and that to maintain an imaginary balance, cling to the bench and to each other, and scream with fear and excitement. In the climax the room is turned completely upside down, and the people feel as if they are hanging, heads down, from the ceiling.

This phenomenon of transference can be displayed in the cinema. In Kubrick's *2001*, a stewardess on a space shuttle walks down an aisle, reaches a hallway and then appears to walk up its curved wall leaving through another exit upside down. In fact the 'stationary' foreground aisle is a revolving drum and it is this part of the set, including the camera, which turns upside down while the stewardess stays upright walking a treadmill.[1] The audience, unaccustomed to a camera roll, naturally assumes that it must be the (circular) hallway rather than the (rectangular) aisle which moves. The same technique was used for Fred Astaire's dance up the walls and across the ceiling in Donen's *Royal Wedding*, and to help Jeff Goldblum hang upside down on the ceiling and run down the walls in the 1986 remake of *The Fly*. Another unusual camera movement, swirling, is also used to produce a transference effect, usually to indicate fainting or vertigo.

Another departure from reality is that in tracking-shots, especially forward tracking-shots, which are often elevated above the ground, there is a strange sense of dream-like power. The camera can be moved in ways which are denied us in real life. There are vertical tracking-shots up the face of a building or cliff. There is the opening of Wilder's *The Lost Weekend*, when the camera moves smoothly over the skyscrapers of New York to finish at the window of a flat where a flask of whisky is hanging. One of the earliest and most celebrated of tracking-shots is at the beginning of Murnau's *The Last Laugh* (1924). The shot begins in the street, moves in at the spacious hotel entrance past the lordly doorman (Emil Jannings) and finishes in the manager's office. Equally impressive is the long ride into the city in Murnau's American film, *Sunrise*, as the young couple take a tram. This is one case in which a tracking-shot is literally life-like: both trams and cameras move on tracks. A further good example of tracking is

1. Plate 11.

in Renoir's *La Grande Illusion*, where the camera moves round von Rauffenstein's room picking out the objects which typify his Prussian, aristocratic background (the part is played by von Stroheim) – riding-whip, gloves, perfume, and so on. The result in the one case is quite unlike someone walking into a hotel, and in the other case unlike someone going into a room and examining the objects in it – but both are undeniably effective.

Panning movements may have an entirely subjective effect. They are frequently used in crowd scenes to convey the onset of panic, or in chase sequences to suggest the pursued searching for avenues of escape. A striking example of a subjective tracking-shot is in de Sica's *Umberto D*, where the old man, almost at the end of his tether, looks out of the window. With a sudden forward movement – a zoom-shot[1] – of the camera, the stones of the pavement rush up at us. We get a vivid expression of the old man's thought – merely a thought – of suicide. In Steven Spielberg's *Jaws* there is an intricate combination of tracking-shot and zoom,[2] a 'triple-zoom-reverse' shot, which refines the similar effect used by Hitchcock to suggest James Stewart's *Vertigo*. As Roy Scheider, the police chief, thinks he spots a shark's fin in a sea packed with bathers, Spielberg's camera tracks in from the distance towards Scheider – at the same time as the lens is zoomed backwards. The actor is kept in constant size, framing and perspective while the camera rushes to within inches of his face. By distorting the background during the shot and changing the viewer's relationship to the actor and his setting, Spielberg creates a unique frisson of suspense and shock.

In Costa-Gavras's *Z*, about a courageous liberal politician (Yves Montand) who is struck down and killed after a political meeting, the camera looks down on the crowd from the meeting-hall, then moves among the excited throng with a strong feeling of involvement, of violence, jostling, of imminent danger. Then when he has been fatally clubbed, the swaying movement and blurred focus carry us with him on his last journey. Hitchcock is celebrated for his camera movements and there is an unusual one in *Frenzy*. The

1. See page 52

2. See page 52 for the relationship of zoom and tracking-shot.

story involves a murderer who lives in a flat near Covent Garden. We have already seen one woman strangled by him in horribly close detail. A second time would be too much, and as the murderer ushers his second victim into the flat the door shuts and the camera tracks back, down the stairs, out of the front door and into the street as if from something it cannot bear to look at. It then pans up to the window of the flat, and cuts to a comedy scene with the detective sadly preparing to tackle his wife's attempt at French cooking.

In *Brief Encounter*, directed by David Lean, when the heroine nearly commits suicide and leans towards the rails as the express train comes in, there is a light spiral movement of the camera which expresses her feeling of giddiness. Then, like slaps on her cheek, we see the lighted windows of the train flicker across her face while the draught of the train blows her hair, cuts her breath, and brings her back to reason. In Sternberg's *The Blue Angel*, Emil Jannings, dismissed and disgraced, sits in despair in his empty class-room gazing on nothing. The camera draws back foot by foot as if following his gaze, as if measuring the void he sees before him. In Cocteau's *Les Parents Terribles* when Sophie, feeling she has lost her son, is stealing out of the drawing-room where her husband, her sister, and her son, Mic, are gathered round Mic's resplendent young fiancée, the camera backs away with her, expressing her withdrawal from a world she feels has rejected her. In this case the lighting (light and gay on the group, sombre and tragic on Sophie) reinforces the effect.[1]

Subjectivity may go further. Following the camera, the spectator may move like a sick man, or a runner, or he may trip, fall, be jostled, trodden on; he may become a rolling stone, a flying arrow, a diving aeroplane, a striking axe, a bird, a top, a projectile. The theme of *The Hill* is a brutal punishment camp where men are given literally killing fatigues, climbing up and down a steep hill in blazing sun in full kit with gas-masks on. To express their agony the director Sidney Lumet includes shots taken through the eye-piece of a gas-mask with an unsteady camera. Edgar Anstey in *Granton Trawler* used shots in which the camera had fallen over with its mechanism still running and recorded nightmare gyrations

1. Plate 16.

of deck, masts, and flying clouds, to convey the intensity of a violent storm. In *Napoleon*, Abel Gance had his cameras thrown as snowballs, fired as cannon-balls, dropped from a cliff into the sea, fixed to the saddle of a cantering horse, and mounted on a swinging platform during a scene of a stormy meeting of the Convention during the French Revolution, to give the scene the movement of a raging sea.

As equipment has improved, fluent and expressive camera movements have become easier to achieve. If this statement suggests that art is dependent on technology, it should be borne in mind that the relationship is by no means always in that direction. As has been noted already, technological development also responds to the demands of the artist. Stanley Kubrick's exacting specifications have consistently resulted in the discovery of new ways of working. George Lucas set up his own special effects company, Industrial Light And Magic, to provide answers to the questions his fantasy productions continually raise. Back in 1923, scriptwriter Carl Mayer induced photographer Guido Seeber to build a special tripod which would move on rails in order to be able to film certain scenes Mayer had written for *New Year's Eve*. A year later, whilst preparing the script for *The Last Laugh*, Mayer consulted photographer Karl Freund to discover how far it would be possible to go in filming long sections with a continuously mobile camera. At Mayer's instigation, Freund researched new ways of achieving such a style and Mayer rewrote his script to enable director Murnau to explore it to the full.

The modern camera is lightweight and mobile: it can be mounted in helicopters, on speeding boats, carried in various ways and be made independent of the operator, who controls it by computer, viewing through a monitor not fixed to the camera itself. Aerial photography – nowadays by helicopter, though D. W. Griffith used a balloon – has become almost a cliché, though striking effects can still be achieved. Kubrick flew his camera over the Hebrides and Monument Valley to create the 'Stargate' sequence for *2001*. For the opening shots of *The Shining*, he hired a specialist aerial photographer and sent him to Glacier National Park in Montana to create the ominous mood of Jack Torrance's car journey and to emphasize the isolation of his eerie destination, the haunted Overlook Hotel.

The French-invented Louma camera (like a camera on the end of a fishing rod) was first used by Polanski when making *The Tenant* in 1976. It is ideal for use with miniatures where the lens needs to be as low as half an inch above the ground, or for snaking between heads and shoulders of a crowd, or in confined spaces like those encountered by Wolfgang Peterson when filming *The Boat* almost entirely inside a German U-boat. Spielberg made effective use of the Louma in *Raiders of the Lost Ark* for a five-minute take inside a crowded Nepalese bar during Karen Allen's drinking contest, and he was so impressed with it that he used it as his main camera for both the live action and special effects shooting of his hectic comedy *1941*. At the opening of *To Live and Die in L.A.*, William Friedkin used a Louma to film his secret service agent standing on a bridge. It enabled him to move from behind the man looking down into the water below; go over his head showing the huge drop below; and then to swing out above the water and turn back to show the man's face – objective and subjective points of view fused within a single fluid shot.

Another significant development has been the Steadicam (invented by Garrett Brown) and the similar Panaglyde. These are systems of springs and balances which take all the unsteadiness out of hand-held camerawork. This allows smooth tracking-shots to be achieved in places where tracks cannot be laid or where they would be seen by the camera, and enables the operator to run, climb stairs, turn round and so on without jerky results. Brown himself operated the Steadicam shooting in *The Shining*, notably shots of the small boy racing his tricycle around the hotel's endless corridors, and the climactic deadly chase through the snow-covered maze. In Malick's *Days of Heaven*, the young couple played by Richard Gere and Brooke Adams discuss the marriage proposal made to her by her employer (Sam Shepard). The whole scene takes place as they wade around in the river and was largely improvised without set movements. Only the Panaglyde used by Nestor Almendros could have followed their every movement – just as later in the story, it could trace the unpredictable progress of a fire in the wheatfields, going right up to the flames with dizzying, dramatic movements. The Panaglyde was used for shooting as much as sixty per cent of John Huston's *Under the Volcano*. The recently introduced Skycam is a further evolution: a design of poles and wires from which are suspended a camera, gyroscopically and radio controlled, combining characteristics of the crane, the Steadicam and the helicopter.

Even without such devices, modern lightweight cameras offer unprecedented flexibility. The low-budget horror movie *The Evil Dead* forced its makers to improvise. In place of a Steadicam, director Sam Raimi fixed a camera in the centre of a plank fifteen feet long. Two men simply held each end and 'ran like hell' to achieve the very effective final shot as an unseen power (the camera takes its place in a subjective shot) stirs in the forest, races down the hillside, through a house and right up to the back of the victim who barely has time to turn and scream. The film ends on a huge close-up of his startled face. In other shots the director carried the camera (weighing only ten pounds) strapped to one hand.

A master of the more conventional tracking-shot is Brian de Palma. His *Dressed to Kill* is virtually an essay on tracking, the whole effect of which depends on the audience's familiarity with the accepted conventions. The film's major sequences are all variations on the theme of surveillance, developing the notion so disquietingly proposed by Hitchcock in *Rear Window* - the cinema spectator as helpless voyeur. Each scene from *Dressed to Kill* challenges the viewer's assumption that he, like the camera, is 'following' the action. Repeatedly we believe we have interpreted the action correctly, only to have our expectations shattered. In the bravura museum sequence, as the doomed heroine (Angie Dickinson) follows a curious stranger, she (and we) are continually unsure of his whereabouts and are nonplussed by the unexpected, disembodied hand that retrieves her fallen glove at the end of the scene. Slowly we realize that it was Angie herself (and us) who were being followed. Later, in a subway chase, we are taken by surprise when the killer suddenly appears because we think we have seen him in another part of town. The shock is doubled when the fleeing heroine (now it is Nancy Allen) is rescued by a character we have not previously seen in the chase, and do not expect to be involved. Here the shocks are achieved by cuts, showing that de Palma is as adept at manipulating his audience through this technique as through camera movement. As we have indicated before, neither process is necessarily more 'truthful' or 'real' than the other.

The comments and examples given show that camera movement

can (though in each case with a difference in flavour) perform functions similar to cutting – scene changing; elimination of unwanted material; building up a picture; creating by juxtaposition affinities and contrasts. Like cutting, camera movement can also enrich and amplify the spatial qualities of a scene. If cutting usually remains the glue that holds most narrative films together, it is no longer thought of as the indispensable essence of film art: camera movement is clearly just as expressive. At the same time, it is true that whereas many films have been made without camera movement it is harder to conceive of a film without cuts. Hitchcock's *Rope* (see next chapter) comes closest and it remains a unique experiment. Jim Jarmusch's *Stranger than Paradise* consists entirely of a few long takes, each separated by four seconds of blank screen, so that conventional cutting is absent. Angelopoulos's epic *The Travelling Players* consists of only about thirty shots in its nearly four-hour duration, and camera movement is used not only to indicate a change in space but also changes in time. In single continuous shots the director includes episodes from different decades as he constructs a complex allegory of recent Greek history. A few films (Warhol's *Empire* for example) appear to consist of one long static shot.

But these are exceptions that prove the rule – camera movement cannot replace cutting as a technique for film narration. It is, on the other hand, frequently indispensable for indicating spatial relationships within a scene. In *The Emerald Forest*, the young man, Tommy, (played by director John Boorman's son Charlie) needs to reach his parents who live at the top of a high-rise building. Brought up in the Amazonian jungle he knows only one way to accomplish this task – by climbing the outside of the skyscraper. Various strategies were used to make the climb convincing but it is the first shot that is crucial. Starting on Tommy's face, the camera tilts and tracks as he climbs the first three storeys in continuous action. Cutting would have destroyed the audience's belief that the boy was really climbing: by tilting upward the camera also showed the whole height of the building and the scale of Tommy's task. Having won over the audience, the director could then complete the scene without his son having to clamber all the way up.

Worth noting finally is Fassbinder's *Chinese Roulette*, a film which charts the course of splintering relationships almost entirely through camera movement. The breaking up of family ritual is reflected (literally) in mirrors, which fracture the seamless images of Fassbinder's elegant tracking-shots in a way that comments on relationships as no style based on cutting could hope to do.

FRAMING

The fragmentation of space in the cinema is accentuated by the limitation of the cinema screen with its sharply-defined 'frame'. The picture in the cinema is a fixed rectangle which shows us only a section of reality. This limitation has in the past been regarded as a disadvantage and attempts have been made to overcome it by using larger and larger screens, the ideal being an unlimited screen whose vast expanse would give the spectator the sensation of being immersed in reality itself. In 1900 Grimoin-Samson tried to do this with his cineo-rama; in 1959 the American circarama, and later the Russian circlarama, by using a screen which curved round behind the audience, succeeded in surrounding it with images, if not reality. Many pleasure parks now offer short cinema shows on giant screens, though nobody has yet found anything very interesting to show on them. Currently the best large projection format is the IMAX 70-mm system, a Canadian development which uses a screen forty-five feet high by sixty-two feet across. There is an example at the National Museum of Photography, Film and Television, in Bradford.

But it is not fundamentally a question of size. Reality exists all round us; above, below, in front, behind. In real life we do, in a way, frame what we see by directing our attention, but as soon as we concentrate our attention on, say, the left limit of what we can see, our eyes and our head move involuntarily and the limit moves with them; the same happens on the right, above or below. Any screen must have some edge, if not at the sides, then at the top or bottom.

In any case, the frame of the cinema has artistic uses. First, it allows film-makers to choose, to isolate, to limit the subject, to show only what is mentally and emotionally significant. Unnecessary or irrelevant material can be eliminated and the camera concentrated on what is essential.

Secondly, the frame forms a basis for the composition of shots by giving them an architecture, an equilibrium, a meaning. The rectangle of the screen constitutes a frame of reference from which to organize and orientate the contents of the picture. Like the proscenium of the theatre, it provides an area of plastic composition as well as a centre of dramatic action. A chapter could be written about the composition of the film image in relation to the frame. Here there is space for no more than a few words. One notes the constant use of stairways in the cinema to provide diagonal lines of movement contrasting with the rectangle of the frame. In many films the camera has stressed the dominating vertical structure of the modern city overpowering its inhabitants. In the 'Superman' films the horizontal shape of the cinemascope frame is used to reflect the vast horizons, both physical and psychological, that its hero's powers can encompass. Similarly, in Peter Bogdanovich's *Paper Moon*, the wide screen is well suited to the open stretches of the Middle West travelled by the fraudulent Bible salesman and his precocious companion (Ryan and Tatum O'Neal). Another example is Rossellini's *Paisa* in which the endless flat expanses of the Po marshes are brilliantly used.

Thirdly, any picture isolated by strongly marked boundaries has the property of attracting attention. The main function of a telescope's tube is to hold the magnifying lenses – but if we look through a tube with no lenses, we can still see the tiny field it covers more clearly than with the naked eye. Furthermore, the very act of *framing* by itself can begin to create a work of art. The frame does more than isolate a picture; it pushes it together and gives it a unity it would not otherwise have. By isolating part of a landscape and transferring it from its natural setting to another setting – a house or museum – a painter presents this section of reality under new conditions of vision which bring out artistic values that its natural surroundings would hide or neutralize. The spectator sees it with new eyes. I. A. Richards saw a like effect in poetry:

> Through its very appearance of artificiality metre produces ... the 'frame' effect, isolating the poetic experience from the accidents and irrelevancies of everyday existence.

Similarly, by extracting a fragment of reality from the chaos of nature and projecting it on to the screen, the cinema enables us to see beauty and meaning in it which otherwise would be hidden by utilitarian commonplace.[1] There are innumerable examples of unexpected delights of this kind in the cinema: the play of light on water in a filthy gutter, washing drying on the line, a smoking chimney, the pattern on a dilapidated wall, a hand occupied in some skilled task, the curve of a cheek ... Without being isolated, set in a frame and magnified in size, such mundane, such sordid objects would never attract us. In fact they are not beautiful in themselves. It is the way in which first the artist and then, through his eyes, the spectators look at them that makes them beautiful.

In most films the shape of the screen remains fixed throughout. The relationship of width to height is known as the 'aspect ratio'. Early on this was set arbitrarily at 4 horizontal to 3 vertical and became known as the Academy ratio, usually expressed as 1.33. Since the 1950s, a variety of wider screens have been in use. In America and Britain, widescreen normally means 1.85 (roughly 7 to 4), on the Continent 1.66 (5 to 3). Both are achieved by not showing on screen the top and bottom of the film frame. The anamorphic system which uses lenses to 'squeeze' the picture during filming and 'unsqueeze' during projection can produce an even wider picture – Cinemascope and Panavision are 2.35 (roughly 9 to 4). All these widescreen systems involve blowing up the image more to fill the bigger screen with consequent loss of quality. This can be overcome by using a wider film (e.g. 70-mm), but this then requires special projection equipment.

Whatever the shape of the screen it can, of course, be changed by masking. In early films the frame was frequently transformed into one or more smaller vignettes of any shape – circular, triangular, irregular. The practice fell out of fashion though it had a revival during the French 'new wave' when Truffaut, in particular, utilized masks as a form of homage to the pioneers. Nowadays the device is usually restricted to those occasions when there is a narrative explanation – a character looking through a telescope or binoculars, or peering through a keyhole. More common is the practice of splitting the screen into multiple images. This is now an almost constant feature of some forms of television programme – notably sports, where it is often helpful to see the general situation

1. Plate 18.

and a particular detail at the same time. In the sixties directors who had graduated from television introduced such techniques into the cinema. In *Grand Prix*, John Frankenheimer split the cinemascope screen into three for some sequences with exciting results. In *The Thomas Crown Affair*, directed by Norman Jewison, different accomplices coming together for a hold-up under the telephone control of a mastermind are shown simultaneously on different parts of the screen. Later in the same film we see a polo match with multiple framing used to give the partial, fragmented views of a casual spectator. The widescreen in fact often causes problems for directors seeking intimacy in a particular scene. One answer is to mask off the screen not through an external device but by framing the image in such a way that a blank wall, for example, fills up one side of it.

On the other hand, directors have occasionally sought even more space by using double or triple screens. The most famous triple screen movie is Abel Gance's *Napoleon*, in which the two 'wings' showed action complementing and reinforcing the central screen. Gance developed his experiments with polyvision in a short film, *Quatorze Juillet*. Andy Warhol's *The Chelsea Girls* is a double-screen movie which can be shown with two 16-mm projectors working simultaneously. The film consists of long static shots of people in hotel rooms, lounging about, lying on beds, which makes it easier to take in the two images at the same time. There are also interesting relationships between the two screens, sometimes using the same actors, sometimes showing similar scenes at staggered intervals.

Dramatic Use of Framing

The splitting up and delimitation of space not only enables the artist to choose the essential, and to concentrate the spectator's attention; it can be used to obtain powerful dramatic effects, of contrast and surprise.

An interesting example of framing used to bring together dramatically contrasting elements is to be found in Cocteau's *Les Parents Terribles*. In a burst of joy, Mic – the son – tells his mother, Sophie, that he has met the girl of his dreams. Mic is behind his mother, his arms round her, his chin on top of her head. At the beginning of the conversation the camera frames the two faces alternately, then at the crucial moment the camera is placed so that it frames the lower part of Mic's face with its radiant smile and the upper part of his mother's face, her eyes filling with bitter suffering and jealousy. The dramatic force of the scene is enormously increased by the framing. There is a vivid shot in Kurosawa's *Dodeska Den* in which a man's face is cut off horizontally so that the camera can concentrate on the expression of his eyes, while at the same time the unusual appearance of half a face immediately attracts our attention.

Framing is normally designed so that the centre of attention is within the frame. There are many examples in which, to create suspense and dramatic tension, a framing is used which deliberately excludes the central action.[1] It is effective because it is unusual, because it arouses the spectator's curiosity, and because suggestion can be more powerful than direct statement. The film *In Which We Serve* shows the captain of the cruiser *Torrin* on leave and having a picnic with his wife in the peaceful English countryside. Then we hear the sound of planes fighting in the sky. We never see the planes and the camera remains fixed on the picnic party, but for all that, the fact that this is total war is brought dramatically home. There is a famous scene in Wyler's *The Little Foxes* in which Herbert Marshall, as the husband, dies of a heart-attack which his wife (Bette Davis) has deliberately engineered. The camera, instead of following him as he staggers to the stairs to get the medicine she has refused to fetch, remains fixed on her as she sits motionless in the centre of the scene. The effect is to express very powerfully her strong indifference, as if neither the camera nor the heroine even 'turned their head'.

In Griffith's *Birth of a Nation*, the bloody, heroic sequence of the battle of Atlanta opens with a shot of a peaceful, rural scene, with young women and children sitting picnicking on a hillside. Then the frame moves, following their gaze, and down in the valley we see armed men, troops, moving up. The battle sequence begins, far more dramatically effective for the contrast with the peaceful shot which opens it. This sort of dramatic surprise is common in Westerns. From a shot of the villian on horseback making off with

1. Plate 19.

the unwilling heroine, the camera suddenly swings, and we see the sheriff and his posse coming up at a gallop on another road.

In Jean-Pierre Melville's film, *Léon Morin, Prêtre*, there are two interesting examples. The setting of the film is a French town occupied by German troops. In one scene the heroine is cycling along a road with her little girl. Suddenly she seems agitated, stops and gets off the bicycle, hurries the little girl off the road and, pushing the bike, starts to go through the fields. We wonder what it is all about. Then the camera swings and shows us in long-shot a German road-block with troops lounging about. The dramatic effect depends on the fact that at the beginning of the shot the German troops were shut out by the framing. In another scene the heroine has just walked near a level-crossing and turns off on a rough track by the railway line. Suddenly a shout from outside the frame of the picture startles her. She turns and is overshadowed by a German soldier, a menacing figure, who threatens her and points to a notice forbidding civilians to go near the railway. The treatment is different in the two scenes but in both its effect is dependent on framing. In the first the director arouses our curiosity. Something is up, but we cannot tell what, because we are shut in the frame of the picture and cannot see what the heroine sees. Then the camera pans, and the suspense is resolved. (A cruder example of this is when, for example, in a horror film, the 'Thing' from outer space is out of frame, and all we can see is the horror on the faces of the actors.) In the second example, because we are shut in the frame of the picture, we share the shock of the heroine at the sudden voice off. In the first case the heroine knows, we do not; in the second case neither of us knows.[1] Near the end of *The Red Shoes*, directed by Powell and Pressburger, occurs another good example of dramatic framing. Lermontov, disappointed in his love for Victoria, is leaving Monte Carlo. We see him in a medium long-shot, on the platform wearing dark glasses. He turns towards the camera then stands still in surprise. What is it? The camera tracks back, widening the field of vision, and in close-up in the bottom of the frame the back of a woman's head with a shock of red hair

1. A third type of suspense when the audience knows and the actor does not is mentioned on page 118.

comes into view. It is the red-headed young dancer in love with Lermontov, who cannot let him go without saying good-bye.

In Hitchcock's *Torn Curtain* there is an effective shot when the camera concentrates on the hands of a communist agent round the hero's throat. The hero manages to get the agent's head into a gas oven and we see the hands gradually letting go their hold, waving in the air, collapsing. It is more striking than if we saw the whole of the body.

The frame is of course shared with other arts: painting, photography, the theatre (in the form of the proscenium arch). The difference is that, although the cinema frame is fixed, what it contains is highly dynamic. It is as though the whole proscenium arch could be moved at will and scenery changes could be effected in the blink of an eye. The cinema frame can also tilt – or rather, if the camera is placed at an angle, the on-screen image will reflect the fact. Known as 'oblique framing', this can be used to convey meaning.

Early examples of oblique framing are found in *October*, directed by Eisenstein and Alexandrov in 1928, where they are used to make the crowd movements more dynamic. There is one shot, depicting Bolshevik civilians who have just collected their arms, as a mass leaning forward, seeming to stream downhill and giving the impression of an irresistible river-like force.[1] Other shots, such as that of Lenin addressing the crowd, use the same means to give an urgent feeling of imbalance.

In Francis Coppola's *Rumblefish*, the director creates expressionist compositions by tilting the frame alarmingly to turn buildings into precipices and streets into dangerous alleys. At the same time he uses accelerated motion (see Chapter Four) to send clouds careering across the sky in an ominous fashion and painted long shadows on walls to suggest further the sense of uneasiness. A quite different effect was sought by Bill Forsyth for the closing moments of his comedy *Gregory's Girl*. The awkward adolescent hero and the girl with whom he has been matched are 'hand-dancing' on their backs in the park while the sun sets romantically behind them. Gradually the whole picture starts to tilt until they are both vertical, an effect that gives a charming impression of their

1. Plate 20.

mutual happiness. Ken Russell had a similar idea when, in *Women in Love*, he had his lovers, walking naked in a field, photographed at right angles so that they appear to float lyrically in the air.

A very different effect is created in suspense films, when oblique framing is used to suggest the abnormal and menacing, tipping the shadowy streets and sewers of Vienna slightly off-centre in *The Third Man* to suggest a twisted universe, or increasing the bewilderment and terror of Tippi Hedren slumped on the floor after the aerial assault in *The Birds*.

It is possible to distinguish two rather different attitudes towards the frame. Hollywood film-making in the thirties and forties (what might be regarded as the classical period) tended to regard it more like a picture frame in that the subject or action was generally kept inside it and the focus of attention remained near the middle of the picture. Increasingly, and camera mobility is again a factor here, this form of 'closed frame' has been replaced by more open forms. Actors are no longer kept at the centre of the screen, or even in the picture at all. They may wander off, only to return a little later: the camera may cast its eye around a location quite independently of any action, or lack of it. Open framing may take the form of compositions that emphasize the presence of the world off the edge of the screen – actors moving away out of the picture or simply looking off-screen, inert objects placed in such a way that the eye is continually led away from the centre, by a line of trees or a road or a building. Antonioni's studies of alienation constantly stress the spaces between people, and his widescreen compositions reflect this with the viewer's attention being drawn away from screen centre – 'things fall apart, the centre cannot hold ...' The final moments of *The Passenger* offer an example. The penultimate shot is a seven-minute take which opens with the defeated news reporter, Locke (Jack Nicholson), in a seedy hotel room with a girl. Telling her to leave, he lies down on the bed, framed in such a way that he is decapitated. The camera slowly turns to the window and moves out towards the desultory scene in the street outside. The main body of this lengthy shot then shows us various activities going on in the street, only some of which relate, ambiguously, to the fate of the reporter. We do hear sounds that could be coming from the hotel, and one that might be a gunshot, before the camera eventually turns full circle and looks back in through the window as the, now dead, body of Locke is discovered. As a death scene, this long, continuous shot, which avoids picturing the critical action in any way, captures all the pathos of a futile life draining away, yet not without elements of spiritual transcendence conveyed by the movement from the dingy room to the sunlit street.

The special nature of the film frame means that we see the image as both rigidly bound and dynamic and free at the same time. Though what we see at any one moment is a restricted rectangle, we are aware that space exists beyond these confines and that a camera movement might at any time bring it into view, reveal 'what happens next' in spatial terms. This point was interestingly illustrated in a series of films on art. In the first documentaries on painting, the pictures were presented as we would look at them in a gallery, on the wall, as exterior objects. The camera might move in to stress some detail – like a visitor going up to a canvas – but one never forgot the general set-up – a picture limited in space and hence an isolated object. But, about 1947–8, certain film-makers (Luciano Emmer, Enrico Gras, Henri Storck, Alain Resnais, and Gabriel Pommerand) developed a new technique in such films as *Il Dramma di Cristo*, *The World of Paul Delvaux*, *Van Gogh*, and *Légende Cruelle*. The camera from the start is set right inside the painting, as if it were a real world. It never goes outside the canvas and we never see the picture frame. The painting – or paintings – is cut into fragments, which, by rearrangement, contrast, linkage and visual synthesis are built up into a new total effect. Further (a point developed in the chapters on Time), the spatial relationships of the painting become, in film, relationships in time. The film-maker dissects the painter's work, organized in spatial immobility, transforming it into a moving temporal unity by cutting, montage, and camera movement.

The result of the camera never going outside the painting is that it appears as unbounded in space. This is due to a curious psychological effect. Instead of the spectator's vision being limited by the frame of the painting which he knows is real, it is limited only by a boundary which he regards as conventional – the edge of the screen. By substituting its own frame for that of the painting, the cinema substitutes *film space* for pictorial space; and by this trick it assimilates pictorial space into the unbounded space of

nature which the camera usually shows us: proof that our concept
of space in the cinema is arbitrary.

The graphic composition of the film image is more than a question
of merely framing the picture, but is connected with it, and we may
appropriately consider it – very briefly – at this point. In a general
way, composition in the cinema will follow similar rules to those of
painting or photography, with this difference – that graphic composition in the cinema is basically mobile. Both the movement
within each shot, and the movement created by changes from shot
to shot, introduce dynamic considerations unknown in a static
composition. Thus, ideally, the director should not only achieve
proportion and equilibrium in his composition of each shot, but
should also ensure the composition which will best suit the
relationship between the shots as they follow one another. It is
clear, in the extreme case of camera movement, that there would
be little meaning in trying to compose or to analyse such a
movement in terms of static composition, since there is an infinite
series of framings and reframings, an infinite and ever-changing
series of compositions.

There is always some danger in laying down rules for artistic
composition and here, such is the complexity of the factors (aspect
ratio; vertical and horizontal planes; depth; oblique, curved and
straight lines; masses; light and shade; texture; proportion; colour
– and all in movement), it would be particularly difficult. Short of a
long and complex discussion, one can only point to the examples
from the work of great formal directors – Eisenstein, Renoir, Ford,
Welles, Satyajit Ray, Antonioni, Bergman – whose films present
not merely individual compositions of formal beauty but a flow of
images interrelated in terms of composition. Watching their films,
we are conscious of a visual rhythm, something apart from the
meaning, the drama, the emotional content, the music, and the
dialogue – although, because the art of the film is so heavily laden,
often submerged by them – which, if we can train ourselves to see
it amid the confusion, can give us as much aesthetic satisfaction as
a good painting or a fine piece of sculpture.

Once more, it seems clear from our discussion of cutting, camera
movement and framing, as from our analysis of other elements,

that the cinema depends on a constant tension resulting from the ever-changing relationship of the image to the real world. Any film is in a position of balance between what is shown and the way it is shown, between the opposing pressures towards credibility and towards shape and significance. It is never possible simply to show 'objective reality': every decision taken by the film-maker implies an attitude towards his material and will lead his audience towards certain interpretations and meanings and away from others. However, he is free to choose how far he goes in any direction, constrained only by the need to use 'language' that will be understood by the audience. Within the relevant conventions he can choose and compose his scene; emphasize features that would be lost in nature; alter the scale by enlargement or reduction of details so as to enhance their value as visual symbols; and/or establish visual relationships which by their novelty will stimulate the audience to see things anew and with deeper meaning. To a greater or lesser extent his work will be one of personal interpretation and re-creation. Like any art the cinema is man-made. But unlike most arts it combines a high degree of artificiality with a compelling realism.

So far as space is concerned, it is clear that film space has a structure and properties which distinguish it radically from physical, sculptural, pictorial, theatrical, or any other kind of space. Film space forms a wholly conventional world of its own. The director completely re-creates the natural world and the spectator regards it as real only by accepting certain conventions. Film space lacks such characteristics of physical space as tangibility, density, weight, expanse, depth, and continuous existence. But on the other hand it affords possibilities which real space does not. The camera can move at any speed in any direction. It can divide objects and give significance and unity to a small, chosen section of reality. It can analyse space by fragmenting it, then re-forming it into a new whole.[1] The camera can abolish distances, can make objects as large or as small as it likes. It can accentuate, abolish or distort

1. This is most commonly seen in single sequences built up by montage – a race, fight, meeting, conversation – but it also applies to films on art, architecture, etc.

perspective.[1] Finally the camera can control (by setting, by lighting, by camera-angles) forms, volumes, and appearances.

The camera can also repeat events and multiply objects as in the example in Plate 21. This shows repetition in the same image designed to lend brilliance to the dancing. There is another type in a curious scene from *Zabriskie Point* in which a naked couple, one a violent boy, make love on the dusty ground. Immediately the whole desert landscape is peopled with interlocked couples. It is an ugly scene, as is presumably intended, and much of its emphasis is achieved by repetition. In the same movie there is an example of events repeated. The heroine is running away from a luxurious country residence and looks back to see it, in a striking slow-motion shot, blown to pieces by a great explosion. Then the explosion occurs again – and again. The sequence forms a strong symbol of the girl's rejection of the existence of the idle rich. Films quite often evoke memories in which characters think back repeatedly over past events which are then shown several times. Nor do the repetitions have to be identical – rethinking a scene may add subtle differences. In Antonioni's *Blow-up*, a gun is finally seen and a possible crime uncovered, only after the photographer hero has studied and restudied, processed and reprocessed his film. De Palma's *Blow Out* records a similar series of events: here the hero is a sound recordist, painstakingly isolating a gunshot on a crowded soundtrack. Both films are concerned with the ways in which film and recording tape can lie. Loosely related is the *Rashomon* construction, in which a series of witnesses tell the same story from their point of view and the camera shows us different versions of the same event. A simpler example of straightforward repetition is a striking scene in *Z*, when the grief-stricken wife is going over her husband's last hours and the unsuccessful attempt to save him by brain surgery. One dramatic action – that of throwing a sheet over the body as it lies on the operating table – is repeated several times,

1. Interesting examples of distortion are the war scenes in *Jules et Jim* (1963) and *Lenin in Poland* (1966), in which documentary film taken on the battlefield forty-five years ago is stretched out to cinemascope width. The figures are dehumanized, the terrain becomes unearthly and, with the grainy texture of the old film, this sequence gives us a unique combination of abstraction and realism, a grim, telling picture of war. In *Seconds* the distorted image of a fish-eye lens represents the viewpoint of a man going under an anaesthetic. See Plate 22.

depicting the way a sorrowful mind goes again and again over the same ground.

Space in the cinema, then, is not an intractable, solid thing, but something almost like a fluid substance; something which can be handled on the screen with the same omnipotence as we manipulate physical space in thought, imagination, or dreams. Thus it has the properties of abstract space, yet at the same time it identifies this abstract space with the reality of the sense world. This peculiarity of cinema has possibly led to more freedom of approach in other media, particularly graphic arts. It also relates to ideas about space which modern science has brought into our concept of the universe. The cinema can demonstrate visually what science proves empirically: that the space we experience through our senses in everyday life has only an illusory tangibility. This is a point dealt with more fully in Chapter Five, on space–time in the cinema.

CHAPTER FOUR

Time in the Cinema:
Physical, Psychological, Dramatic

ON the Continent the cinema is sometimes called the seventh art. Canudo, an Italian writing in the twenties,[1] regarded it as a fusion of three arts of space – painting, architecture, and dance – and of three arts of time – music, theatre, and literature. Canudo's proposition has been used to show that film is not an art in its own right; but the argument is not convincing. The cinema is not just the sum of these six arts, but something new and different from them all. Nevertheless the list is useful in illustrating the complexity of the film, and as a brief catalogue of the elements which compose it. Here it is interesting to note that time ranks equally with space in the analysis. Our discussion would be incomplete without considering the different aspects of time in the cinema, the way in which a film modifies the time of the real world, and the importance of time in its dramatic and rhythmical structure.

Here we look at time in the cinema from three aspects: physical, psychological, and dramatic. For the purpose of our analysis we can define them as follows: *Physical time* is the time taken by an action as it is being filmed and as it is being projected on to the screen; *psychological time* is the subjective, emotional impression of duration which the spectator experiences when watching the film; *dramatic time* is the compression (or sometimes expansion) of the actual time taken by the events depicted, which occurs when they are made into a film. This division into physical, psychological and dramatic time, suggested by Bela Balazs,[2] is useful and

1. Ricciotto Canudo, *L'Usine aux images*, Chiron, Paris, 1927.

2. *Theory of Film*, Dobson, 1952.

logical. But, as in the case of space, it should be pointed out that the different kinds of time merge into one another and, in the films we see, they all form part of the total effect and operate as a whole. Consequently although it is necessary for analysis, there is a certain artificiality about dividing the concept of time in this way. It follows that, as in the case of space, some of the examples given are suitable as illustrations for more than one section of the argument.[1]

PHYSICAL TIME

A film to all appearances perfectly reproduces the movement of the physical world in its temporal aspect. We see a man walking, a tree waving in the breeze, or a horse jumping, at exactly the same speed on the screen as we would in real life. But the two phenomena are very different. In the cinema a series of still photographs is projected on the screen, twenty-four being shown, twice each, every second. While one photograph is being changed for another the screen is dark for one forty-eighth of a second. Thus, at the normal projection speed of twenty-four frames a second, there are pictures on the screen for half the time and for the other half the screen is dark. Due to the fact that visual impressions on our optic nerve persist for a fraction of a second, we are conscious of the next picture before the impression of the last one has had time to fade.[2]

The illusion of the cinema depends on the imperfection of our senses. Just as our sense of touch cannot distinguish between a grain of powder and a molecule, and our sense of hearing cannot distinguish the individual vibrations of a sound, so our sense of sight cannot discriminate between still photographs following each

1. See footnote 1 on page 44.

2. Wertheimer's theory of the 'phi-effect' proposes that the illusion of movement stems not from the overlap of successive stimuli on the retina but from the combination of direct impulses to the brain, like a short-circuit. Video of course works quite differently, with the retina never stimulated as a whole but at a single tiny point every 400,000th of a second in a constant current from one side of the screen to the other: no single image is ever perceived in its entirety by the eye which sends a very different sort of message to the brain compared to that sent when stimulated by film.

other at a certain speed, and continuous movement. The reproduction of movement is therefore quite artificial and time can be stood
still (by repeating the same still photograph), reversed (by showing
the still photographs in the reverse of the natural order), slowed
down, or speeded up.

The artificiality of the reproduction of movement in the cinema
is illustrated also by the fact that its effect is different on different
sizes of screen. For instance large movements will flicker across a
very big screen in quite an unreal manner. We may note in passing
that the size of the screen has a general psychological effect on the
viewer. The viewer cannot get the feeling of being absorbed in the
spectacle with too small a screen, even if he sits relatively close to
it, and it may detract from a film. On the other hand, too large a
screen destroys the illusion, because movements have to cover such
a great distance in the same time.

Although we now take it for granted, the cinema's reproduction
of movement is a remarkable mechanical achievement. At the same
time, the important thing about the cinema is not its ability to
reproduce movement in time. Many pre-cinematic devices succeeded in doing this. It is rather to have inscribed and fixed time
on such a flexible material as film (and now videotape), one which
can be technically manipulated so freely, on which different time
values can be recorded, and different moments of time isolated and
reassembled to form new wholes.

Time Variation within the Shot

Fast or slow motion in a film is as new a phenomenon as the
microscope or telescope, and demonstrates in the most forceful
way the relativity of time. It was early applied to plant growth and
the flight of birds in the work of Percy Smith, begun in 1908. A
speeded-up documentary on plant growth may introduce us to a
universe whose rate of movement is fifty thousand times faster than
the one we know, a temporal universe as incommensurable with
solar time as ultra-microscopic worlds are incommensurable with
visible space.

This order of variation is so great as to be of scientific rather
than artistic interest, but less violent variations can be effective,
though at first they were little used. While the scale of image in
space from long-shot to close-up was constantly varied in every

film, speed of movement, which is the corresponding factor in the time dimension, was almost invariably constant.

Time variation was in fact suggested by Pudovkin (in *Film Technique*) before 1928 in a passage quoted by Ernest Lindgren in *The Art of the Film*; Pudovkin describes a sequence of a man scything grass – which he proposed to make for experimental purposes – in which almost every shot reproduced motion at a different speed. Pudovkin goes on to say that the idea proved sound in practice, and in fact he and Dovzhenko use variable motion in several films – *Storm over Asia, Zvenigora, Earth*. But subsequently both accelerated and slow motion were sparingly used until more recent times, when the latter in particular has become almost a cliché as a stylistic device for representing experiences as varied as romantic passion and bloody death. This suggests perhaps that in graphic movement, time variation is both less necessary and more powerful in effect than variation in space.

Accelerated Motion

Accelerated motion has been occasionally used, from the very earliest films onwards, for comic effect. There are examples in the farces of Mack Sennett, Max Linder, Buster Keaton, Charlie Chaplin, and in the funeral scene of René Clair's *Entr'acte*. We know how often it is used in cartoons, and the film of a train speeding from London to Brighton in a few minutes has been shown repeatedly on television. It is more difficult to accommodate easily in feature films for other than comic effect. Richard Lester uses accelerated motion in several of his films, notably in *The Knack* and *A Hard Day's Night*. In *The Three Musketeers* it is used in an exaggerated way to ridicule the swashbuckling and sword-play of both villains and heroes. Not only is the effect funny in itself but, since accelerated motion is obtained by filming at slower than the normal rate *while the actors move at their normal speed*, the split-second timing on which so much slapstick depends seems to be achieved at a much faster pace than is really the case. It lends a brilliance to the action which could not be obtained by any other means, or in any other medium. Woody Allen shot large parts of his comedy *Zelig* at eighteen to twenty frames per second, not, in fact, to achieve a comic effect but to make his new footage match the silent film clips he incorporated in his film and to give the whole a dated atmosphere.

Accelerated motion can also be used, less obviously, in adventure and action films to add excitement to chases and getaways by very slightly speeding up the movement. In Spielberg's *Indiana Jones and the Temple of Doom* a whole arsenal of techniques, including accelerated motion, were employed to suggest that the trolley in which the main characters are escaping is travelling at breakneck speed. In reality it was going round and round a circular track at no more than 10 miles per hour but the camera was undercranked to little more than half speed and the fact that the trolley was shot parallel and very close to the rock wall was sufficient to create an impression of great speed (as experienced on underground trains for example). The electrifying chase through the redwood forests on speeder bikes in Marquand's *Return of the Jedi* was achieved by the simple process of a Steadicam operator walking through the trees shooting at only one frame per second. Shown at normal speed the result was a hair-raising sequence with the proximity of the towering trees to the camera making it appear that the bikes were sure to crash at any second. Even in the most serious films accelerated motion may be used imperceptibly to underline some effect: the movement of a crowd, a battle-charge, or an expression of anger, fear, enthusiasm or rapture. In Cassavetes' *Shadows*, where the boy suddenly becomes aware of the girl's colour, the whole film leaps and the tone changes completely. More obviously, mortality and decay, the themes of Peter Greenaway's *A Zed and Two Noughts*, are illustrated with shots of various dead objects being consumed by insects and turning to dust before our eyes.

Slow Motion

Slow motion used to be associated with tragedy, with events drawn out to accentuate the unbearable and inevitable sadness. Over the years its accepted meaning has changed and broadened. It was much used in Leni Riefenstahl's *Olympic Games* where it conveyed the poetry of the athletic movement. More recently, the memorable opening sequence of Hudson's *Chariots of Fire* with its group of runners training on the Kentish beach similarly gives a lyrical impression of the ecstasy that can accompany the sweat and effort of reality. The use of slow motion later on in the race sequences was less successful since the essence of racing is speed rather than grace, but sprints lasting a few seconds would have appeared insignificant if shown in real time. If it fails to reflect the speed, slow motion can at least accentuate the effort and beauty of movement visible in even the most brutal of sports. Scorsese used it to achieve an almost surreal, emotionally intense atmosphere in the opening credit sequence of his film, *Raging Bull*, where the smoky, black and white images of boxer Jake La Motta (Robert de Niro) warming up before a fight are slowed to the rhythm of Mascagni's 'Cavaleria Rusticana' intermezzo on the soundtrack, emphasizing both the power and the isolation of a man caught in an egoistic macho world which will destroy him. Later, in the fight scenes, camera speed was varied even during shots so that, for instance, the water thrown on the boxer's face in his corner between rounds runs down over his body at 96 frames per second and the camera gradually slows to 24 frames per second for the fight sequence that follows.

Some extraordinary slow motion shots are included in King Hu's metaphysical martial arts epic, *A Touch of Zen*, notable also for use of split-screen and negative shots. At the film's climax the prodigious leaps of the warrior monks give them more than a touch of mythical splendour. A less obvious example can be found in Tarkovsky's *Mirror*, in which just a few frames of the printing-press scene were filmed in this way so that the change of speed is barely perceptible but enough to convey a vague feeling of something strange. The technique is a way of bringing out a state of mind through means other than acting.

More often slow motion is used to enable violence and death to be more than a split-second event. In *Bonnie and Clyde*, Arthur Penn's climactic use of slow motion in the ambush and shooting of the hero and heroine convey a real sense of horror and tragedy, but its copying *ad nauseam* by less talented directors has lessened the impact. Once the technique becomes commonplace, the viewer's reaction is different and its effect is to give wounding and death a spurious glamour and grace. The later films of Sam Peckinpah are filled with such moments (*The Wild Bunch, Straw Dogs, The Killer Elite*) and their legitimacy is much disputed.

In Nicolas Roeg's *Don't Look Now* we see a drowned child in slow motion under water while on the father's drawing board spilled ink spreads a red stain. Later in the film when the child's mother (Julie Christie) happens to meet in a restaurant a medium who has 'heard' her dead child and as a result faints at the luncheon table, the scene of her collapsing and pulling the laden cloth to the ground is shown in slow motion. Not only is it beautiful in itself and expressive of her fainting, but it adds to the macabre atmosphere of the movie. In Alan Pakula's *The Parallax View* the assassination of a politician is shown in long-shot and the distant little figures moving in slow motion express helplessness and dismay.

Slow motion is often used for dream states. In Buñuel's *Los Olvidados* there is a touching sequence of a young boy's dream, in which his mother is kind to him and feeds him as she never has in his waking life. In Cocteau's *Orphée*, when the poet accompanied by the chauffeur, Heurtebise, is going to his rendezvous with death, the grace and slowness of his movements remind us of some ghostly under-water diver. There is the famous dormitory sequence in Vigo's *Zéro de Conduite*, with boys in their white nightshirts and the air full of feathers from a pillow fight. They look like angels floating in a heavenly snowstorm.[1] In Jacques Demy's *Lola* there is a charming scene in which a good-natured American sailor takes a little French girl for a ride on a merry-go-round. As they get off, a shot in slow motion perfectly expresses the little girl's mood of dreamy delight. In this case, because of the context, the slow motion has a lyrical rather than a tragic effect. In René Clair's *Un Chapeau de Paille d'Italie* a bridegroom at a wedding is worried by a threat that all the furniture in his flat will be thrown out and smashed. We then see furniture coming out of the flat window in slow motion and other furniture being carted away by men in top-hats. The whole sequence is fantasy, but it is the slow motion which most takes the edge off reality and marks the scene as imaginary. In the 'war dream' sequence of Tarkovsky's *The Sacrifice*, Sven Nykvist's camera is shooting a crowd fleeing in terror. Slowly it tilts downwards until it is looking straight down at the heads of people immediately below. At the same time the camera speed changes so we see the useless panic and chaos of their flight in very

1. Plate 23.

slight slow motion. The combination of angle and camera speed conveys the meaning of the shot.

Reverse motion is comparatively rare and too eccentric an effect to be very often appropriate. In the early days it was used plainly, without any pretext, as a magic or comic effect (broken china mending itself, a wall rising out of the dust, a diver springing back out of the water). Eisenstein used it in *October* to show symbolically the restoration of the *ancien régime* – a statue of the Tsar previously smashed to pieces is miraculously restored. In Cocteau's *La Belle et la Bête* it is used on several occasions – when pearls and precious stones come to fill the hands of the Beast; when Beauty passes through the wall of her room using a magic glove; and at the end, when the lovers are drawn up to a fairy paradise. Chaplin uses it as a trick in *Pay Day* to make it seem as though he is catching bricks in impossible positions. It has been used to fake knife-throwing scenes, the knife being pulled out of the wall with an invisible thread, and the shot reversed. It is used in Richard Lester's *The Knack* with comic effect. An egg broken into a pan climbs into its shell again to the dismay of the straw-hatted cook.

A slightly different use of reverse motion was seen, but probably not recognized as such, in Terrence Malick's *Days of Heaven*. The film, though shot in Canada, is set in the grain-producing Texas panhandle. At one point a swarm of locusts descends on the area, destroying the crops. For some shots real insects were used but for others they were impossible to handle. Instead, peanut shells and seeds were scattered from above by helicopter. Malick used a camera that could shoot with the film running backwards and he instructed his actors and tractor drivers to do likewise. When the film was projected the people and machines moved forward normally, while the seeds (locusts) could be seen flying upwards from the crops as they were disturbed.

Reverse motion is now most commonly seen in the popular martial arts genre where fantastic leaps are apparently made. These highly choreographed action movies do occasionally reach balletic heights in the hands of the more ambitious directors, notably the ubiquitous Jackie Chan.

Finally, a most striking example, in which the whole film is in reverse motion, is Walerian Borowczyk's *Renaissance*. From chaos and darkness a group of broken objects – a stuffed owl, a euphonium, a hamper, books, a doll, a plate – slowly, slowly reconstitute themselves to the sound of trumpet music. Suddenly at the climax there is a great explosion and chaos again. It is the reverse motion which gives this film its strange, unearthly atmosphere.

Stopped Motion

Stopped motion is used here by analogy with accelerated, slow and reverse motion as a general term to cover the 'freezing' of the action of a moving picture or the use of still photographs.[1] Stills can be included in an otherwise moving film or they can even constitute the whole film. They may be introduced for practical reasons: for historical reconstructions (e.g. of Victoriana), and where authenticity is important, staging impossible, and movie material not available (e.g. photographs of the victims, in films about concentration camps). Moreover, some films have been deliberately made entirely from still photographs, because they give the finished production a special quality quite different from a moving image: the work of Ray and Charles Eames (*House, Parade, Death Day, Toccata for Toy Trains*) is perhaps the best known. In Chris Marker's short film *La Jetée*, stopped motion, in the form of stills, grows naturally out of the subject. The film is science fiction and the characters are survivors of an atomic war who try by telepathy to establish contact with the past, to capture 'images' of a lost era, 'moments of time' from a dead world. Consequently, the use of stills, animated only by music and commentary, is both appropriate and telling.

In *Chinatown* Polanski uses stills to point up his theme of voyeurism – all have some form of sexual content. The film even opens with a series of such photographs, of a couple during intercourse. The groans that accompany these images turn out to be uttered by the cuckolded client to whom private eye Jake Gittes (Jack Nicholson) is showing the fruits of his inquiries. Later we

1. The terms 'stopped motion' or 'stopped-action photography' are used more particularly to refer to a technique of faking in which the camera is stopped to enable a 'magic' transformation to take place; also for animation in puppet films, and for 'pixillated' photographic effects.

actually see Gittes at work, spying on a couple. He produces his camera and his face disappears behind it. In the lens we see the distorted reflection of the man and woman, a perfect expression of voyeurism. The passive Gittes is reduced to studying photos in his efforts to unravel their sexual mysteries. They tell only part of the story; their lack of movement suggests his impotence and predicts his ultimate failure. Joseph Losey also used stills in an appropriate manner in *King and Country*, where they presented suitably grisly images of corpses and death.

A different technique is that of 'freezing' the action during an otherwise moving sequence by printing the same frame over and over again. This became a popular way of ending a film after Truffaut's celebrated freeze-frame, in *The Four Hundred Blows*, of the young Jean-Pierre Léaud as he looks back at the camera as his flight from reform school is cut off by the sea. Another striking example was in Milos Forman's film *Peter and Pavla*. Here, the father of the young people who form the subject of the film, tries to play the heavy parent but his pontificating is hindered by his inability to express himself. A friend who has come to visit his son says, on going, that he has enjoyed himself because 'it's so interesting here'. The father is indignant at this remark – 'It isn't interesting,' he says, 'it's . . .' As he tries to think of the right word there is a long frozen motion shot of him with his mouth open. The film ends and leaves him trying to think of the right word for the rest of time. The same type of ending has been used in subsequent movies, for instance in *Elvira Madigan* in which a lovely frozen shot of the young heroine in a cornfield reaching out to catch a butterfly coincides with the sound of the shot by which her lover kills her before shooting himself.

A freeze-frame concludes *Butch Cassidy and the Sundance Kid* as the two cornered heroes are in the act of making their last suicidal break for freedom. Freezing need not be at the end of a film. Many films start with a frozen image that subsequently springs into life, others have frozen images at the introduction of important characters. Stopped motion had a specific narrative function in Marcel Carné's *Les Visiteurs du Soir*. Two emissaries from Hell, whose mission is to part a pair of lovers, watch them dancing at a ball to celebrate their engagement. Using their infernal power they make time stand still. The music dies away, the dancers are transfixed, time and space are frozen. In this interregnum in time, the 'visitors' take their victims by the hand, animate them with a dream life and drag them into the shadows to sow the seeds of estrangement between them. After a time the two couples return to the ballroom, life starts again, music breaks the silence, space and time unfreeze. The whole thing happens in the twinkling of an eye.

This sequence gives a concrete manifestation of the polyvalence of time and shows its relative, subjective nature. From another point of view it expresses the intangible – the realm of pure spirit – in a dimension of time. Just as the cinema can express time in terms of space – as we see later – so here the intangible, spiritual world is expressed by means of duration. There is also a suggestion in the sequence that the outer physical world of the senses is an empty, automatic world – the dancers are stopped and restarted like mechanical toys – and it is the inner life which is real.

A final, rarely used technique is that produced by 'step printing', the repetition of several frames to give a jerky effect. In his television series *France/Tour/Détour/Deux/Enfants*, Godard used the process to draw attention to simple movements that would otherwise pass unnoticed. In his film *Slow Motion*, he intermingled such meditative, momentarily frozen frames with natural movement to suggest the relationship between artifice and nature, and to comment on the images of women which his shots portray.

Montage and Physical Time

With the exceptions we have mentioned (slow, fast, stopped and reversed motion), the temporal structure of each individual shot is entirely realistic. But it is a very different matter when we come to what André Bazin has called 'the abstract, intellectual imaginary time of montage'. *Within* the shot, time on the screen is as fixed and unchanging as in nature; but from shot to shot, time is completely free. The relationship of one shot to another may be *from* any tense (past, present, or future) *to* any tense (future, present or past). The change may be to another dimension or another universe of time, to the time of a nightmare, a daydream or a vision, or – as in the example from Carné's film which involves cutting as well as stopped motion – to the time of Heaven and Hell, to the time of eternity. Or the relationship may not be a time one at all: time may have nothing to do with it. In a sequence showing different aspects of a room, or a woman sewing, or a crowd in the street, or the architecture of a church, it does not matter which shots were taken later and which earlier. And on the screen they are not shown in the same temporal order or arranged in the same temporal pattern; quite other structural considerations – rhythm, contrast, the building up of a pictorial climax, etc. – are the determining ones. When, as in Fritz Lang's *Fury*, we see women gossiping and then hens cackling, the temporal relationship is not significant; the hens are inserted as a metaphor, a symbol. When, in a film on the bombing of London, we see shot after shot of burning buildings, the juxtaposition is for the purpose of repetition, emphasis, crescendo, and time does not come into it. Again, cutting from one shot to another may merely be ellipsis – the leaving out of the unimportant – an essential feature of any art.

The film has often been compared with literature – by Cocteau,[1] by Bresson[2] and by many others; the camera likened by Astruc to a pen; and the structure of a film compared with the grammar of writing. The main difference between the two – the fact that literature uses abstract symbols while film consists of concrete images – is discussed in Chapter Nine. But it is also interesting to compare the way these two different media present the dimension of time.

Both film and literature, in narration, can deal very freely with time, more freely for instance than the theatre. Both have forms (essay/documentary; text-book/technical film) in which time is largely irrelevant. In story-telling, as Malraux points out in his 'Esquisse d'une psychologie du cinéma',[3] the cinema started out divided into continuous parts more like the theatre, but developed the flexibility of the novel with the development of cutting. But there is a permanent difference, in that writing has more exact, readier means of pin-pointing, of describing time relationships. '*Before* he came into the room . . . *Since* I have been here . . . *Then*, as a last resort, he went to the police . . .' Film has no words like

1. *Cocteau on the Film*, Dobson, 1954.

2. Quoted in *L'Art du cinéma*, Seghers, Paris, 1960.

3. 'Esquisse d'une psychologie du cinéma'. *Éditions de la Nouvelle Revue Française*, Paris, 1945.

these; film has no tenses – past, present, or future. When we watch a film, it is just something that is happening – *now*. We may know that it is the sinking of the *Lusitania* in 1915, but those people struggling in the water, clutching at the hull as the doomed ship sinks, are in a sense drowning before our very eyes. The immediacy of what a film shows us consequently surpasses anything in other arts, and it can have a terseness and a pace that literature cannot match. But there is a real problem of communication. In general, the cinema is enabled to tell a story because there is a convention that – unless there is some indication to the contrary – the order of shots on the screen is the order of events in the story. To a certain extent the same convention exists in literature and the famous lines: 'I came, I saw, I conquered' may be taken as an example of it. But it could equally be regarded as an ellipsis (which incidentally enhances the vividness of the writing) with the word 'then' or 'and' omitted.

The Flashback

'Unless there is some indication to the contrary . . .': such indications are used to introduce a flashback and may take many forms. There may be explicit reference in the dialogue: 'Remember darling . . .' (in Carné's *Le Jour se Lève*) – and we know that the next shot is a reminiscence, not the next event in the story. There may be merely a fade-out and -in or a dissolve, the soundtrack may become blurred or there may be a tune which recalls the past. These days, audiences are so skilled in following complex narration, so adept at 'reading' how a story develops however often it may jump backwards and forwards in time, that there may be no indication at all.

The exact structure of a flashback may not be apparent until it is over. In *Variety*, a convict, aged and bent with long years in prison, comes before the governor for discharge. Then we cut to the story of the film, ending in the climax when the deceived lover (Emil Jannings) kills the unfaithful woman. We then return to the first scene – the convict turns to show us the face of Emil Jannings, grown old and worn, and only then do we realize that the whole film has been a flashback from the opening sequence. This pattern has been used many times since. In Billy Wilder's last major film, *Fedora*, the story is told in flashback after the suicide of the apparently ageless film star. At her lying in state, Detweiler, a producer (William Holden), recalls how he tracked her down to an isolated estate after her mysterious disappearance. In the middle of the story he writes a letter to Fedora and we return (a flashback within a flashback) to their first meeting thirty years before when, as a young assistant director, his task had been to cover her breasts with water lilies to satisfy the censors. Later in the film we discover not only that Detweiler's interpretation of events was wrong, but that the whole film has been a flashback from a point several weeks later. Sergio Leone's *Once Upon a Time in America* is based on a similarly complicated flashback structure. It chronicles the life of a Jewish gangster, Noodles (Robert de Niro), from adolescence in the twenties, through the following decade of manhood and success culminating in the traumatic circumstances in which he apparently betrayed his friends and was obliged to go into hiding, only to find thirty years later that he has been duped by his best friend, Max, into years of wasted life as a fugitive. In one scene a bag carried by the ageing Noodles in 1968 is snatched from his hand by the young Max of 1931. In another, Noodles disappears through a doorway, reappearing from the same spot, now markedly redecorated, decades later. Not surprisingly, when the film's American distributors tried to shorten the film and present the story in chronological order, the result made little sense. The meaning of the film was embedded in its structure.

The writer, Dennis Potter, is adept at weaving tales through complex temporal patterns. In *Dreamchild*, his story about Lewis Carroll and his real-life Alice, the present is the 1930s when a widowed Mrs Hargreaves (Alice as an old lady) is invited to attend a ceremony in New York in honour of the centenary of Carroll's birth. On board the liner she both reflects on her friendship with the writer (flashback) and is assailed by nightmares from the darker side of *Wonderland* and *Through the Looking Glass* (fantasy). Potter's television series *The Singing Detective* centres on a writer marooned in hospital with a crippling skin disease. His present, past, dreams, fantasies and fears, the story he is writing, a story he once wrote, even the fantasies of characters in these stories, all combine to the extent that it becomes impossible to decide exactly where reality lies. Only the disease itself and his earliest childhood memories finally seem painful enough to be true. As all these various stories interweave we realize that they are all to some extent figments of the writer's imagination.

Less convoluted is Bergman's *Wild Strawberries*. The main protagonist is Isak Borg, a dried-up academic (Victor Sjöström) who revisits the haunts of his childhood and 'sees' his younger self and his contemporaries reliving his memories. We watch the old man contemplating his earlier life and realizing his mistakes, but the figures from the past are oblivious to his presence. In more recent times two films, Robert Zemeckis's *Back to the Future* and Coppola's *Peggy Sue Got Married*, both transfer their characters bodily back into the past, the one to alter the course of his parents' marriage, the other to save her own.

The flash-forward is less common for obvious reasons: it can hardly be used to visualize memories unless time itself is really less linear than we believe. An example of seeing the future can be found in Roeg's *Don't Look Now*, in which Donald Sutherland and Julie Christie play a couple who have gone to Venice to recover from the loss of their small daughter. But neither can quite accept the fact of the girl's death and continue to search for her in their different ways. The wife is drawn to two old ladies, one a blind mystic. One day the husband sees his wife and the two women, dressed in black, gliding down the canal in a large boat. Only at the end of the film is this shot explained – he has seen his own funeral with his wife accompanying his coffin. In fact the whole film is full of indications that time is flexible – the first two images are of a pond where the girl *will* drown and what proves to be a rain-spattered window in Venice. There is also the well-known sequence in which the couple making love is intercut with their dressing: different events happening at different times are brought together in time on the screen. We do not know which is 'now' or which was then, or which has yet to occur. Roeg returned to the point in *Insignificance*, in which he had his Marilyn Monroe character explain relativity of time and space to Professor Einstein using toy trains and balloons.

The flash-forward to an imaginary version of the future is more common. An early example is in Harry Langdon's *Long Pants* (director Frank Capra) – there is an amusing flash-forward in which, harassed by a regiment of women and unwilling to 'go through with it' he plans to shoot his overpowering fiancée. The imaginary flash-forward in which everything goes according to plan is then contrasted with the real event in which all his wicked intentions are foiled and he is dragged to the altar. At the end of Huston's *The Dead*, Gabriel thinks forward to the death of the old lady whose party he has just left and sees her corpse and mourners.

Laslo Benedek's *Death of a Salesman* and Alf Sjöberg's *Miss Julie* are two films in which past, present and future are freely mixed. In the first film, in an atmosphere of hallucination and subjective mental states, Willy Loman is playing cards with his neighbour Charley. Looking at a portrait of his dead brother Ben brings back the past, and Ben appears and interrupts Willy's conversation with Charley without Charley being aware of it. When Charley leaves, Willy joins Ben in the past.

In another sequence Willy Loman is talking to his wife in the kitchen of their house, and asks her a question. She laughs but we hear a louder, more vulgar laugh, and through the door of the kitchen – now open – we see a woman in a hotel bedroom getting dressed. It is this woman who answers his question as Willy walks into the room and – in the past – takes her in his arms. After a brief love scene, he returns to the kitchen and to the present, and we hear his wife answer the question he asked an instant before.

In *Miss Julie* the heroine becomes the mistress of her father's valet, Jean. During the night they exchange reminiscences about their childhood. There is a shot of the little boy Jean being chased for stealing apples (past), then the camera pans to grown-up Jean and Julie walking together in the same orchard (present). We see little Jean being whipped (past), then the same shot pans to the assembled servants and ends with a close-up of grown-up Julie's face (present). When Julie drinks to forget the shame of her liaison, and recalls *her* past, we see the little girl Julie and her dead mother (past) in the same shot, and alongside, the grown-up Jean and Julie.[1] Towards morning, when Julie has decided to run away with Jean, and is taking money from a desk, she hears her father come back, and imagines the scandal. We see her in the foreground, while her voice (off) relates what is enacted in the same shot in the background – her father finding the theft, calling the police, and so

1. Plate 24.

on ... Here the present appears in the same shot as the future, and a purely imaginary future at that, since she commits suicide to escape her anticipated disgrace.

The treatment of time in Alain Resnais's films is very striking. In *Hiroshima Mon Amour* the main story is a brief love-affair between a film star and a Japanese architect; but there is the freest interchange between this and the same girl's experiences – or her memory of them – during the war, when she had a love affair with a German and suffered terribly, as a result, at the hands of her French compatriots. There is so much interchange between past and present that the two are at times almost fused. The script-writer, Marguerite Duras, and the director together succeed in creating in terms of film the philosophical and emotional world of such writers as Marcel Proust or Rainer Maria Rilke.

In *Last Year in Marienbad* time values are intentionally left completely vague. Robbe-Grillet, the scenario-writer, suggests that the cinema is 'the pre-ordained means of expression for a story of this kind'. He sees Alain Resnais's work as an attempt to get away from the linear plots of old-fashioned cinema which are content to reproduce the continuous sequence of real events. In opposition to such conventional films Resnais aims to construct a purely mental time and space and to follow the mind which goes faster, or slower, than reality – dodges, skips, doubles back, lingers, repeats, and creates imaginary scenes, parallels and possibilities. It is only necessary to think of *Marienbad* to appreciate how exactly this applies.

One would agree that reproduction of every detail of ordinary actions would be intolerably dull, and all films modify reality to some extent. The question is: how far can modification be taken? *Last Year in Marienbad* goes further and succeeds better in enabling the spectator 'to come to terms directly with subjectivities', than anybody might have thought possible before it was made. One might also say this film constructs a poetic as well as a mental time and space, and is virtually the first film conceived as a poem, that is, in which the traditional dramatic construction is replaced by non-narrative construction.

Resnais's films correspond with a view of time suggested in these chapters, and constitute a vindication of the cinema's natural freedom in temporal construction. It is apparent that the lack of time prepositions and conjunctions, tenses and other indications may be an advantage as well as a drawback and can leave the film free to reach the spectator with an immediacy which literature is unable to match. It can also make for speed and economy in a narrative. We see too that the problem of communication between the artist and his audience is not a simple one: it depends on what is to be communicated. Difficulty in communication, demanding an effort to follow on the part of the audience, may not be due to any fault or perversity on the part of the film-maker, but rather to the fact that he is trying to communicate something deeper or more complex. Referring to another medium, Browning wrote of 'Feelings that broke through language and escaped.'

We have said (on page 71) that cutting may be an ellipsis leaving out the unimportant. What is left out may be time as well as space. When we cut from a shot of a woman dressing to go out to a shot of her dancing with a young man at a ball, a good deal of time as well as space has been eliminated compared with the physical reality – although not necessarily compared with subjective reality. Camera movement also, though not quite in the same way, may be thought of as abbreviating time and space. We talk of the speed of an aeroplane annihilating time and space, and fast camera movement will do something similar. When the camera moves at a moderate pace, the intervening space and the time of its movement will have the same value as they do in everyday life. But the faster the camera moves the more it compresses the intervening space and shortens the time, until with the fastest movement (zip-pan and zoom) we approach annihilation of space and time. The same consideration applies when the intervening space is blank, neutral or non-existent (if the camera moves to a wall and away again; up to the clouds and down again; down to the ground or to water and up again; from one set to another adjacent to it; and so on) and what is ostensibly a single camera movement may, so to speak, contain a hidden 'cut'. All this goes to show again that time and space in the cinema are not corporeal but mental coordinates having an illusory physical appearance.

To summarize the argument of this section: we have said that the cinema can repeat, prolong, abbreviate, or reverse the events on the screen. Past, present, and future time can be mixed in any order. A film breaks up the continuity of time in the real world, and out of the physical time of reality creates an abstract *film time*.

PSYCHOLOGICAL TIME

We have seen in the discussion so far that the cinema can either imitate exactly the time of the physical world, or can modify it radically. By modifying it, the cinema can, as Robbe-Grillet suggests, assemble on the screen, by various means, but principally by montage, something more like the time of our mental than our physical life – a mixture of future, past, and present, passing over some events in a flash, dwelling on others, returning to others. Something less continuous, less predictable, less inflexible than the time of the physical world.

We have included this roving of the mind under physical time because although a psychological phenomenon, it is one which the cinema can manifest physically on the screen. And we have reserved the term 'psychological time' for another mental phenomenon – our subjective sense of duration. Most of our knowledge of the universe comes, in one way or another, through our senses; but our knowledge of duration seems innate. We are still conscious of the passage of time even when we are alone in dark and silence, and virtually without any tactile sensations.

Our feeling of duration may be connected with subconscious awareness of bodily rhythms – heart-beat, pulse, breathing. Over longer periods, our feeling of time may be connected in some way with the knowledge of our own age and expectation of life. Perhaps it is significant that our feeling for rhythm and tempo, which is related to our sense of time, is also something innate and dependent on recurrent bodily rhythms.

Being subjective, our sense of duration varies considerably in comparison with clock time. If we are preoccupied and happy, 'times goes quickly'. If we are bored, idle, and unhappy, 'time hangs on our hands'. If we are looking forward to some future event, whether with apprehension or with impatience and longing, that is, if we are in *suspense*, time will 'go slowly'. Variation is even more pronounced in abnormal states such as dreaming, fantasy, madness, or on the borders of sleep or unconsciousness.

In the real world, our mental state determines the way time goes.

In the cinema, it is the other way round: the way time goes on the screen will affect our mental state. By making time go quickly – using quick cutting, loud or lively music, dynamic composition of the images, and rapid action (comic or thrilling) – the film-maker can induce in the audience moods of exhilaration and laughter for a comedy, excitement for an adventure film, horror and dismay for a tragedy. By making time go slowly – depicting quiet uneventful scenes, using soft, soothing music, static composition of images and slow cutting – he can induce moods[1] of lyricism, contentment, sadness, nostalgia, or grief; the exact mood evoked will depend largely on the context and nature of the film.

Suspense

Our sense of duration is affected in a special way when we are held in suspense by a work of art. Suspense does not follow the general rule given above, for although time goes slowly, unbearably slowly, we are still highly excited – held and absorbed by the tension of the situation. Suspense consists in delaying the resolution of a situation so as to arouse and maintain the spectator's interest, and it is something common to all the narrative arts. It will be useful to quote a classical example from Scott's *Ivanhoe* which illustrates very clearly the use of long-drawn-out suspense.

In Chapter 22 of *Ivanhoe* the wicked Norman, Front-de-Boeuf, is about to torture the Jew, Isaac, in the dungeon of his castle when he is interrupted by 'the sound of a bugle, twice winded without the castle'. In Chapter 23, instead of telling us who blew the bugle and why, we go to another part of the castle where De Bracy (another wicked Norman) is trying to seduce Lady Rowena, a beautiful Saxon – until he also is interrupted by 'the horn, hoarse-winded and blowing far and keen'. One might think that Chapter 24 would bring us to the bugle and its blower but, again, we move to another room in the castle where Brian de Bois-Guilbert (*another* wicked Norman) is making advances to Isaac's daughter Rebecca, a beautiful Jewess. He also has to break off at the end of the chapter because, as he says, 'that bugle-sound announces something . . .' Not until Chapter 25 do we discover the true role of the

---

1. Impatience or boredom are also possible.

bugle first mentioned in Chapter 22 which is, of course, to bring help to Isaac, Rowena, and Rebecca. Scott could very well have left all mention of the bugle until Chapter 25 but by bringing it in earlier, he creates a situation which requires resolution, and retains the reader's interest.

Another literary device is to end a chapter at a crucial point and carry on in the next chapter with another part of the story as, for example, in Charles Morgan's *Sparkenbroke*. This device is very similar to the parallel cutting of the cinema which takes us from the heroine in the hands of the thugs to the hero trying to get the police to take up the chase. Suspense may consist in withholding something (in a detective story the identity of the murderer) from the reader or the audience; or it may consist in withholding something from one of the characters in the film – *we* see the policeman ready with a big stick but Charlie Chaplin does not, and we wait with bated breath for him to be arrested.[1] Hitchcock gave his own interpretation of suspense as follows: 'A curious person goes into somebody else's room and begins to search through the drawers. Now you show the person who lives in that room coming up the stairs. Then you go back to the person who is searching, and the public feels like warning him, "Be careful, watch out. Someone's coming up the stairs." Therefore, even if the snooper is not a likeable character, the audience will still feel anxiety for him. Of course, when the character is attractive, as for instance Grace Kelly in *Rear Window*, the public's emotion is greatly intensified.'[2] Surprise then is a bomb exploding; suspense is knowing that it is about to explode and being, like all cinema audiences, unable to intervene in the action.

Our subjective sense of duration is partly a relative matter. A flurry of quick cutting, of violent action, of loud music or noise will be all the more effective if it comes after a slow, quiet sequence and acts with a sudden shock. Slow cutting needs some variation to relieve it. Our sense of time will also be affected by camera movement and not only by the absolute rate of movement, but by a change in the

1. Plate 25.

2. François Truffaut, *Hitchcock*, Martin Secker & Warburg, 1968.

rate and whether it is accelerating or decelerating. Generally, camera movements are held rigidly to a steady rate and there is something emotionally satisfying about this. But there seems no reason why the camera should not excite us by getting faster in its movements or soothe us by gradually slowing down. The same applies to cutting – the psychological effect of a sequence in which each shot is shorter than the last (*accelerando*) is more exciting than a whole string of short shots. Our sense of the duration of each shot will also depend on its dramatic content, its scale, its emotional significance, and the complexity of its composition; and all these will have a relative as well as an absolute value.

The objection may be made that, as the audience is mostly unconscious of shot-change, it will be unconscious of the duration of shots, and the intended effect will be lost. But the fact that it is not conscious of the duration of shots does not matter. Subconscious reactions may be just as important, if not more important, than those the audience is aware of. There are many effects in art which are appreciated without the audience being consciously aware of them – the rhythm of a poem, the balance of a painting and so on. There is indeed something in the view that analysis spoils a work of art, something in the complaints that enjoyment of Shakespeare is spoiled by studying his plays at school. Analysis which leads to better understanding will in the long run increase appreciation and hence enjoyment, but at the time, in respect of the particular thing being analysed, it will tend to limit emotional participation, because of the concentration on reasoning which is necessary. Several film examples discussed here are from sequences which are erotic in their effect when seen in the cinema – but they lose their eroticism under analysis.

Rhythm and Tempo

Our mental sense of the passage of time can be affected by the rhythm of any work of art in which time is an integral element – music, dance, poetry, drama, film. But rhythm exists also in static arts – painting, sculpture, and architecture. It is a different rhythm in a way, but there are affinities – certainly movement and time are concerned. For, although a statue or picture does not move, we who look at it do not grasp it all in one moment. We take time to explore it, to move round it, or around inside it – movements which may be merely subconscious or imaginary, but can also be the actual movements of the eye. If the building does not move, *we* move – mentally if not physically – when looking at it. We can compare this building of a picture by mind and eye with what we have described the cinema as doing when it constructs a composite picture of a scene, a character, a building or a work of art.

The remarkable thing about film is that it works in both space and time, and combines static and dynamic rhythms. Soviet director Andrey Tarkovsky believed that time and rhythm are at the heart of film-making. While the tempo of a piece of music or a play are not predetermined but can vary with each performance, time in the cinema is integral to the structure of a work. So time becomes the very foundation of the cinema, as sound is of music, colour of painting, character of drama. The director's task therefore becomes, in Tarkovsky's phrase, 'sculpting in time'.

It is often argued that rhythm derives largely from montage, from the editing process. Tarkovsky however holds that it is 'rhythm and not editing . . . that is the formative element of cinema'. By this he means that the time running through the shot makes the rhythm of the picture. It is this distinctive time imprinted in the frame which dictates the rhythm of the montage.

Whether we accept Tarkovsky's position or not, we can certainly agree that editing and the material to be edited are in constant interplay. As in other arts, rhythm in film is a matter of relationships: proportions and equilibrium. In a very general way rhythm will grow out of the content of a film. The duration of shots will depend on their visual and dramatic content.[1] A simple image needs less time to grasp than a complex one, a close-up less than a long-shot; a fixed frame less than a moving frame; a strongly dramatic image less than a neutral one; a shot in strong contrast with the previous one less than one similar to it. But all these are no more than guiding principles, there to be broken. In a film the number of rhythmical elements is very large. Quite apart from music, dialogue, natural sound and colour, all of which may have rhythms of their own, there is the composition of lines, masses, light, and shade, the movement of persons, objects, and light, the

1. Shot duration – time – is therefore affected by spatial considerations, another interrelationship of time and space.

1. (*right*) Leni Riefenstahl's *Triumph of the Will* spread the Nazi cult (p.17).

2. (*above*) Flaherty's films stem from direct contact with a way of life (p.23). *(Nanook of the*

3. (*above*) Film production is a heavy industry (p.23). (*The Diary of Anne Frank*)

4.(*above*) The first film-makers were content to register mechanically the actual world (p.31). (*Peek Frean Biscuit Factory,* 1906)

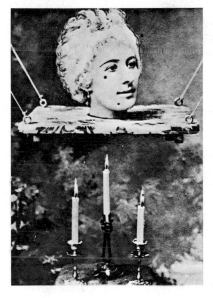

5. (*left*) The fantastic imagination of Méliès (p.32). (*The Magic Head*)

6. (*above*) Relative scale is indicated by
the size of human beings (p.37).
(*Greed*)

7. (*left*) Human beings can be
presented as larger than life – or
smaller (p.38). (*Brats*)

8. and 9. Shooting angle can bring out an object's essential nature (p.39). (*above*) The low angle is used to express the authority and isolation of imperial power. (*The Last Emperor*) (*below*) The low angle close-up emphasizes both the stature and helplessness of the fallen warrior who dwarfs but is looked down on by the (unfocused) figures behind him. (Kozintsev, *King Lear*)

10. (*above*) The only way to show a crowd's size is by shooting at a downward angle (p.40).
(*Prisoners of War*, 1918)

11. (*above*) The stewardess appears to walk up the curved wall of the space shuttle (p.78). (*2001*)

12. (*above*) The camera's exaggeration of contrasts in size can combine realism and symbolism (p.49). The judge is huge, the pleaders tiny, in *A Matter of Life and Death*.

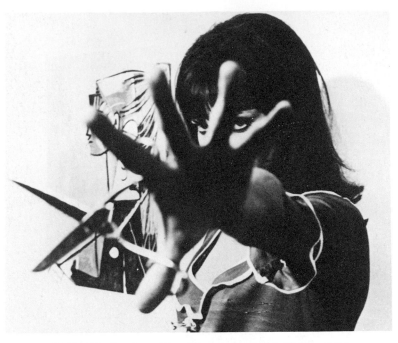

13. (*above*) The short-focus, wide-angle lens overstates depth (p.52). (*Pierrot le Fou*)

14. (*above*) The telephoto lens flattens the image (p.52). (*Buffalo Bill and the Indians*)

15. (*above*) In *Citizen Kane* ~~scene~~ after scene used setting in depth (p.56).

16. (*above*) In *Les Parents Terribles* Sophie steals out of the drawing room and the camera backs away from her (p.80).

17. (*above*) The cinema can show actors' faces large enough for us to see every detail of their expression (p.73). (*Ivan the Terrible*)

18. (*above*) By extracting a fragment from the chaos of nature the cinema helps us to see it with new eyes (p.87). (*Strike*)

19. (*below*) A framing which deliberately excludes the central action (p.89). A scene of childbirth from *Stagecoach*.

20. (*above*) In *October* oblique framing is used to make crowd movements more dynamic (p.91).

21. (*above*) Film can multiply objects or scenes (p.96). (*Top Hat*)

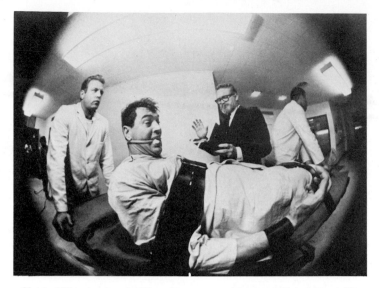

22. (*above*) Distortion, through a fish-eye lens, to create a sinister, paranoid atmosphere (p.96). (*Seconds*)

23. (*above*) A famous example of slow-motion (p.104). (*Zéro de Conduite*)

24. (*above*) We see the young Julie and her mother (past) in the same shot as the adult Julie (present) (p.113). (*Miss Julie*)

25. (*above*) We see the policeman ready to make an arrest, but Charlie does not (p.118). An example of suspense from *The Kid*.

26. (*above*) Photography brings out the time aspect of a rifle shot (p.133). A bullet breaking an electric bulb, taken at one millionth of a second.

27. (*above*) Painting has tried to copy the movement of film (p.134). *Dynamism of a Dog on a Leash*, Giacomo Balla, 1907.

movement of forms caused by shot-change or by camera movements, the duration and relationship of shots, the rhythm of the narrative, and variations in dramatic intensity. As Eisenstein pointed out, each of these elements will form both a 'melodic line' of its own, and also be related simultaneously in harmony or discord with all the others. One could compare film to a piece of counterpoint containing a dozen or more 'voices', all on different instruments. René Clair distinguished three factors which, he begins by saying, would make the metre of shots as strict as that of Latin verse: the length of each shot, the alternation of scenes, and the movement within each shot. But he saw at once that none of these factors was capable of definition or measurement, and that it was impossible to lay down laws. Film rhythm could not be achieved by reason; it was a matter of sensibility, flair, and taste. 'I am resigned', he concluded, 'to find neither rules nor logic in this world of images. The primitive wonder of this art enchants me.'[1]

The complexity of elements in a film is both an advantage and a handicap. The cinema's richness, the variety of its form, the range of its styles, the multitude of its subjects, may make other art forms seem poverty-stricken, but this complexity makes it (paradoxically, in view of its origin and growth as a popular art) one of the most difficult of all arts both to practise and to appreciate. We have already mentioned the viewer's difficulty in distinguishing the pure rhythm of movement amid the welter of other elements. It is just as difficult for the film-maker to control every element and achieve perfection in each. This is why simplicity, spareness, austerity, can be such virtues in film – the music should not be as rich as in a symphony, the dialogue not so copious as in a play, the visual compositions not so subtle as in a painting, the plot not so involved as in a novel, the acting less showy than on the stage. One has only to think of the films of Robert Bresson to find examples of this taken to its logical and perfect conclusion – the apparent observation of life shorn of all exaggeration and artifice.

Of course the rhythm and tempo of a film should be appropriate to its subject and to the audience. The rhythm of a teaching, a demonstration or a reportage film will follow its objective reasoning, and be such as to make the meaning plain before anything else. A

1. René Clair, 'Rythme', in 'Les Cahiers du mois', *Cinéma*, 1925.

fictional film, however, will follow an emotional pattern and a dramatic rhythm to suit the action. What matters in both cases is that the spectator should accept the film with his head or his heart, and that its rhythms should be effective and appropriate. *Lord of the Flies*, directed by Peter Brook, is a film which attempted strong rhythmic effects which were sometimes successful – the first appearance of the 'hunters' dressed in long cloaks and marching along the beach chanting *Kyrie eleison*, or the slow pan upwards from the feet of the rescuing naval officer – but at other times failed. One reviewer wrote that the film was 'too slow in the establishing shots, too flurried with action shots'.

Once again it is clear that the classic Hollywood style had its own very distinct conventions concerning rhythm. Framing, movement within or of the frame, and cutting were all subservient to the action. Each shot and each scene tended to follow a similar plan whereby interest was established, reached a peak and ended shortly afterwards. The only crime in such a style was to prolong any element in case boredom or impatience set in and attention flagged. The modern cinema is less bound by such restrictions. Directors like Antonioni in the example from *The Passenger* quoted earlier have demonstrated that attention does not necessarily fall if a shot is held – on the contrary, the viewer starts to see further into the image, seeing both 'more' and 'differently'. Polanski's *Tess* is full of shots of Nastassja Kinski which are held long after their purely narrative significance warrants – but important for their function of making us see Tess in a certain way. At the other extreme, influenced by advertising and 'rock video' and by a now more sophisticated audience, scenes barely need to be established at all. Each shot can be reduced to the central movement of maximum drama, and a new style of montage cinema has been produced. The average shot in *Rambo II* lasts for just 2.9 seconds.

Inevitably, to audiences weaned on action movies and comedies based on styles derived from TV advertisements, rock videos and cartoons, many older films appear slow. Audiences everywhere have cultural expectations that may make works from a different time or place difficult or frustrating. The rhythm of silent films often appears wrong to modern audiences (though this may owe something to incorrect projection speeds as well as to other factors). The influence of television notwithstanding, cinema audiences are now prepared for directors to take longer to tell their stories if necessary. The classic ninety-minute feature implied a measure of economy and the maintenance of a steady rhythm. The director today has the option of being more indulgent with the possibility of long, slow passages where narrative takes second place to character development, subplot, thematic subtext, etc.

Films from cultures alien to our own have different rhythms and structures. India and Pakistan produce around nine hundred features a year, most of which confound the expectations of Western audiences with their switch from energetic action to lengthy song and dance numbers, looking odd to those accustomed to other conventions. The same applies in reverse, and relatively few foreign language films are shown in India. There, the family audience is still dominant and the vast majority of films are rated 'U'. American films fall foul of this social phenomenon and pictures like *Rambo* are banned altogether. Directors like Satyajit Ray and Mrinal Sen who have absorbed 'Western' styles to some degree (and the same applies to Akira Kurosawa from another culture again) find that their films are applauded more in the West than at home.

DRAMATIC TIME

For thousands of years the tragedies and dramas of the real world have been re-enacted for the edification or entertainment of an audience. In the most primitive of these representations, dramatic time was very little different from the time which the events themselves would have taken in actuality. The interminable length of medieval mysteries indicates the difficulty which writers of the period had in altering the time-scale. A drama which did not take virtually as long as the events it depicted would not have commanded the spectator's belief or attention.

In more sophisticated drama, some *condensation* of the time of actual events became permissible. According to one of the three dramatic unities, laid down in classical times and respected by classical dramatists of the seventeenth and eighteenth centuries (but not by Shakespeare), twenty-four hours was the maximum period which could be compressed into the three or four hours which a play lasted. Nowadays, the dramatist is entirely free and we have plays depicting different generations, or the life of a man from the cradle to the grave shown in a series of episodes.

The cinema has descended from modern, not medieval, drama and only a handful of films have tried to keep exactly the same time-scale as reality: Hitchcock's *Rope*, Wise's *The Set-Up*, Zinnemann's *High Noon*, Varda's *Cleo from 5 to 7*, Warhol's *Empire*, Malle's *My Dinner with André*. *Rope* is a curiosity, a film using camera movement exclusively and apparently without a single cut from beginning to end. In fact, a movie camera can only hold about ten minutes' worth of film, so Hitchcock was forced to 'cheat' and there are breaks when the camera moves to a dark surface. In *The Set-Up* and *High Noon*, the fact that the events of the film take just an hour and a half is indicated by including shots of clocks which show the time. But these films cheat too and include a mass of incident occurring *in different places to different people* during this time which (if laid end to end) would in reality take far longer. In other words, space has been substituted for time.

Other films, while not keeping exactly to real time, have maintained it for long periods, and the films themselves are usually enormously long as a result. Andy Warhol's six-hour *Sleep* is made up of three hours of ten-minute segments, each shown twice. Chantal Akerman's *Jeanne Dielman, 23 Quai du Commerce, 1080, Bruxelles* runs 195 or 225 minutes (there are two versions) and consists of its housewife-prostitute heroine mostly doing mundane tasks in real time. In fact the action covers two days – and right at the end she murders a client, possibly less for any real motive than simply to end the film. Jacques Rivette's *Out One* ran for thirteen hours and was publicly shown once. Described by its director as 'something of a documentary about the modern experimental theatre' it included many long takes of the actors left entirely to themselves. It was later re-edited into the four-hour *Spectre*. John Cassavetes has also experimented with real time in films like *Faces*, where his method involves keeping his performers as people rather than letting them become actors, a characteristic shared by many such films. The result for the audience is either boredom or (gradually) fascination.

Most films however either condense or expand the time span of ordinary life. Yet although the director has freedom to deal with time as he likes, an attempt to distil too great a time period into a film can cause a loss of dramatic power. In Griffith's film *Intolerance* for instance, which ranges over the whole of history from the Babylonian empire to the present day, the various episodes never really form a single unity and the film is not as dramatically effective as the same director's *Birth of a Nation*, which covers the few years of the American Civil War. Preminger's *Exodus* would have been a better film if it had not tried to combine two entirely separate sections – one in Cyprus, the other in Israel. In Pasolini's *Oedipus Rex* the ancient Greek tragedy is set between modern prologue and epilogue. Not only are the modern sections less powerful, but they blend uneasily with the antique settings of the main section.

In the case of a film whose story is in two widely separated parts, unity of time (and place) can to some extent be preserved by means of a flash-back. Instead of showing the beginning and then the end ten or twenty years later, the film can start with the second period, flash back to the first period, then return and finish in the second period. Thus the main containing action forms a unity based on the present and the structure is symmetrical as in *Le Jour se Lève*, *Citizen Kane*, *Hiroshima, Mon Amour*, *Heat and Dust* and innumerable other films. In some cases the present is limited to a few minutes at the beginning and end of the film, the whole story being set in the past. Ulu Grosbard's *True Confessions* consists almost entirely of the memories of two brothers (Robert de Niro and Robert Duvall), who meet in the tiny desert village where one, the priest, is dying. In flashback, they contemplate both their pasts and the downfall of the once powerful cleric through ambition. Only at the end do we return to the present, aware now, sadly, of how the decaying village reflects a ruined life. Roland Joffé's *The Mission* opens and closes with a letter being written by the Pope's envoy in which he is reporting back to the Vatican, helpless to do anything but recommend a politically expedient decision that he knows will destroy the evangelical work of the Jesuits to whom he once belonged. The main body of the film, showing the missionaries at work and the rapacious, slave-owning adventurers who want them removed, highlights the dilemma with which the envoy is faced and how he is forced to make what he knows to be the wrong decision.

Perhaps the most audacious expanding of time occurs in Coppola's *Godfather* films in which *Part Two* both encompasses and recalls *Part One*. It takes the story of the Corleone family back in time before the start of the first film, and carries it on through the next generation.

Part One is part of the structure of the second film through the memories of the viewer. The texture created by the interplay of periods is indicated by the inferiority of the television version, which imposed a chronological order on roughly the same material.

We have already mentioned that cutting from shot to shot may be a means of shortening time and leaving out the inessential. Because a film is composed of hundreds of bits of time joined together, it can effect this condensation of time continuously from the beginning to the end of the film. The theatre has steadily grown more flexible in this respect by abandoning elaborate stage settings, and allowing changes of place or time to be represented by moving a spotlight from one side of the stage to another, or by changing a cardboard tree for a cardboard street-lamp, and so making it possible to have far more changes of scene. But the theatre is still not so flexible as the cinema.

How much can be left out, how quickly the narrative can proceed, is something which the director should have carefully in mind. If too much is left out, the sequence of events may be difficult to follow. As in the case of space, more can be left out between sequences than within the same sequence, and the various transition devices which have already been discussed (in Chapter Three), just as they carry the spectator over a change of place, will carry him over a change of time.

Two unorthodox time transitions in John Schlesinger's first feature film *A Kind of Loving* are fitting examples. There is a long sequence in which the young man persuades his girl to make love to him. It ends on a quiet, a curiously quiet, note, both of them inwardly still . . . Then suddenly by a straight cut we go with a bang into a raucous, violent dance scene – the band playing as loudly as possible, the girl being manhandled by a clumsy oaf of a partner. It is about a month later and the girl is worried that she is going to have a baby. The transition is very successful, no doubt because of the strong contrast in tone from *pianissimo* to *fortissimo*. Later in the film we see the same couple on their honeymoon. The camera (long-shot) is looking out from the hotel bedroom at them on the beach at dusk, as they turn to come to the hotel. Before this shot quite ends *we hear their voices in the hotel bedroom* in low intimate tones, and only then does the camera pull back and pan over to the couple lying in bed. This transition, achieved in a single shot, is a striking illustration of the cinema's ability to telescope time. Again, in Terence Young's *Dr No*, time is neatly telescoped in the following sequence. A beautiful spy plans to decoy James Bond by asking him up to her bungalow in the hills. She rings him up and as she gives him directions over the telephone we dissolve to Bond actually in his car driving and obviously following the directions which her voice goes on giving . . . Another example of ellipsis with a sound link is in *The Godfather*. Near the end the Mafia leader (Marlon Brando), playing with a small boy in some raspberry canes, falls to the ground. As the small boy runs off and the camera watches the man lying there, a bell begins to toll. It is only on the second or third stroke that the camera cuts to a visual image corresponding to the tolling bell – the Godfather's funeral.

Instead of condensation from real time to dramatic time there will sometimes be expansion. This can take two forms: either the film concentrates on a particular occurrence, repeats it, gives different aspects of it, stretches it out; or else there may be inserted a sequence which in thought takes place in a flash but in the film takes many minutes. An example of the first occurs in Michael Curtiz's film *The Charge of the Light Brigade*, in which the charge lasts more than ten minutes, although in reality the horses galloped less than two miles. Tony Richardson's more recent *Charge of The Light Brigade* could equally well be taken as an example.

An example of the second from *Death of a Salesman* has already been quoted. In the fraction of a second between Willy asking his wife a question and her answering it, he thinks of an affair with another woman; in the film the time is expanded to allow the love scene with the other woman to be played out. There is an experimental film *The Last Moment* by Paul Fejos which opens with a figure struggling in the water and a hand reaching up. The film follows the chief character's boyhood, youth, first love-affair, war service, unhappy love-affair, decision to commit suicide. Then the opening sequence is repeated, the hand gradually sinks into the water and the film ends. Two films of this kind have been made from an identical Ambrose Bierce story: *The Spy* by Charles Vidor (1932) and *Incident at Owl Creek* by Robert Enrico (1961). A man is being hanged under martial law during the American Civil War. The hanging takes place on a bridge and, as he drops, the rope breaks, he plunges into the stream and, by swimming under water, escapes. There is a long sequence of him making his way through the forest to his wife and home – then suddenly we are back at the bridge, the body dangling at the end of the rope. The main part of the film has occurred during the fraction of a second of his fall – a flash of wish-fulfilling thought.

Also stretching real time in a different way, is the technique of holding the camera on a person or object longer than normal, simply to make the audience look at it. In Huston's *Life and Times of Judge Roy Bean*, the judge is set upon by a gang of ruffians who slip a rope round his neck and drag him behind a horse. Fortunately the rope breaks before he is strangled and the gang ride off. At this point the camera dwells insistently on the broken end of rope as if it had more than special significance. As indeed it has. For the incident makes a change in the judge's life, since he regards himself as saved by divine providence and given the mission of bringing law and order to the Wild West – a mission which forms the theme of the movie. At the end of Fassbinder's *Effi Briest*, after her death, the camera stays on a scene of Effi's parents in their garden long after they have finished talking. It acquires an air of finality which brings the film to a close as effectively as the long-held, final chord of a symphony. An extreme example of camera insistence is Andy Warhol's *The Chelsea Girls*. The film is made up of interminable, static camera shots at close to medium range, of people in hotel rooms – men, women, children; standing, sitting, in bed; cutting their nails or hair, drinking, skylarking, taking drugs; talking, talking, talking. Like the 'almost real time' epics discussed previously, it sounds intolerably boring, but once again, the more one sees, the more one becomes involved, whether in sympathy, revulsion or astonishment. One becomes conscious of the wrinkles in the blonde's trousers, the wart on her chin, the fat girl's dirty feet, the worn patch on the upholstered chair and so on. These details acquire the same importance by holding them in the dimension of time, as a close-up would give by magnifying them in the dimension of space.

We have already alluded to changed attitudes towards running times. Bela Balazs held that films in practice could not last longer than an hour and a half because for physiological reasons the viewer could not watch for longer than this. 'This predetermined length', he wrote, 'is itself a style which the artist must master.' If ten thousand feet was the limit of length when Balazs wrote, it is certainly not so now, and the number of long films, two hours, two and a half hours and more, is sufficient to show that the spectator's physiology is no bar. At the same time there are limits. It was reported of a special cinema showing of the *Forsyte Saga* (which in one-hour, weekly episodes formed easy and popular viewing for millions) that the projection opened with a packed auditorium, but even with breaks for refreshment, finished some twenty-four hours later with only a dozen or so hardy viewers still in the cinema. Tyranny of length arises sometimes from commercial considerations and films are still cut down or stretched out to fit into programmes. Buñuel's son said of his father's film, *The Exterminating Angel*, that it was slightly too short for commercial exhibition, so he simply repeated a sequence at the beginning! The guests come into the hall of the house, mill around for a moment or two looking for the servants (who have gone) and then go up the grand staircase. Then the whole thing is repeated. Certainly it is an odd repetition without any clear symbolic meaning (as there is in other parts of the film) so the explanation given may be correct. Balazs is right in counting length as part of the style. It should be part of the total conception of the film and will largely depend on the content – what the artist has to say. Because of the pattern of commercial exhibition the most neglected form in the cinema is the short-story film and many short-story ideas are padded out to feature length. Short documentary films are not much seen in cinemas, either, but at least they flourish in the spheres of education, industrial sponsorship, film societies and television.

As a medium with different viewing conditions, television has provided an outlet for work of varying lengths, notably the (roughly) sixty-minute TV play. Over recent years, however, the distinctive one-off play, grouped into seasons like *Armchair Theatre* and *Play For Today*, has given way to other forms. A short vogue for the mini-series with its (usually) romantic drama lasting several hours and broadcast on consecutive nights, has given way to a mixture of long-running series and TV movies. The former (*Dallas et al.*) are guaranteed a regular audience which can be delivered to the advertisers in predictable numbers. Also profitable is the low-budget TV movie, Hollywood's answer to the obsolete 'B' picture and now, ironically, the main sustainer of the major studio stages. Non-commercial television in Britain, Italy and Germany enables the companies to invest in productions with some substance and style. Where advertising dominates, notably in America, the TV movie tends to be a glossy but cheap production, made at top speed and aimed at the middle-of-the-road audience for whom so many cinema films are now thought to be unsuitable. Pioneered by Universal in 1964, over one thousand had been made in America by 1980. A handful have risen above the general level and several have had theatrical release outside the USA (e.g. Spielberg's *Duel* of 1971).

In Europe, with TV an increasing source of feature film finance in many countries, the gap between TV movies and cinema films is narrowing – though budgets remain restricted. However the small screen does offer directors a chance to depart from the accepted feature-film length. Though scheduling often demands that a film be a certain length to fit a particular 'slot', the possibility remains for very long and very short dramas. If the fifteen to thirty second advertisement and the three minute rock video are the most obvious examples of the latter, experiments with five minute playlets have occasionally surfaced, and other shorter pieces can be slipped into schedules later in the evening when the rigidly ordered prime-time has passed.

At the other extreme, television can offer film-makers the chance to explore ideas which expand beyond feature length. Roberto Rossellini has made a whole series of historical dramas, some of which would be an unwieldy length for theatrical release (e.g. *The Age of Cosimo de' Medici*, which consists of three parts totalling four and a half hours). In Britain outstanding examples are Ken Loach's *Days Of Hope* (four episodes running in all nearly seven hours) and Les Blair's *Law and Order* (four episodes at seventy-five minutes each), plus two series written by Dennis Potter, *Pennies From Heaven* and *The Singing Detective*. Other successful series such as *Gangsters* and *The Boys from the Blackstuff* grew out of single plays. In America a one-off TV play will only be made if it is a pilot for a series.

In some cases shorter film versions have been produced of longer TV originals (*The Prisoner's Song, Sybil*) but the result is rarely satisfactory unless an artist like Bergman consciously works with two end-products in mind, as he did for both *Scenes from a Marriage* and *Fanny and Alexander*. Finally, there are projects which are, in most respects, feature films but whose sheer length makes TV transmission the most suitable form of presentation. Fassbinder's *Berlin, Alexanderplatz*, Edgar Reitz's sixteen-hour *Heimat* and Claude Lanzmann's nine and a half hour *Shoah* are recent examples.

In general, however, television is too competitive and ratings-conscious to allow such luxuries except as rarities. To keep its huge audience the TV image must be constantly on the move, fearful always of boredom and channel-hopping. Its rhythm is naturally restless, its attention-span too often limited to the short period before the next advertising break. Its open-ended form of drama is inimical to the cinema's need for an event that can be fitted into an evening.

CHAPTER FIVE

SPACE–TIME IN THE CINEMA

HAVING for convenience of analysis discussed space and time separately, it remains to restore their fundamental unity and consider them together as cinematographic space–time. The space–time of the physical world forms a four-dimensional continuum in which all our sensory experience takes place. The space–time of the cinema is likewise composed of the same four dimensions and within them the film world, its people and events live and move and have their being. To this extent they seem to be the same. But we already know how different the components of the two worlds are. There are the same fundamental differences between film and reality when it is a question of space–time, as there are in the case of space and time separately. The differences can most conveniently be considered under two heads – within the shot and between shots. Under the first head the significance of cinematographic movement is considered, and the movement of the cinema compared with the immobility of the static arts. Under the second head the essential nature of montage is discussed.

SPACE–TIME AND CINEMATOGRAPHIC MOVEMENT

All movement in reality has space and time dimensions. However, in ordinary life, if the space dimension is comparatively very small, for instance in the growth of a plant, we think of it as something occurring in time only. Conversely, in the everyday world a rifle shot is just movement in space – the time it takes is infinitesimal and we disregard it.

Movement in reality is continuous but movement on the screen is discontinuous and is achieved by showing very quickly a series of still photographs. Because film movement is artificial in this respect, the dimensions of space and time can be manipulated (by slow and accelerated motion) in ways not possible in reality and so as to create new worlds of experience. In the case of a plant growing, the cinema, by increasing the relative value of the space dimension, shows us that this is movement in space as well as time. In the case of the rifle shot, photography, by increasing the time dimension relatively to that of space, can show the bullet stationary in time.[1] Slow and accelerated motion, discussed in Chapter Four under time, thus have a bearing on space as well.

Of course, in these two cases both the time and space dimensions exist so far as science is concerned, and it is interesting to note that the cinema can demonstrate visually what science has discovered empirically or theoretically. We can say that a film, by varying the time dimension, in the one case substitutes space for time and in the other substitutes time for space, and thus the cinema is able to demonstrate that space and time alike are dimensions of the same continuum.

All movement has space and time dimensions, but what if there is no movement? This is a theoretical extreme in which the time dimension is infinity and the space dimension zero, and it gives us a new way of looking at the static arts. For they approach, at least, a state of perpetual immobility and their value in human eyes depends to some extent on this quality. They are immortal, eternal, unchanging. 'Forever wilt thou love and she be fair' wrote Keats of figures on a Grecian urn. Because of the sharp contrast with movement, this quality of 'frozen harmony' can well be appreciated in a still image suddenly occurring in the middle of a film.

Static Arts and Cinema

Because of their durability, sculpture and painting have been used from the earliest days for commemoration and for representing the immortality of gods. The Egyptian painter was referred to as 'one who keeps alive'. The Renaissance artist, commissioned to paint a

1. Plate 26.

crucifixion, put a portrait of his patron at the foot of the cross. However, since its invention in the last century, photography (the snapshot, the studio portrait) has largely replaced painting as a means of perpetuating the memory of the past.[1] There were several reasons for this: photography was cheaper than painting, it required less skill to get a likeness, and (human fallibility being more or less eliminated) it had great authenticity. Painting, relieved of the need to provide an exact likeness of reality, has been set free to indulge in the abstractions and experiments of the last seventy years – expressionism, surrealism, cubism, and the rest.

Cinema and video can go further than the photograph in preserving the past for, although they present a moving image, it is one that can, with care, be perpetually preserved and renewed. A film can perpetuate not only an instant but a period of time. Film and video home-movies rival the holiday snapshot. Films of important people and events are an established part of historical record.

The advantage of being able to fix a period rather than a moment of time – or to make a durable record of movement – seems to have been appreciated millions of years ago, and throughout its long history static art has tried to imitate movement. Recent research, by filming and animating successive cave drawings of bison, has shown that put together they represent a continuous movement. The same technique applied to a Greek vase shows us an acrobat doing a somersault – a moving picture created over two thousand years ago! Then there are medieval and Renaissance paintings showing successive incidents in the life of a saint on the same canvas, paintings in series (Hogarth's *Rake's Progress*), sporting prints of a day's hunt, and strip cartoons. Early in this century the futurist painter Giacomo Balla experimented with the rendering of movement by painting in such canvases as *Dynamism of a Dog on Leash*,[2] *Rhythm of a Violinist* and *Abstract Speed Wake of a Speeding Car*.

This reaching out of static art for movement cannot in the nature of things be successful and in a sense it is not intended to be.

1. Plate 28.

2. Plate 27.

Besides the advantage of being able to contemplate it at leisure and come back to it, the still image has a particular flavour of its own, which may even lead to its being used from choice in the cinema itself, as illustrated in the section on stopped action.

We see then that, even within the single shot, the space–time of the cinema is different from that of reality. It introduces us to a different world which may range from the immobility of the still image to accelerated motion as fast as the eye can follow. A world too which can vary the space–time dimensions of the real world for its own purposes.

SPACE–TIME AND MONTAGE

The differences from reality which occur within the shot illustrate the subjective nature of space–time in the cinema, but this gap between the reality of the object and the reality of the image becomes even greater when we start to consider the relationship *between* shots.

In the ordinary world of experience every event occurs in a framework that is homogeneous, continuous, and irreversible. For example, if from his window a person sees two men talking in the street and wants to go near so that he can hear what they say or see who they are, he can walk outside and go up to them, but he cannot do so instantaneously. He has to go through the door, down the steps, across the street. He has to move through the space that physically separates him from them. He is dealing with concrete space. It is the same in the case of time. He cannot see what the men will be doing ten minutes later. He has to wait for the full ten minutes to pass.

In the cinema it is very different. Space and time can be divided, expanded, contracted. Scenes from different times and places can be brought together, distances abolished and time abbreviated, without the spectator being in the least disturbed. The observer mentioned above who is looking through the window can be with the two men in the street in an instant. In the same instant he can be in Paris or Pekin. The film audience can see a figure in the distance and then close to, they can jump from one day to the next, see what happened yesterday then tomorrow. They may even be shown, in the same sequence, shots which, on the face of it, have no determined space–time unity whatsoever. The silent cinema would frequently use this method, depicting a spring morning, for instance, by a succession of images that showed: the sun rising over the trees; birds singing in a wood; a flower opening; a young woman pushing up her bedroom window with a smile at the new day. In a dramatic film the action can be split up, one incident alternated with one or more other events, or with past or future happenings. To do all this it is only necessary to join one piece of film to another. Thus, unlike the physical world the cinema allows breaks in the continuity of space and time which give it an abstract character suitable for artistic creation.

There are limits to the liberty of montage. Film-makers and audience must be in tacit agreement about how far from reality the film can be allowed to depart. The terms of this agreement vary – with different cultures, different times, and different genres or types of film. The classic Hollywood film, for example, allowed some ellipses: by observing certain rules of cutting and camera placement an actor could be made to cross from door to table more swiftly than he could in real life. As we have seen, the 'new wave' broke the limitations of this convention, deliberately making characters jump from one place to another. Nowadays, viewers have accepted much less adherence to reality in this respect. We also more readily accept such superficially surreal elements as repetition and slow motion. Correctly filmed, the audience seeing a gun removed from a holster twice in succession will not necessarily start wondering where the second gunman has come from. The repeated shot is immediately recognized as a figure of speech, a comment on the significance of the action. The repetitious shot of the lovers' lips meeting in a kiss is interpreted as just one moment that will be relived in their memories – the kiss and the memories are combined in the same images. If, as so often, the shot is shown in slow motion, it reflects the lovers' feeling that 'time is standing still'. Conventions – the terms of agreement between film-maker and audience – change, so that films that looked true to life when they were made in the thirties now look stylized, with obvious sets, dated décor, unreal sources of light, theatrical delivery of speech, etc.

What is acceptable will differ from one picture to another depending also on the 'convention of reality' determined by the subject and style of the film. As, in mathematics, the nature of a theorem will depend on the initial axioms laid down, so, in a film, will the freedom with which space–time can be treated. For instance in a didactic film the abstract logic of the argument will determine the arrangement of shots and the space–time continuity of the film. As long as the argument justifies it, space and time can be split up without losing verisimilitude. To show that early training may inculcate militarism, a shot of boys playing soldiers can be shown next to a battle scene. In the two shots, space and time are independent and the scenes are joined by a conceptual link. In a fiction film another convention of reality is adopted and the continuity is a dramatic and psychological one. Such a film can perfectly well show, in a few seconds, a man ringing a bell, a woman in a sitting-room who hears the bell, a servant going to open the door, and the man going into the house. This sequence is quite unlike any series of events which one human being could experience in the space–time of the physical world, but it follows a psychological continuity, a psychological reality, and it appears physically possible because there is a dramatic unity which justifies the splitting up of space and time. A third example is a dream sequence of a film whose whole action is subjective, in which reality becomes entirely mental and abstract. Space–time continuity can then be completely different from physical reality. A character can move in a flash from one place to another, or a gesture be endlessly repeated.

Theories of Montage and Realism

In previous chapters we have considered the fact that a film is made up of single shots, using the word 'cutting' to describe the process. The same process can be seen also as one of synthesis, the joining together of separate elements, often known by the French term 'montage' from *monter*, to assemble. The separate shots must be combined into a meaningful whole and it is this process that formed the basis of early film theory.

Pudovkin described an experiment devised by Kuleshov in which an actor's expressionless face was intercut with a series of other shots – a bowl of soup, a small girl, a body in a coffin. Pudovkin noted that the unchanging expression of the actor was variously interpreted by audiences as suggesting hunger, tenderness or grief according to the shots which preceded and followed it. His conclusion was that montage is a process of building, of laying bricks, and he went on to identify a number of ways in which this process worked. Until then, film editing had used montage simply as an incidental feature of narrative with no formal significance of its own. Pudovkin, by showing that audience reaction flowed from the juxtaposition of shots, gave montage a new significance – but he still believed that the main aim of montage was to support the narrative.

It was Eisenstein who took the new theory a stage further. He rejected the brick by brick analogy and argued that the process was more akin to Japanese character writing in which the whole is more than the sum of its parts. For example, the Japanese character for 'dog' plus the character for 'mouth' together make, not a character meaning 'dog's mouth', which would be simple addition, but a character meaning 'bark', a new concept.

Eisenstein's thought was much influenced by the philosophy of 'dialectical materialism' which proposes that artistic creation, like political progress, comes about from the interaction of contradictory opposites: the dialectic process of thesis – antithesis – synthesis. He argued that montage should be seen, not as a process in which the viewer reacts first to one shot and then to another, but as the creation of a third concept arising from their combination.

There are objections to this theory: not all montage involves new concepts and two elements in a single scene can form a new meaning without montage. Even so, there is no doubt that Eisenstein's analogy illustrates an important aspect of cinema. The *Gestalt* psychologists insist that we react to organized wholes which are something more than the sum of the parts into which they can be analysed. As I. A. Richards wrote: 'It is the organized whole which has artistic communicability,' and Tarkovsky (a severe critic of montage cinema): 'No one component of a film can have any meaning in isolation: it is the film that is the work of art.' The isolated image is not perceived, and does not function, by itself; the individual shots are brought to life by their context. Thus in every film there is enrichment of meaning by mental association, and this enrichment is achieved to a considerable extent by montage.

This notion of montage has been called 'expressive montage'. Its most radical form, what Eisenstein called the 'collision' of opposites, shows a clear contrast with the 'invisible' cutting of straightforward narrative montage. Examples abound in Eisenstein's own work, notably in the celebrated Odessa steps sequence from *Battleship Potemkin* for which the editing was planned in advance, and the film photographed to fit the scheme. The impression given is one of constant movement and confusion with a gathering tension that finally provokes a strong emotional response. Into the scenes of general chaos are inserted sudden details which dramatize the violence – the shooting of the nursemaid, the runaway pram, the small boy trampled underfoot. In *October*, grotesque bourgeois women are contrasted with an innocent young revolutionary, Kerensky's militia are compared to wine glasses and tin soldiers, the *ancien régime* symbolized by shots of medals and uniforms, and Kerensky himself compared to a peacock.

It is not hard to find further examples. In Chaplin's *City Lights*, the film shows a crowd of commuters, then a flock of sheep; in Lang's *Fury*, we see women gossiping, then hens cackling; in *Strike*, workers are shot down, then oxen slaughtered. The technique seems rather artificial now, but it can still be effective in appropriate circumstances. In *King and Country*, directed by Joseph Losey, the camera cuts away from the hero, Hamp, in the mud of the trenches, as he describes his peacetime background, and illustrates his words with brief shots of characters in England. These shots are too short for flashbacks and are a visual presentation of his thoughts, a kind of expressive montage. They succeed in the film because they contrast strongly with the main sequence and also because they have a primitive pictorial quality which illustrates a central theme of the film, the naïve simplicity of Hamp's character.

In Truffaut's *Shoot the Pianist*, one of the gangsters uses a stock phrase, 'May my mother die if I'm telling a lie,' and the film cuts momentarily to a shot of an old woman collapsing. In *The Fallen Idol*, Carol Reed cuts from a bullying housekeeper in one of her bad tempers to an angry lioness in the zoo. There follows a scene showing the little boy who tells the story, at the zoo with a friend. Buñuel's *The Phantom of Liberty* doesn't take place in a zoo at all, but the final shot, quite unexpectedly, is of an ostrich peering nervously around. The image is a comment on liberty itself and on the audience. More provocatively still, in *WR – Mysteries of the Organism* the Yugoslav director, Dusan Makaveyev, cut from a shot of Stalin to an erect penis, to illustrate the argument that 'politics is for those whose orgasm is incomplete'. At the same time he is making a comment on the dictatorial element in expressive montage – it forces an interpretation on the viewer.

Some commentators tend to criticize expressive montage where the comparison is with an object not already part of the narrative, preferring that an image be credible in story terms before it becomes significant. They considered the symbol a flaw in the film's integrity, and held that meaning should be contained within the image rather than imposed upon it. At first sight, narrative montage seems closer to this ideal – until we remember that the camera is not necessarily any more impartial than the editing table.

In the fifties and sixties, in general theory, there was indeed a reaction away from montage as the ruling principle of film language. In part it stemmed from the adoption of a different ethical perspective, the search for truth rather than the imposition of ideas; in part from technological changes. The development of deep-focus photography and the new mobility of the camera had changed the nature of the shot itself, giving it a greater variety, the ability to hold more information and the possibility of moving from one set-up to another without a cut. These changes gave rise to theories which devalued montage and reasserted the primacy of the image. Siegfried Kracauer maintained that the revealing of reality was the natural goal of film, and 'realism' the principal criterion of aesthetic value. 'The realist tendency is at one with the very essence of film.'

But, as we have already seen, no photograph is ever a neutral recording of reality. Kracauer did take this into account, suggesting that man's interference could 'help and substantiate' the realist tendency – thus modifying the absolute basis of his realist position. But he did not go on to consider the role of the viewer in relation to his pure (or now, not so pure) reality. André Bazin recognized this problem and, as a working critic, grounded his work on textual analysis. Unfortunately this led him into a contradictory position. Inspired by Italian neo-realism, he followed Kracauer in seeking pure photographic realism, at its most perfect in the documentary. But, wishing also to be able to include manifestly fictional films in his theory, he constructed a second form of realism in which real object and film image share, not reality itself, but their spatial context. It is the *viewer*'s 'normal conception of space' which links the object itself and its filmed image. Since both montage and artificial expressionist décor destroy natural spatial unity, Bazin concluded that they were therefore 'anticinematic'.

Clearly Bazin's two positions are not easy to reconcile: one holds that image and object are identical, the other that they share a common denominator – the structure of space. Further, his exemplar of spatial realism was Orson Welles, a director whose films can be overtly expressionist and whose use of the camera is by no means faithful to the object. His florid, at times self-conscious, camera movement can be as dictatorial as the most frenetic cutting. What Bazin did clarify was the role of the viewer in the process. His realism based on deep focus and camera movement implied a viewer more actively involved in the film, making 'a positive contribution to the action in progress'. Whereas montage 'by its very nature rules out ambiguity of expression', the realist image is essentially ambiguous and open to interpretation.

If Bazin distinguished between 'directors who believe in the image and those who believe in reality', Jean-Luc Godard brought them back together and, as a film-maker himself, stressed that, in practice, montage and *mise-en-scène* are interlinked. 'Montage is above all an integral part of *mise-en-scène*. Only at peril can one be separated from the other. One might as well try to separate the rhythm from the melody . . . Knowing just how long one can make a scene last is already montage, just as thinking about transitions is part of the problem of shooting.'[1]

Of course this does not entirely resolve the problem. There are different ways of handling montage and *mise-en-scène*, there are radically different approaches to the film medium. But the two concepts are closely linked, and they are bound to be because cinematic time and space are inseparable. We have already seen how, through fast or slow motion within a shot, film can substitute space for time and time for space. This is even more apparent from shot to shot. As a result of montage a complex assimilation of space and time values occurs. This peculiar space—time structure forms a characteristic, most curious feature of the cinema. For one thing it corresponds to the scientific assimilation of space and time into a space—time continuum. In scientific thought a hundred years ago time was quite apart from space and the two belonged to different

1. Tom Milne, *Godard on Godard* (pp. 39–40), Martin Secker & Warburg, 1972.

orders – space solid, Euclidian in structure, time an endless flow. In science today, space and time are combined to form a framework on which the universe is built; we may move about in time much as we can in space, and space has some of the flowing quality of time. 'Physicists have been forced by virtue of the character of their own subject matter to see that their units are not those of space *and* time, but of space–time.'[1]

Firstly the cinema leads to a *temporal organization of space*, a term originated by Erwin Panofsky.[2] In real life, in the plastic arts and on the stage, space is for practical purposes static, motionless, unchanging. It stays put while we move about in it, either physically or mentally. In the cinema, space loses its static quality and acquires a time-charged dynamic quality. Parts of space are arranged in a temporal order and become part of a temporal structure with a temporal rhythm. The close-up for instance is not just a large scale picture of a part of space – it is a stage to be reached in time just as much as a *fortissimo* passage in a musical composition. In any composite film picture (of an individual, a group, a landscape) shots of different aspects of space follow each other in an order in time and could be put together in a different time-order to give a different result. Pudovkin pointed out that alteration of the order without any alteration in the shots themselves could radically change the meaning of a sequence. *One of the most important aspects of a composite film picture of space is its time dimension.*

We could say that montage in the cinema leads to the *temporalization of space*. The other way round it results in the opposite phenomenon, the *spatialization of time*. Time in real life (except in dreams), in literature and on the stage, has a definite directional trend of development. In the cinema, time loses this directional trend and (as will be apparent from what was said in Chapter 4) in a film we are free to move about *in* time, as in real life we are to move about in space. A film can go backwards and forwards, can show separate events together, can show simultaneous events separately. Time loses its uninterrupted continuity and irreversible

1. John Dewey, *Art as Experience*, Allen & Unwin, 1934.

2. Erwin Panofsky, 'Style and Medium in the Motion Picture', *Critique*, 1, New York, January 1947. Reprinted in full in *Film, an Anthology* by David Talbot, Simon & Schuster, New York, 1959.

direction. Neither literature nor the theatre are able to mingle brief moments and phases of time to the same extent as the cinema.

There is another way in which the cinema spatializes time, connected with the fact that in film every shot is in the present tense – every picture we see is just something happening. Our sense of time is different from other senses in being direct and subjective. Most of our knowledge of the world we acquire through specific sense organs but our sense of time derives from the biological clock with which we appear to be born. As soon as we wish to objectify time or measure it in concrete terms we can only do so in terms of space – clock, hour-glass, sun, stars, tide, growth, etc. This is exactly the case with the cinema. The cinema expresses different times by showing us different parts of space. As Élie Fauré said: 'The cinema makes duration a dimension of space'.[1]

The fact that cinema shows us time by a series of different positions in space, stems from the basic principle of moving pictures – that they consist of a series of still photographs of space which (the other face of the coin) *are arranged in time*. Since a film is a series of still photographs, it follows that (from certain points of view) the difference between the succession of each frame within the shot, and the succession from shot to shot is a difference of degree rather than one of kind. In fact in an animated film, which is created frame by frame, a cut from position to position of a single movement is exactly the same technically as a cut from one scene to another.

In this second way then, the cinema spatializes time, expressing duration by a series of positions, both from shot to shot and also within each shot. The latter case (within a shot) will include camera movement; and camera movement has the additional property of showing a series of different parts of space even if there is no movement in the setting. Normally in camera movement, say a panning-shot, the different parts of space will be related to a continuous period of time – successive instants immediately following one another. But camera movement can also be used by the artist to make large and dramatic time changes (e.g. from the present to the past as in the examples from *Miss Julie*, *Death of a*

1. *L'Arbre d'Éden*, Éditions Crès, Paris, 1922.

Salesman and *Wild Strawberries* already described). We can even have – in thought or dream – the man and the boy-the-man-used-to-be in the very same shot. Different periods of time are clearly expressed by different parts of space. In Bruce Beresford's *Crimes of the Heart*, there is a scene in which two sisters (Sissy Spacek and Jessica Lange) discuss their absent sister, Lenny (Diane Keaton). As one tells the story of Lenny contacting a dating agency the camera pans away and the Lenny of several years before bursts in to tell of her forthcoming date.

There is yet another way in which the cinema substitutes space for time, that is by multiplying, intensifying, and enriching the time the film runs, by deployment of space. It is rather like travelling on a holiday whose few days or few weeks may contain as much as months of ordinary life because they are crammed with experience – new places, new sights, new sounds. We try when on holiday 'to make as much of time as we can'. The time we spend in watching a film is similarly supercharged; it is ninety minutes of intensive experience. This is something common to all the arts, but the means are different, and in other arts it is not space that is used to enrich time but other things – in the theatre as much as anything it is language and the force of personality, in literature it is the magic of words. The cinema cannot match the words of literature or the personal presence of the theatre – but its command of space and all that it contains (sights and sounds) is unsurpassed.

One last point. Quite apart from all the considerations we have been discussing, there can be an emotional flavour about time and space as we experience them in the cinema. From this aspect the variations from reality which occur in time and space are not of such direct significance, and what matters will be the feeling they give us. John Dewey in *Art as Experience* makes the point of art in general when he says:

> As science takes qualitative space and time and reduces them to relations that enter into equations, so art makes them abound in their own sense as significant values of the very substance of things. Up and down, back and front, to and fro . . . *feel* differently . . . fast and slow as experienced are qualitatively as unlike as noise and silence, heat and cold, black and white.

The important thing here is the communication of experience, the *feeling* of spaciousness, of claustrophobia, of a rush of events, of the dragging tedium of ennui, of the choking unease of suspense. We remember the excitement, the exhilaration (with a touch of fear) as Chuck Yeager crashes through the sound barrier in Kaufman's *The Right Stuff*, and the awe of being in space with the astronauts later in the same picture. We can feel the steel at our throats as Marlon Brando wakes suddenly to Jack Nicholson's words, 'You just had your throat cut,' in Arthur Penn's *The Missouri Breaks*. We can almost taste the parched air of the desert township where the men wait for work, any work, in Clouzot's *The Wages of Fear*. The sight of the burning sledge 'Rosebud' in *Citizen Kane* can still bring tears to the eyes, however familiar, and few can fail to be affected by the death of Bambi's mother, or reduced to nervous exhaustion by the Russian roulette sequence of *The Deerhunter*. Truffaut talked of the cinema's 'privileged moments', those unanalysable happenings when time stands still, space expands and the image seems to communicate directly with the feelings of the viewer. Space and time in the cinema, compared with space and time in science and everyday life, are like every other element, emotionally charged. We come back to the point that art has an anthropomorphic quality, is bound up with the artist's experience.

Film is an art of time and space, and as Pudovkin says, the director builds up his own 'filmic' space and 'filmic' time. Film grinds down space and time until one is transformed into the other in a dialectical interaction. The cinema's freedom is based on a double mobility: that of the camera in space and that of shots in order and duration. The film is free to work with endless variations of physical reality in which the laws of time and space become 'tractable and obedient'. The cinema effects a synthesis. It divests space and time of their everyday, commonsense characteristics and invests them conjointly with the immateriality of thought, associates them together in a new *cinematographic space–time*.

CHAPTER SIX

THE SURFACE OF REALITY:
Décor, Costume, Make-up; Lighting, Soft-Focus, Double-Exposure, Negative Image, Distortion; Colour; Special Effects

IN the previous chapters we have been dealing with space and time as they make up the structure of reality, the space–time continuum, and as they are modified and used, selected and arranged, by the artist, to form an artistic space–time. In this chapter we wish to consider not the *structure* of reality, but the *surface* of reality – the surface quality, the texture and colour of things. These character- istics constitute the flesh which clothes the bones of length and breadth and depth and time; the texture of the image, the beauty that is only skin deep, the bloom on the peach, the polish on the furniture. In the cinema the features corresponding to this aspect of reality can be divided into three main areas. First, the actors, setting and décor, all characteristics which are shared with the theatre but taking different forms and playing different roles in the two media. Second, the circumstances of the shooting – lighting, colour (also shared with theatre) and photography – which combine with the first area to form the *mise-en-scène*. This second grouping is the means through which the first is transformed from pre-filmic object to filmic image. The third group consists of processes which are removed from the setting – optical effects and laboratory processes.

Here, too, the world of the cinema is related to, but different from, the real world. The film-maker has many decisions to make about the creation of his singular world, guided and constrained as always by the conditions under which he works and the style and conventions he chooses to follow.

MISE-EN-SCÈNE CHARACTERISTICS

Décor

There is no doubt about the artificial nature of stage settings which have grown up out of a long tradition – from the amphitheatre of Greek drama, to the apron stage of the Elizabethan theatre, the wooden platform of the mystery plays, the room with one wall missing of the realistic stage (realistic chiefly in including actual furniture and bric-à-brac), and the stark props and lighting effects of the modern theatre. The stage is in essence simply a convenient place for the players to perform, and it is dressed with props and scenery, and lit, partly for decoration and for the rest merely to symbolize or suggest a real place.

In the cinema it is rather different, and it is the particular property of the camera that it is able to give us a photographic reproduction of real locations, real bits of nature.[1] The first films ever made, those of Lumière, had no set décor. The cameraman merely set up his camera and filmed what was there or had his characters enact a simple story in a garden or a field. Then came the elaborate theatrical settings of Méliès and his imitators, but they proved to lead to a dead end. The American film-makers Porter and Griffith led the way back to natural settings and started the vogue of the Western – a genre in which magnificent natural scenery is sometimes the best thing in the film. Similarly, the appeal of a film like *Out of Africa* depends to some extent on the beautiful landscapes of the dark continent, and the conviction of *The Mission* is related to its sensuous evocation of the harsh luxuriance of the South American jungle. Werner Herzog's *Fata Morgana* and Reggio's *Koyaanisqatsi* are plotless, voiceless meditations on various strange land- and city-scapes. The streets of New York, Los Angeles and San Francisco must now feel almost as familiar to European cinema-goers as the highways of their own home towns.

Décor can add to a film by contrast, reinforce a mood, build a period atmosphere. In Ferreri's *La Grande Bouffe* (*Blow-Out*) the obscene gourmandizing and frantic sex are the more shocking for

1. Plate 29.

being set in a lovely old house with fine antique furniture and *objets d'art*. Jean-Jacques Beineix's *Diva* contrasts familiar Paris – the Tuileries, the Place de la Concorde – with unknown parking lots, deserted warehouses, pinball arcades, and sets the cool neo-classical interior of the opera singer's apartment against the empty garret of another character with its huge hyper-realist painting.

Not surprisingly, media images themselves are frequently part of modern décor: directors like Spielberg, Joe Dante and Sidney Lumet often include TV monitors in their settings. Lumet's films continually allude to the influence of the media either through theme (*Network, Power*) or décor (*The Anderson Tapes, The Morning After*). *The Morning After* opens with Jane Fonda discovering the identity of her deceased overnight lover from the television chattering away in the corner. The most extreme example perhaps remains Fassbinder's *The Third Generation* in which the characters, and audience, are constantly bombarded with media sound and images. The TV screens included in almost every scene (images within images reflecting the theme of wheels within wheels) force us to confront a modern world which consists of watching and being watched.

The choice between location shooting and filming on a set is one that raises issues of economics, aesthetics and fashion. The classic Hollywood pictures naturally made every possible use of the readily available studio space. Cheaper, independent films were more likely to prefer location shooting as soon as the appearance of lighter, more flexible apparatus made this an option for indoor as well as outdoor scenes. The studio offers vast technical resources and experienced manpower. It gives the film-maker maximum control of his environment so that every factor can be adjusted to his precise requirements.[1] The location, on the other hand, does away with the inevitable artificiality of the studio set: everything is 'real', the light is naturally there (though it may need supplementing), very little has to be specially built. Everything is more hazardous, however, in such an uncontrolled environment; the director may need to be more flexible, to take advantage of lucky accidents and allow for unlucky ones.

The modern set can be both vast and convincing. Michael

1. Plate 30.

Cimino's notoriously expensive Caspar City set for *Heaven's Gate* covered a huge area and was accurate to a fine degree even though it was actually on screen for a matter of seconds.[1] The Brooklyn set for *Once Upon a Time in America* is on a spectacular scale with a re-creation of the Brooklyn Bridge that deceives the eye – a far cry from the painted backdrop of a liner from a similar studio set for Hitchcock's *Marnie*.

On the other hand, Fellini's liner in *And the Ship Sails On* makes no pretence of realism. The director wants us to know that this is a film set and that the sea is made of black polythene. Similarly Coppola's *One from the Heart* was filmed entirely in the studio, using electronic video equipment, giving him the ability to create a deliberately expressionist setting for his musical.[2] Many film-makers now construct their own temporary studio by hiring an empty warehouse or factory and building sets within it. Kubrick's *Full Metal Jacket* was filmed in this way in the East End of London.

Location shooting can mean anything from the shutting down of an entire city street, the provision of vast quantities of a wide assortment of lamps, reflectors and all the electronic apparatus and power sources to run them, the organization of hundreds of extras and the presence of a huge crew fulfilling all the various Union requirements – to jumping into a van with a minimum of crew and actors and shooting a road movie on the run. This was how Coppola shot *The Rain People*. Both the cheapest and also some of the most expensive pictures have been made on location: whatever the budget, the location director is at the mercy of external conditions, notably the weather. Some of the most inflated of 'runaway' budgets have been accumulated on films shot away from the certainties of the studio (and the close scrutiny of the financiers) – *Heaven's Gate*, *Revolution*, *Apocalypse Now*.

The needs of the artist and the changing state of film and video technology combine continually to alter the equation between studio and location, though in general the trend has been away from the big, fully-manned studio with its heavy overheads: in Britain now there is not a single such studio left.

1. Plate 31.

2. Plate 32.

Paul Schrader's *Mishima* illustrates in one film contrasting approaches to décor and design. The story of the controversial Japanese writer was told in three ways, each of which was shot in a quite distinctive style. The film's present is 25 November 1970, when Mishima attempts to ignite an army revolt and a return to absolute Imperial power. When, predictably, he fails, he commits hara-kiri. This part of the film was shot in a mixture of locations and sets to look as much like newsreel as possible with bleached colours, hand-held cameras and rapid cutting. In contrast the flashbacks to Mishima's childhood were filmed in a more classical style with black and white photography and simple design reflecting the look of previous decades. The most unusual and visually arresting of the three strands was that illustrating three of the writer's stories, which comment on aspects of the writer's life and character in a more revealing way than the more overtly biographical sections. Schrader hired Ishioka Eiko, Japan's leading high-concept fashion designer. She used highly stylized designs, all created in the studio with expressionist settings, brilliant unnatural colours and hard edges emphasized by harsh lighting. The effect is highly theatrical, a fitting evocation of Mishima's vivid and violent imagination.

In David Lynch's films, his characters' physical and psychological diseases are related to his surreal visions of a sinister underworld barely concealed beneath a civilized veneer. Most explicit in *Eraserhead* with its ruined industrial landscapes, clanking machinery and the mysterious radiator, this 'hell on earth' surfaces again in *The Elephant Man*'s squalid backstreets and the abominable machines which mutilate the workers. The cosy world of *Blue Velvet*'s small town is continually cracking open to reveal the horrors lurking beneath, in the undergrowth, through the louvred doors or up the creaking fire escape. At its centre lies the perverted relationship between the singer (Isabelle Rossellini) and the crazed Frank (Dennis Hopper) which is acted out against the repellent purple and brown shades of the former's flat, colours which echo its owner's darker side.

The art director plays as large a part in the look of a film on location as he does on set, though his role may be rather different. As Bernard Evein, a leading designer of the 'new wave' has pointed out: 'Whether filming in "natural décor" or in the studio, our role is equally important . . . Reality must be modified in order to make it "more true than the truth". If you show the public something, say a concierge's lodge, no one is going to believe that it is really a concierge's lodge, and if I show it my home, no one will believe that they are in a decorator's house. To invent décor is to compose a universe.' Or as Alexandre Trauner, perhaps the most distinguished of all art directors, has put it: 'A room which is suitable to live in would not be suitable for a film. Décor ought to be realistic but not naturalistic.'

Cinema realism is, once more, seen as clearly distinguishable from reality itself. The designer sees his job as creating a world which conforms as much to audience expectations as to fact. Again at this stage we can see that the audience influences the way a film is made so that the film-maker is circumscribed by the mores, norms and conventions of the period.

Costume

In everyday life, costume is utilitarian, the word being understood to include functions like attracting the opposite sex and conferring prestige, as well as warmth and protection. In the cinema, as in the theatre or in painting, it has a predominantly aesthetic or dramatic function, distinct from the dictates of fashion or the demands of ordinary life. Film clothes can even become an integral part of the actor's personality. The supreme example is Charlie Chaplin. One needs only to draw a cane, a hat and a pair of shoes to know who is intended. The clothes which Buster Keaton wears differ from film to film, but his style of costume is unmistakable, a fact to which he draws attention in *Steamboat Bill Jr* when he tries on various hats before settling for his familiar flat boater. The identification of a man with his clothes or accessories occurs to some extent in real life (Churchill and his cigar, Harold Wilson with his pipe and raincoat, the Beatles with their long hair) but it seems stronger in the cinema, where clothes may help define the character of the owner, a shorthand way of telling us visually what his personality is like. We not only see the outward appearance, we draw certain conclusions about the inner person.

Alex and his gang of droogs in *A Clockwork Orange* are immediately recognizable for what they are, on their very first appearance in the Korova milkbar. Their braces, codpieces and top hats, along with Alex's single set of painted eyelashes, leave little doubt that ultra-violence is in their minds. In *Blue Velvet*, Frank's gang are a hideous set of grotesques whose lethal insanity is externalized through the outlandish garments which they wear. Francesco Rosi is a director who pays particular attention to costume – perhaps because his wife owns a fashion shop. In *Chronicle of a Death Foretold*, the character played by Rupert Everett is dressed in sombre colours, evoking the mystery of a figure who, in a sense, represents destiny. By contrast the young and handsome victim of the story, murdered on suspicion of dishonouring a young woman, wears white throughout. The girl herself wears clothes that are beautiful without being gaudy, to suggest the modesty of her character.

Costume may be simply utilitarian with no special meaning, or it may be expressive and significant. The costumier must always be as aware of the audience as of literal truth. Spectators of early Westerns would have been surprised to be presented with images showing cowboys as they really were. Elaborate conventions have grown up around the figure of the screen cowboy which owe little to the reality of life on the range. In the sixties these conventions were gradually broken down so that today the cowboy has a different image (not necessarily more accurate) and the well-laundered gunmen of classical Hollywood now look strangely surreal. Musicals have always avoided literalism so that farm workers (*Oklahoma*), factory hands (*The Pajama Game*), New York gangs (*West Side Story*) and so on, can all be glamorized to the extent of wearing gaudy outfits and *outré* styles. Lawrence Langner in *The Importance of Wearing Clothes*[1] suggests that, if shows of this kind were costumed realistically, the audience would be critical of incidents which, in the fairy-tale atmosphere created by the costumes, are passed over and accepted.

Peter Greenaway's *The Draughtsman's Contract* is concerned with the clash between realism and artifice, reflecting the director's own conflict between his training at art school (and the resultant inclination towards Romanticism), and his early career editing documentaries for a government department. Though his film is

1. Constable, London, 1959.

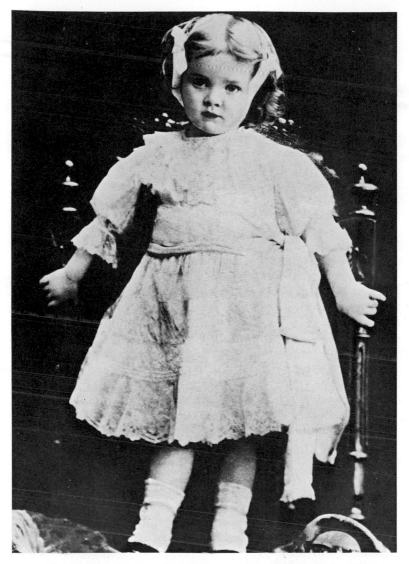

28. (*above*) The photograph took over the function of recording the past (p.134). Marlene Dietrich aged three.

29. (*above*) Natural scenery contributes to the appeal of certain films (p.147). (*Cheyenne Autumn*)

30.(*below*) On the other hand the cinema can make use of formalized décor (pp.148,224). (*The Cabinet of Dr Caligari*)

31. (*above*) The notoriously elaborate and expensive Casper City set (p.149). (*Heaven's Gate*)

32. (*above*) An expressionist setting from Copolla's musical *One From the Heart* (p.149).

33. (*above*) Parodies of the highly artificial styles of the seventeenth century (p.153).
(*The Draughtsman's Contract*)

34. (*above*) Film make-up now utilizes highly sophisticated techniques (p.156). (*The Elephant Man*)

35. (*above*) Star make-up raises daily beauty to the level of a superior, radiant, unalterable beauty (p.154). (*Rancho Notorious*)

36. (*above*) Side lighting gives relief and solidity to a face (p.158). (*La Terra Trema*)

37. (*above*) and 38. (*below*). Painting in Light (p.158): capturing the unique clarity of Indian sunlight (*A Passage to India*); and the carefully contrived backlighting of a French woodland (*Pierrot le Fou*).

39. (*above*) Lighting can give strong effects of depth (p.161). (*Love Me Tonight*)

40. (*above*) Candlelight as the sole source of illumination (p.162). (*Barry Lyndon*)

41. (*above*) Soft (or shallow) focus isolates the boxer from both foreground and background (p.163).
An example of a recent film in black and white. (*Raging Bull*)

42. (*above*) Double exposure was first used dramatically to represent the supernatural (p.164). (*Nosferatu*)

43. (*above*) Multiple exposure unites Napoleon, Josephine and a map of his forthcoming campaign (p.164). (*Napoleon*)

44. (*above*) Distortion with a justifiable source in the frame (p.165). (*Repulsion*). Compare with Plate 22.

45. (*above*) The abstract, formalized expression of a film like *Last Year in Marienbad* (p.167).

46. (*above*) Poster for the first sound film *The Jazz Singer* (p.177). Note how the artist has reproduced the camera's exaggeration of perspecive.

47. (*above*) War reduced to its filthy reality (p.203). (*Kanal*)

48. (*above*) The end of *Le Procès de Jeanne d'Arc* is dominated by the sound of a conflagration (p.209). Also an example of a close-up (p.75).

49. (*above*) A period setting can be very convincing (p.218). (*The Leopard*)

50. (*above*) Documentary-style carries authenticity, through the transfer of belief from the documentary to the fiction film (p.216). (*The Killing Fields*)

51. (*above*) Woody Allen as Zelig appears to clown with forties baseball star Babe Ruth (p.217). (*Zelig*)

52. (*above*) and 53. (*below*) What the cinema shows us may be not only a simple concrete image in its own right – it may represent or symbolize something (p.219). Above, the Stock Exchange symbolizes the capitalist system in *L'Eclisse*: below, the statue is an iconic representation of religion and the scene is a symbolic comment on the place of religion in the modern world. (*La Dolce Vita*)

54. (*above*) The realism of photography can give force to fantastic elements (p.234).
(*Un Chien Andalou*)

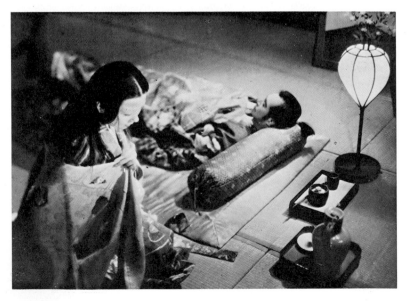

55. (*above*) The most effective ghosts are often the more realistic (p.234). (*Ugetsu Monogatari*)

set in the early seventeenth century, his hero, Neville, is faced with the same conundrum. Invited to draw sketches of the gardens of the handsome Jacobean country house of his patron, his determination to draw exactly what he sees produces bizarre results when items of clothing keep appearing unexpectedly around the gardens, offering clues to a murder mystery. The film is all about appearances – the look of the landscape, of Neville's images of it, and the look of both as we see them through the medium of film. Since clothing is at the centre of the plot (both the murder plot and the plot of the film) Greenaway is careful to make it a central feature. As a result, although his lords and ladies appear to be dressed in accurate period costume we soon realize that they are in fact parodies of the highly artificial styles of the time.[1] No lord ever wore so flounced or powdered a wig, no lady so tall and elaborate a hat. They artfully reflect one of the themes of the film, the artificiality of human intervention into the natural 'experience' of landscape. The draughtsman, the artist, the film-maker can never reproduce simply what he sees; his intellect ensures that what he finally produces is endowed also with what he knows and feels.

Make-up

Make-up in the cinema fulfils a different and perhaps more important role than it does in the theatre. In the vast amphitheatres of the Greek theatre, an actor was a tiny figure whose expression would have been lost to most of the audience. Masks larger than life-size and with emotions depicted in the most striking possible lines were an obvious advantage. Masks have been used, too, with resonant mouthpieces which amplify the human voice. Modern theatre make-up is the heir to this dramatic tradition, and invests the actor with a special authority and a personality suited to the role he is playing. It aims particularly at bringing out the expression, and stressing the lines of the mouth and eyes. While the contemporary theatre may have diminished the role of make-up, it still to some extent perpetuates the hieratic function of the antique mask.

In the cinema, actors can be presented in a great variety of styles ranging from no make-up at all, to a make-up far more elaborate

1. Plate 33.

than anything used in the theatre. At its most elaborate, in other words, in the case of 'star' make-up, the cinema also provides the actor with a mask, a mask which is invisible[1] but more complete than anything known to dramatic art, a mask which may require wig-makers, dentists, and plastic surgeons as well as the usual *coiffeurs*, make-up men, and colourists. It is also a mask with a different function, idealizing, beautifying. In both respects film make-up is nearer that of ordinary life but more skilful and carried to a higher pitch of perfection. The function of stressing expression is not required in the cinema since this can be brought out in other ways, particularly by the close-up. Cinema make-up can afford to be more elaborate than theatrical since there is only one performance. It also requires to be more flawless since the camera will look closer and more searchingly than a theatre audience, but, at the same time, with the aid of flood-lighting and perhaps soft-focus, it can achieve a more complete illusion.

At one end of the scale we can locate the classic star make-up of the Hollywood film which, as Edgar Morin put it,

> does not oppose a sacred vision to the profane life of every day; it raises daily beauty to the level of a superior, radiant, unalterable beauty. The natural beauty of the actress and the artificial beauty of the make-up combine in a unique synthesis.[2]

Star personality and hence star make-up are unalterable in different scenes of a film and even from film to film.

> In darkest Africa as in the filthiest hovel, at grips with hunger, thirst, frostbite, the marvellous Max-Factorized faces bear witness to the presence of the ideal at the heart of the real.

Star make-up is unalterable because it is divine and stars are the gods and goddesses of the modern world. But instead of God making man in his own image, man has fashioned these gods in an idealized, human image to fulfil a dream – a material, juvenile but

1. Cinema may also use the same kind of mask as the theatre: as in *Zardoz* to create the other-world atmosphere of science-fiction; to introduce us to 'men from Mars'; for a race of super-intelligent animals as in Schaffner's *Planet of the Apes*; or to give a picture of blind strength as in the figures in Lang's *Metropolis* and Whale's *Frankenstein*, or Lucas's Darth Vader in *Star Wars*.

2. E. Morin, *The Stars*, Calder, 1960; Plate 35.

perhaps a necessary dream – of fabulous wealth, of everlasting love, of effortless success. Star make-up means depersonalizing the face and creating an unchanging super-personality.

This ideal nature of star make-up, as of star costume, is more clearly visible if we contrast it with the other end of the scale – the films made virtually without make-up, the films of Eisenstein, Flaherty, Dreyer's *La Passion de Jeanne d'Arc*, Visconti's *La Terra Trema*, de Sica's *Umberto D*, Bresson's *Pickpocket*, and so on. These views in close-up, showing the grain of the skin, its shadows, its relief, its thousands of wrinkles, transform the face from the star's smooth mask into the richest and most expressive of terrains. One is accustomed to think that modern film-makers use little make-up but Diane Kurys's *Coup de Foudre* reveals that both the film's stars, Isabelle Huppert and Miou-Miou, actually have faces covered with freckles, 'blemishes' not seen in their other films.

Even without make-up the face is still a mask, although a richer, more expressive one. For it is the property of the camera to turn whatever it alights on into a 'film object'. Depending on the circumstances, looks may be as important as (or even more important than) acting ability and experience. Fellini's films are full of faces and bodies that are immediately recognizable as 'Fellini-esque' – grotesque, often threatening, always highly expressive. Even then, he usually casts established actors in the main roles, transforming them into barely recognizable freaks if necessary, as witness Donald Sutherland as Casanova. Fellini's compatriot, Francesco Rosi, has frequently cast non-actors in major roles. Above everything else he insists that he must find someone who corresponds in appearance to his idea of the character to be played. The result is a mixture of amateurs and professionals. Bresson goes even further, preferring non-professionals at all times, believing that dramatic acting is inimical to cinema which merely requires the person to remain him- or herself. At the other extreme Robert Altman's *Secret Honor* is a monologue delivered by an actor impersonating Richard Nixon in the White House bemoaning his fate. The actor Philip Baker Hall bears no resemblance to the politician at all and there is no attempt through make-up to create any similarity. Here the performance is all and, after a short while, as one watches, the surface discrepancy is forgotten.

The quality which all these performers share is that of being 'photogenic', which can be understood in a wider sense than being attractive or glamorous. The face of Falconetti in *La Passion de Jeanne D'Arc*, a tragic pattern of suffering, seamed with grime and sweat, can be called photogenic. And, again, the artistic value of a shot like this is in its success as a film object, as an artistic entity in its own right, not as a copy of reality. For these film close-ups show us the human face as we would never see it in reality.

Because of the greater control over an actor's appearance which can be achieved in the cinema, it is possible to effect far greater physical transformation than on the stage. A star hardly changes, because it is part of his appeal to be always the same. But an actor like Lon Chaney, in his many roles, or like Alec Guinness, who played seven different parts in Robert Hamer's *Kind Hearts and Coronets*, can change far more in appearance, in voice, in gesture and mannerism. Peter Sellers was a recent master of disguise with his multiple roles in Kubrick's *Doctor Strangelove*, probably his finest achievement. Robert de Niro is the current actor who most completely surrenders himself to his parts, changing both his face and his body to suit the character he plays – most clearly in adding several stones to play the middle-aged, paunchy ex-boxer in *Raging Bull*, having first trained to ring fitness to play the fighter in his prime.

Recent trends in film-making have created a whole new area of make-up in which special techniques are required and which afford the make-up artist an entirely new status. The release of *The Exorcist* in 1973 was the dawn of this era. Dick Smith had been working in the industry for twenty years but his range of prosthetic and other effects in this film attracted unprecedented attention. Smith went on to work on both *Godfather* films, on *Taxi Driver*, *Altered States*, *Scanners* and many other films and his lead was followed by others like Rob Bottin, Rick Baker and Tom Savini. Using latex foam to sculpt faces and bodies that are made mobile by the musculature of the performers they are built on, these make-up men brought the 'realistic' presentation of often gory details to new levels.[1] More, the complex technology involved means that the make-up expert effectively directs the scenes in which his most lurid moments are enacted. Bottin did his own lighting for scenes

1. Plate 34.

in *The Howling*; Savini took complete control at certain moments of Romero's *Day of the Dead*. Often the make-up is so constructed that there is only one way to film the scene without the artifice being apparent – and only the make-up expert knows it.

At these moments make-up and animatronics (the use of models animated by hydraulics and other methods) take over entirely from the actor who may not even be present. This is a field almost outside live-action movies bringing us into the sphere of *The Muppets* and *Spitting Image*.

Here we can only touch on the more synthetic nature of film acting. The cinema brings us so much closer to human beings that stage acting would be overpowering. 'Don't act, think' is what one film director[1] advised his actors. Again, a film performance is far less than on the stage a controlled total effort of the actor, but more a picture painted, stroke by stroke, jointly by cameraman, actor, director, and the rest. A child's smile of welcome to its mother may be directed at an ice-cream. Spencer and Waley[2] tell of a film in which the heroine had to register ecstasy at the return of the hero she supposed dead. The best of the many takes was found to be one caused by the camera over-running after the tea-break had been announced. Actors themselves have a wide variety of approaches to their work, from those who have studied Method Acting and aim to live the part, to those who rely on instinct and spontaneity. Whichever approach is used, and whether the style of performance is mannered or natural, matters far less than the final effect on the audience.

PHOTOGRAPHIC CHARACTERISTICS

Lighting

Film-making has been called 'painting in light' but light is an unusually abstract raw material from which to conjure images. As Brecht wrote in his *Life of Galileo*: 'Sometimes I think I'd gladly be locked up in a dungeon ten fathoms below ground, if in return, I could find out one thing: what is light?' When we watch a film, all

1. Friedrich Murnau.

2. *The Cinema Today*, Oxford University Press, 1939.

we actually see are patterns of light and shadow on the screen thrown by the cinema projector. During the process of filming itself, light has already been involved twice. The object or setting must be bathed in light, and then this light is reflected back and recorded by the movie camera. Light is also involved and can be altered and modified during the development stage when negative becomes positive.

While shooting, the film-maker can utilize natural and/or artificial light. Though film is now sensitive enough to pick up even very low levels of light, feature film photographers (usually known as cinematographers or directors of lighting) nearly always use some form of electric illumination. This can be adjusted along four main dimensions. Brightness can vary from high-key (which throws a strong light over the whole, shadowless scene) to low-key (with most of the frame in darkness and perhaps a few distinct pools of light). Contrast ranges from high-contrast with its bright highlights and deep shadows, to low-contrast where the whole scene is evenly lit with no extremes. Texture can be hard or soft with bright light, for example, throwing clear shadows and giving crisp edges while a more diffuse source will produce less sharp outlines. Finally, the direction of the light is of great importance and most scenes involve a complicated balance between different sorts of light from different directions.[1]

All four dimensions affect the look of the frame, not only in revealing what it includes but also in suggesting emotionally how we are to see it. High-key lighting is associated with optimism and excitement, low-key with mystery or threat; high-contrast tends to be dramatic, low-contrast calmer or even melancholic. Direction can be particularly influential – a face may alter significantly depending on how it is lit. Lighting from above spiritualizes a subject and gives it a solemn or angelic look (religious characters) or an air of youth and freshness. Lighting from below imparts a feeling of unease and gives a wicked or unearthly appearance. Lighting from the side gives relief and solidity to a face,[2] but may make it ugly and show the lines. It may indicate an ambiguous

1. Plates 37 and 38.
2. Plate 36.

personality, half good, half bad, symbolically half light, half shade. Lighting from in front blurs any faults, flattens relief, softens modelling, makes the face more beautiful but takes away its character. Coming from behind, lighting idealizes a subject, giving it an ethereal quality. This sort of lighting is a modern version of the halo of saints or the aura of a medium.

At different periods, film-makers have followed different styles and conventions in the use of lighting to interpret reality. The early silent films used natural sunlight filtered through white canvas, a technique adapted from the painter's studio. The result was a soft, shadowless light. The German expressionists introduced another technique from painting, chiaroscuro, the management of light and shade, which favoured design and allowed the introduction of lighting effects. This developed into the classic Hollywood style that used complex directional lighting to increase the information carried in the frame and to achieve effects that were later to be more easily achieved in colour. As the Cuban director of photography Nestor Almendros has described it: 'For 25 years cinematography, especially that of interiors, had been chained to a series of rules and precepts, that Berlin had created and Hollywood imposed: every scene should be lit from four basic sources: 1) Key light, which modelled the subject; 2) Filling light, to fill the excessively harsh shadows produced by the key light in the subject; 3) Back light, the light that comes from the opposite direction to the camera and that creates a halo round the head or body to detach it from the background; 4) Background light, to emphasize the sets.'[1]

This era of idealized but stylized lighting lasted until around 1950 when neo-realism made a break with both form and content. The key figure appears to have been G. R. Aldo, a still photographer who had no cinema experience and was able to ignore all tradition when he lit Visconti's *La Terra Trema*. In this film, in de Sica's *Umberto D* (also in black and white) and in Visconti's colour film *Senso*, Aldo pioneered the technique of basing the lighting pattern on natural light, adding to it only that limited amount of artificial light that had a justified source in the frame (a window or lamp, for example). This additional light was bounced off walls or boards to give it the softer quality of real daylight. Aldo's ideas were taken up by the film-makers of the French new wave, notably Godard and the photographer of his early films, Raoul Coutard, who sought a completely unadorned style, devoid of dramatic effects.[1]

Verisimilitude has now largely superseded balance, though artificial styles may still be needed for particular situations. Alan Pakula has commented that, for the look of *All the President's Men*, 'I wanted a world without shadows. I wanted a world which was a world of truth, where nothing gets away, where everything is examined under this merciless glare. Also a deep-focus film: everything had to be seen, no mysterious backgrounds.' The lighting therefore was hard and dramatic with the important newspaper office lit by neon strips, a light source that would normally be avoided at all costs. Yet this film was photographed by Gordon Willis, the high priest of subdued lighting. Though a lighting director cannot help but have his own particular style, this should be adapted to the special needs of each particular film.

Lighting fulfils a variety of functions during the shooting of a film. It can reveal the image in such a way that the composition has a unified structure, that attention is drawn to what is important, with irrelevant detail in the shade. In doing so it is instrumental in suggesting the meaning of the image. A dark street is both a dark street and also an image of threat and uneasiness. Lighting therefore sets the emotional tone of the film or of the scene. In pictures like *The Third Man, Last Year in Marienbad*, most 'films noirs' and many horror films, the lighting creates a stifling or even morbid atmosphere which heightens the dramatic effect of what we see. This sort of atmosphere is most easily created in the studio where every facet of film-making is under control, enabling the director to simulate the steamy, unhealthy erotic atmosphere of Fassbinder's *Querelle* or the voluptuously damp and ghostly world of Neil Jordan's *The Company of Wolves*. The second part of Renoir's *La Grande Illusion*, in the château prison, has quite a

1. Interestingly, Satyajit Ray and his photographer, Subatra Mitra, were making the same discoveries as Aldo at almost the same time. Upset by the multiple shadows of Hollywood, Ray also endeavoured to 'simulate available light by means of bounced light'. Ray has mentioned Cartier-Bresson as a major influence so it seems that still photography stimulated simultaneous experiments on two continents.

different emotional tone (confined, dark, cramping) from the third part when Jean Gabin and his companions have escaped. The lighting is an important part of this contrast.

We have noted that, in general, dark lighting is used for tragedy or drama and brighter lighting for warmer, sunnier impressions with an optimistic undertone. Thus many scenes in Bergman's comedy *Smiles of a Summer Night* are in light, sunny tones offsetting the elegant, cynical wit of the story. But Bergman also shows how, by going beyond a certain point, garish lighting can have an unreal, ghastly effect, well-suited to dreams, visions or nightmare memories. In *Sawdust and Tinsel*, a flash-back depicts a humiliating memory of the circus clown, Frost, recalling an occasion when he found his wife bathing naked with a regiment of soldiers and carried her back to their caravan through a jeering crowd. Besides being overlit, this is contrasted with the rest of the film by being filmed silent. Another striking example is in the dream sequence of Federico Fellini's *8½*, a film which uses unusual lighting a great deal. The same means is used to give a harsh satiric effect to a scene from *Doctor Strangelove* in which the air-force general, Buck Turgidson, is summoned from his quarters, where his secretary is basking under a sun-lamp, to attend a midnight meeting in the Pentagon. Besides overlighting, a variable or flickering light can be used to reinforce drama or tragedy. The pulsing light of ambulances and police cars often comes in naturally. In *Last Tango in Paris*, during a quarrel on a Metro platform between the heroine and her film-crazy boyfriend, a flickering light that lasts throughout the sequence adds to the violence of their disagreement.

Lighting affects not only the surface but also the structure of reality by helping to create pictorial and scenic space. By skilful use of light the camera can give the strongest effects of depth.[1] In John Ford's *The Long Voyage Home*, we see one of the sailors in flight through the Cardiff docks at night after being mixed up in a brawl. The scene is filmed facing a strong light, a beacon or lighthouse, which creates very strong counter-illumination. The fugitive runs from the foreground at full speed towards the central light point and seems to be swallowed up by it, while his shadow grows out of

1. Plate 39.

all proportion, stretching along the ground to the spectator. The strong effect of distance is emphasized by using a wide-angle lens.

As in other areas, technology and art go hand in hand. When making *Barry Lyndon*, Kubrick wanted to shoot his eighteenth century interiors using only the candlelight that would have been the sole illumination of the period.[1] Until that point there had been no solution to this problem, but Kubrick and photographer John Alcott discovered that NASA were developing a special lens for satellite photography. Zeiss had made ten such lenses which were twice as fast as the fastest movie lenses then available. Kubrick acquired one and, much adapted, it enabled him to shoot in conditions so dim that it was difficult to read. Of course the definition was imprecise, but this was exactly the romantic effect that Kubrick wanted – at other times he used filters, a veil or tracing paper to soften the light.

Soft-Focus, Double-Exposure, Negative Image and Distortion

The 'soft-focus' of Kubrick's images mentioned above resulted from the inability of even the fastest lens to achieve a precise image in very poor light. But soft-focus is also used deliberately in perfectly adequate light to take advantage of the inherent limitations of the camera lens. It first became popular at the beginning of the century in still photography. Soft-focus produced a flattering portrait and introduced an expressive, 'artistic' element into what was widely being interpreted as a mere mechanical copying of nature. Impressionist painting may also have been an influence. In film, soft-focus soon became a means of visual idealization, though it could also convey a mood of pathos, mystery, poetry or fantasy. Its romantic character is best expressed in the many soft-focus close-ups of female stars in classic Hollywood pictures – though here gauze and other forms of diffusion were also used. The device is frequently employed to express subjective states – of fainting, for example, as Ingrid Bergman is overcome by a drugged cup of coffee in Hitchcock's *Notorious*. It is often used to introduce a flashback or memory, but as a rule these artificial uses of the device are becoming less common.

1. Plate 40.

More familiar is the use of soft-focus over a part of the image only. Sometimes called shallow-focus, it conveys the opposite effect to deep-focus, strengthening the contrast between background and foreground.[1] As André Bazin expressed it, 'As soon as the film space ceases to be homogeneous and is split into intellectual and dramatic parts, the art of *mise-en-scène* consists as much in hiding as in revealing. Soft-focus is a means of stressing the plane on which the camera is focused; it translates in terms of plastic composition the dramatic relationships which montage expresses in terms of time.' In a film about American politics, *The Best Man* by Franklin Schaffner, there is a very subtle example. The film depicts a struggle between two men, William Russell and Joe Cantwell, to win the 'primary' election and be chosen as presidential candidate. Cantwell, an oppressive bully, is planning to 'smear' Russell by publicizing an exaggerated report of a nervous breakdown he had a year ago. The President of the United States, who is campaigning for Russell, interviews and draws out a witness who can prove that Cantwell is a homosexual. In a situation rapidly growing tenser, the President and the witness are talking on a couch, while Russell stands pensive, saying nothing, in the foreground. Suddenly the President and the witness go out of focus and the camera concentrates sharply on Russell. It seems at the time completely wrong. Surely the key people are the President and the witness who, in effect, control the election, and the camera ought to focus on *them*. But as the plot develops we find out that Russell's conscience will not let him use the evidence against Cantwell *and it never is used*. The camera, in focusing on Russell struggling with his conscience and ignoring the others, has given us a glimpse of things to come.

Double-exposure is another editorial technique which allows the film-maker radically to alter reality. In fact, the phenomenon does occur in the real world when we see a reflection on glass at the same time as seeing another image through it, or in a mirage where a freak reflection is superimposed on a real landscape. The property of glass to show two images at once has been frequently assimilated into films, most often perhaps in the form of reflections (of trees or

1. Plate 41.

city lights) on car windscreens, and other examples have already been indicated in our discussion of mirrors in Chapter 2.

Like reverse motion, double-exposure began as a simple visual curiosity with no expressive component and, like soft-focus, it was pioneered in still photography in which there was a vogue around 1865–70 for the 'spirit photograph'. Georges Méliès used it in his films as early as 1904 but it was as a dramatic evocation of the supernatural that it first gained popularity. It was used by Victor Sjöström in *The Phantom Carriage*, in Murnau's *Nosferatu*[1] and in Dreyer's *Vampyr*, and the technique is still sometimes seen. In Boorman's *Zardoz* there is extensive and showy use of multiple images, kaleidoscopic effects, reflections, faces floating in the air, magic writing emanating from a crystal ball that indelibly covers different surfaces.

Double-exposure may be used to introduce a symbol or visual metaphor. In Gance's *Napoléon*, a stormy session of the Convention is accompanied in double-exposure by scenes of a great tempest. When Napoleon is leaving for the Italian campaign there appears, through a map of Europe which fills the screen, the haughty silhouette of Napoleon and the enigmatic visage of Josephine.[2] Some close-ups of the hero are decorated as if by a water-mark with shots of his eagle, the motif which represents his soaring ambition.

There are other uses of the technique. It can be a way of suggesting inner thoughts with the character's face superimposed on images of what is passing through his mind, or as a dissolve it can be treated as a means of transition, linking the images of two different places or times. The advent of memory-linked camera systems which allow camera movements to be endlessly repeated to the accuracy of ten thousandth of an inch, has given double-exposure new importance as a means of including numerous different elements on the same piece of film. In Nelson's *The Black Hole* there is a sequence in which people are seen leaving a lift. As the camera pulls back we see them going into an observatory and a tilt reveals the vast domed roof. It looks like a massive set – but no

---

1. Plate 42.

2. Plate 43.

such set ever existed. The whole sequence was built up from eleven separate exposures, including live action, miniatures and painted backgrounds, all put together in the camera.

We should also mention briefly the uses of negative images and of distortion. The negative has been effectively used to evoke the other world, a spectral realm in which living things become skeletons, a demonic, macabre anti-world. Murnau used it in *Nosferatu* for the arrival of the hero, in Count Orlock's strange carriage with its black curtains, in the country of ghosts. Cocteau employed the device in *Orphée* for the appearance of the motor-car in the no-man's land of death. Godard used negative sequences to suggest the dead quality of life on the other side of 'inter-sidereal space' in *Alphaville* ('Capitale de la Douleur'). But, on the whole, the negative image is too extreme, too obtrusive an effect to be used very often. The same applies to distortion unless there is a justifiable cause of it in the narrative, as in Polanski's *Repulsion*, where we see distorted images reflected in the polished surface of a kettle, and see faces through the distorting lens of a door peephole.[1] The visual deformity which results, reflects the inner deformity of the heroine's repressed personality.

Once again glass can be used as a medium for distortion, permitting a visual comment on a theme. In Zeffirelli's *Otello*, as Iago spins his web of deception, distorting events to fuel Otello's jealousy, the two characters move around the latter's study passing behind various lenses that Otello has been using, which magnify and distort their faces. More subtly, Arthur Penn filled the flat of his private eye hero in *Night Moves* with mobiles of distorting glass which reflected the fractured state of his mind. For the war scenes in *Jules et Jim* Truffaut obtained an extraordinary effect by using documentary film shot on the battlefield with normal 35 mm lenses but stretched to cinemascope dimensions. Less satisfactory is the characteristic distortion of the moving wide-angle lens which has no meaning in terms of the shot or relevance to the action.

Colour

One of the most important of the surface characteristics of film, as of reality, is colour. From the earliest days of the cinema, the

1. Plate 44.

inability of the original photographic processes to reproduce colour was considered a serious drawback. Compared with other more subtle deviations from reality this was such an obvious disadvantage. As a result, a great deal of research has been undertaken from the very beginning in an attempt to invent a workable colour process. In addition, the world's film archives are full of productions, which were common forty or fifty years ago, made on tinted film-stock: blue for summer days and for idylls; green for landscapes and seascapes; red for fires and murders; and mauve for night scenes and romantic agonies. There are also reels of early film which have each frame coloured by hand – the work of thousands of hours and of armies of anonymous workers. The first processed colour film, shown in 1910, was in Kinemacolor, a two-colour additive process, which proved unsatisfactory in use. In 1925–6 a Technicolor two-colour subtractive process was introduced, the only surviving film which used it being *The Black Pirate*, with Douglas Fairbanks in the lead. In 1935 came the first successful three-colour picture in Technicolor: *La Cucaracha*. From this date onwards, the colour film was established commercially; improvements followed, and various other systems were developed: Agfacolor, Ferraniacolor, Dufaycolor, Sovcolor, and so on.

Early attempts at colour were abandoned partly because of failures and financial disasters but also because people soon came to accept monochrome as a satisfactory form of expression. The photographic image was not just a picture that *lacked* colour: it was something positive with its own artistic qualities. The still photograph and the black and white film both developed as new forms of visual art. They were new because the half-tones of the photograph are just as different from the black and white of any of the graphic arts – whether etching, woodcut, pen and ink, charcoal or Chinese brush – as they are from reality. Photography was a form of painting with light, particularly in the case of film, since film with its method of projection could achieve a more luminous image than photography.

At the same time continuous technical improvement played its part – better lenses, better lighting, better film-stock. The film image showed a higher degree of delicacy in rendering tonal values, and the range of intermediate shades between black and white became richer and more subtle. On the screen there flourished a fairyland of light and shade creating those symphonies of chiaroscuro which enchanted Bardèche and Brasillach and formed some of the greatest triumphs of the young art. Black and white is able to reveal the world differently from colour. Peter Ustinov made *Billy Budd* in black and white and said, 'Colour beautifies everything and I feel you never get the conditions of people in colour.' In *Uncle Vanya* (1974) Konchalovsky took some scenes in monochrome because 'they could not be interpreted adequately in colour'. In *Heimat* Edgar Reitz alternated colour and black and white seemingly at random and explained that 'the casualness of colour over-determines the images you see and freezes the imagination. Whereas black and white ... encourages you to take a more active part in the film.'

When colour was introduced widely on a commercial scale in the late thirties, it was expected to kill the black and white film stone dead, just as sound had made the silent film a historical curiosity. But this has not happened. Though colour has become the norm and it is hard now to find laboratories that can process monochrome film adequately, black and white is by no means extinct as films like *L'Enfant Sauvage*, *The Last Picture Show*, *Veronika Voss*, *The Elephant Man*, *Manhattan*, *Raging Bull* and many others attest, not to mention the continuing life of older productions on television and video. Black and white is beautiful in its own right and enables a stylization and formal composition that colour may dissipate. The abstract, universalized atmosphere of Resnais's *Last Year in Marienbad* would have been impossible in colour.[1] The striking last shots of Renoir's *La Grande Illusion*, with the black dots of human beings against the white loveliness of the snow, and the faint hint of symbolism, would have been less effective in colour. The harsh, unreal, science-fiction atmosphere of Stanley Kubrick's *Doctor Strangelove* is dependent on its use of black and white. In Orson Welles's *Macbeth*, the sombre tones are needed to conjure up a brooding air of medieval conspiracy, and, in Bergman's *The Silence*, the use of black and white helps to create the stifling emotional climate of the film and underline the morbid psychology of the characters. In other films the differing qualities of colour and monochrome are worked into the very structure of the work. In

1. Plate 45.

Tarkovsky's *Stalker*, the everyday world through which three men journey in search of 'The Zone' is shot without colour. When the Zone itself is reached the film suddenly changes to colour, indicating that the Stalker sees the Zone as his real home, his goal. When the scene reverts to the bar where the men first met, the photography likewise reverts to monochrome. The Stalker's wife comes to take him home. On their way back the pictures are again momentarily in colour. At the very end as we see the couple's crippled daughter apparently causing a tumbler to move across the table through psychic power, the colour returns as if the girl too has reached her own Zone, a place of inner peace and the fulfilment of her wishes.

In *Nostalghia*, Tarkovsky used sepia and colour to distinguish the present from other times and places, whether of memory or dream or death. As the film progresses the clear division between the two worlds crumbles, the inner world overlapping with the real.

A number of monochrome films have included a brief moment of colour. In *Raging Bull*, the boxer's amateur home movies are shown in grainy, blurry colour which makes it look less 'natural' than the pristine black and white that surrounds it. In Coppola's *Rumblefish* only the tiny red and blue fish and the flashing light of the ambulance at the climax are in colour. In Varda's *Cleo from 5 to 7* there is only one shot in colour, the tarot cards which predict the heroine's fatal illness. Many films have used the device of opening in black and white to establish the period, before changing to colour for the main body of the narrative.

While black and white is still a perfectly viable form today, the pity is that, as cinematographer Ghislain Cloquet has pointed out: 'For a long time I had to do films in black and white that would have been better in colour. Now you do films in colour that would have been better in black and white. I think it is a shame that this is done for commercial reasons. The real reason should be that a film is interesting in black and white or in colour.'

Though colour now seems natural to us on screen it should not be thought that it is necessarily realistic. While colour systems have improved immeasurably in a short period of time, there will always be divergencies from nature. Even if this discrepancy between object and image could be overcome, the result would still not, on screen, be a literal duplication of nature. The conditions of viewing, in a darkened auditorium, are different from everyday life, and the colours on screen inevitably have a luminous quality because they are produced by light shining through a translucent material. The aim of the film-maker is not to imitate but to recreate on screen the impression made by the object in life, imbued with the film-maker's attitude towards it. A painter will not necessarily try to reproduce on his canvas the profusion and incoherence of natural colour. Consciously or unconsciously he will shape what he sees to the requirements of his purpose through a process of selection and presentation.

It is instructive to note how frequently film-makers refer back to painters when planning the colour design of their films.[1] When making *Moby Dick* in 1956, John Huston overlaid the three colour negatives with a fourth grey image which gave the whole picture the appearance of an old aquatint. Nestor Almendros has spoken of looking at Victorian paintings with Truffaut before making *Les Deux Anglaises et le Continent*, and of studying German romantic art for Rohmer's *The Marquise of O*. In America he sought inspiration from artists like Maynard Dixon and Edward Hopper before making *Goin' South* and *Still of the Night* respectively. When designing *Round Midnight*, Bertrand Tavernier's story of a jazz veteran, Alexandre Trauner chose a blue and grey colour scheme intended to evoke old monochrome photography, even though it was to be shot in colour. In his earlier *Sunday in the Country*, Tavernier told the story of an elderly painter contemplating his life and art. The director reflected this theme in his design and suggested the interrelationship between painting and art by reproducing the fine effects of early autochrome colour prints which had had a marked influence on impressionism and pointillism in painters such as Seurat and Signac.

If the period of a film is relatively recent, the film-maker has old photographs and, later, moving images themselves as guides. The skating sequence of *Heaven's Gate* fades to muted browns, yellows and pinks, recreating the effect of tinted photographs and emphasizing that the way of life represented is about to pass into history.

1. Many films about painters have naturally reflected their work in the design of the films themselves – Huston's *Moulin Rouge*, Minnelli's *Lust for Life*, Shengayala's *Pirosmani* and Derek Jarman's *Caravaggio* are examples.

Walter Hill's *Southern Comfort* followed a group of part-time
soldiers on an exercise, lost in the swamplands of the Louisiana
bayou. Cinematographer Andrew Laszlo restricted his palette to
drab olive colours in imitation of David Douglas Duncan's combat
photos from Korea in which 'all you'd notice is their steel helmets
and maybe just a glint of light in their eyes.' In *Sophie's Choice*, the
'present' of 1947 (filmed in familiar Technicolor) was contrasted
with the earlier war-time scenes in Germany in which the colours
were desaturated, softening the tones, so that these flashbacks
resembled German Agfacolor films of the period with their relatively pastel shades.

Desaturization is now a common technique, for as Douglas
Slocombe has pointed out, 'Restraint is the keyword. I was able to
conjure up the cold, dank atmosphere of a twelfth century castle
for *The Lion in Winter* far more satisfactorily than I should have
been able to do in black and white. I carefully avoided any 'pure'
colour here, it would have been an intrusion. I tried to let tints
glow through palely. The secret is to photograph places and objects
less colourfully than they would appear in real life.'

Again, the director's artifice may give a more realistic effect than
precise imitation. It is now easy to avoid the picture postcard look
but only by careful sleight of hand. An indication that successful
colour in film-making is not to be found in mechanical reproduction of nature lies in the fact that colour is so effectively used in the
musical and in the ballet film. In this field it *has* ousted black and
white, partly for the reason that a musical demands the gaiety of
colour, but also because the musical is a highly artificial form in
which all the factors can be completely controlled. The colours of
the décor, the costumes, the properties, can all be chosen to film
well, and to combine into an effective colour composition. From
Singin' in the Rain to *Grease*, from *The Red Shoes* to *All That Jazz*,
one can think of many films in which the handling of colour has
been a major part of their appeal.

Dramatic Use of Colour

Colour may be used emotionally for its symbolic or dramatic effect
either in a single scene or to help give a tone to the whole film.
Eisenstein said that 'we should think of the *meaning* of colour.'
Mention has already been made of the tinted film-stock of the early

days in which the whole scene took on a shade appropriate to its character, blue for summer days and idylls, red for fires and murders and so on. The case of Huston changing the colour throughout *Moby Dick* has been mentioned. His success in that case has rarely been repeated. He himself tried the process again in *Reflections in a Golden Eye* in which he effected a washed-out golden aura, but the film was never released in that form. Joshua Logan tinted certain sequences in *South Pacific* in violent shades but the result was not widely appreciated. More acceptable is the sort of combination we have already discussed in which monochrome and colour are used for different sections. *The Wizard of Oz* was an early example of this with its introductory and concluding sequences of reality in monochrome contrasting with the colourful fantasy of Dorothy's tornado-induced dream.

It should be recognized that colour can be related to emotions only in the most general way. Much will depend on the context and meaning of the film, much on other elements such as music and tempo. Red may be just as suitable for the gaiety of a musical, the excitement of a battle or the violence of a murder. In Hitchcock's film *Marnie*, the heroine is violently affected by red, and the red of a storm, a sunset or a dress causes her to have a nervous upset. This strange reaction turns out to be due to a violent childhood experience buried in her subconsciousness. Her mother had been a prostitute and the child, molested by one of her mother's customers, attacked him with a poker and (as she thought) killed him, her principal memory of the event being the red of his blood. Red, once more, is the key colour in Nicolas Roeg's *Don't Look Now*, where it is associated with love, sex and death at various moments. The red of the drowning child's macintosh is matched by the spreading stain of red ink which destroys her father's artwork at the same moment. Later he glimpses the red macintosh in a back alley in Venice and pursues it to his death in a spreading pool of red blood. In *The Red Desert*, Antonioni used frequent colour and focus distortions to signal the heroine's alienation, her inability to adjust to society. Living unhappily in an industrial district, she is shut in a mental prison of loneliness, and the predominant shades are muddy blues, greens and greys – in one scene a whole fruit-stall is sprayed a uniform grey. The only bright colours are the sulphurous yellow and rust red of waste fumes and refuse dumps.

There is a temporary change to rich red in a hut where a group of friends join in a drinking and necking party, and to soft pink when the woman meets a lover she hopes will open a new world to her. At the same time Antonioni cuts her off from her surroundings by the use of shallow-focus, the blur around her expressing her isolation.

In *The Godfather* colour is subdued. The world of the Mafia family is a dark one, but at its centre in *Part One* we find a warm golden glow, symbolizing the security provided by the power of the Don. In *Part Two*, however, this same golden light is used to different effect: it often augurs violence against the family. As the strength of the Corleones is challenged the family becomes a source, not of security, but of danger and threat. In the early part of *The Shining*, Stanley Kubrick uses warm yellow as an indication of stability and well-being. Later, red, white and blue dominate, the red increasingly associated with blood, white and blue with cold and the isolation of madness. The whole can be seen as a metaphor for the breakdown in human contact and relationships in American life. *American Gigolo* is another film that weaves patterns of red, white and blue as an ironic comment on the American flag.

West Side Story uses colour with striking effect in many sequences. Early in the film there is a transition from the hero, Tony, working in the street, to the heroine, Maria, in a dress-maker's shop, which depends on the shimmering colour of semi-transparent material. In the street scene, the washing on the line grows rapidly more glamorous in colour and texture, the camera concentrates on it and then dissolves to the dress material in the shop. The transition is made by a pure colour dissolve. After the lyrical dress-shop scene, and before a violent scene, there is a brief sequence, in abstract reds and blacks, of figures turning and changing, which helps the transition from one mood to another and presages the conflict to come. In the dance-hall scene Maria wears the only white dress, which both stands out prominently against the other strong colour, and also conveys an obvious symbolic meaning.

As a final example, one can mention the successful use of colour for poetic and dramatic ends in Albert Lamorisse's *Le Ballon Rouge*. The balloon is the chief character in the story and, to ensure that it has the principal dramatic part, it has to occupy the most promiment place on the screen. The director achieves this by painting it a splendid red and, what is more, showing it against a background of neutral greys and biscuit colours. Besides the dramatic emphasis given by the contrast, the colours also have a symbolic function. The neutral backgrounds represent the poor district in which a little boy lives, the unromantic, ordinary workaday world. The red balloon on the other hand stands for the splendour and magnificence of the life he aspires to, the fairy-tale world he floats towards at the end, carried up to the sky by a whole collection of gaily coloured balloons. The film should be noted both as an artistic and as a technical achievement for, as in all colour films, the effect is not finally obtained until the film leaves the laboratory. A recent illustration of this last point was Visconti's *The Leopard*, which was praised for its colour in the original Italian prints, but criticized for the colour of subsequent prints made by a different process for exhibition in England.

Sadly, the increasingly subtle and sophisticated effects which film-makers struggle patiently to achieve during production, are rarely matched in the release prints which are mass-produced for public showing. By the time the film is seen on television or video further processes have intervened and the choice of colour rests very much in the hands of viewers who are accustomed to see on their sets the garish flat lighting of the TV studio. The recent introduction of 'colorization' (whereby films conceived and shot in black and white are tinted in shades devised by computer) is another development which destroys the original intention of the film. Had these movies been shot in colour the whole design and photography would have been fundamentally different. A final problem worth noting is the instability of modern colour dyes which threaten the survival of films made since 1950. In 1980 Martin Scorsese led a campaign to draw attention to this threat, noting that 'all films made in the Eastman colour process are about to deteriorate beyond repair'. The answer is to preserve separate reels, each recording just one of the constituent colours of the film, and to store them at low temperatures in special vaults. This expensive process is not a solution that is likely to be widely applied. Ironically, videotape is not thought to suffer from colour fading.

Special Effects

This is a highly specialized area of film-making to which many books and magazines have been devoted as public awareness of, and appreciation of, the achievements of technicians has grown. Of course the history of special effects goes back to Méliès and it has been said that up to eighty per cent of some reels of *Citizen Kane* included such effects. The difference is that today, in certain types of film, they are more visible, whereas in the past an effect was successful only if it were unnoticeable.

Purely physical effects – rain, explosions, bullet wounds, stunts, etc. – are created at the time of shooting. We have already mentioned various in-camera effects such as double-exposures. Fades and wipes are processes achieved in the laboratory using a device known as an optical printer. This is also used for manipulating the image within the frame. In *Citizen Kane*, for example, the close-up of the burning sledge, Rosebud, could not have been achieved simply through camerawork. The printer could enlarge the image, bringing the viewer closer to it than the camera could have done.

One of the earliest laboratory processes was the use of glass shots, in which a background (or part of the set) is simply painted on a glass and placed between camera and set. Many buildings have consisted of a lower part constructed on set and impressive upper portions painted by the studio artist. In this process it is essential for the camera to remain stationary. An alternative method of providing backgrounds is through *mattes*, a device pioneered as early as 1903. From the French word for mask, a *matte* blanks out part of the screen so that, for example, a shot of live action can be combined with a painted area of static buildings or a moving one of spaceships. The travelling *matte* changes its shape, position and size from frame to frame, allowing the actor to move anywhere in front of the background and also freeing the camera to move in panning or tracking shots.

Another commonly used technique for providing a background to live action is back, or front, projection. Again this is an old idea that has been much refined so that it is no longer as obtrusive as it used sometimes to be – Hitchcock was notorious for poorly executed back projection. The effect is achieved by photographing the foreground action in front of a screen onto which is projected the, already shot, background action. Back projection is simpler but has the drawback that the foreground is always brighter than the rear. Front projection overcomes this problem but requires a more complicated set-up involving a two-way mirror. Much of Superman's flying involves front projection with the actor suspended on the end of a hidden pole, but a variety of techniques were used to make us believe a man can fly. Sometimes he hung on wires, sometimes a *matte* was used, at other times a model figure stood in for Christopher Reeve, the actor.

Miniatures are now an integral part of many films and sophisticated processes are used to make them look real: from computer-operated cameras to models so complicated that they easily deceive the eye. Science fiction films are full of such miniature work – but not all models are small. The main model for *E.T.* was three feet tall and required up to twelve operators to manipulate the eighty-five movements of the numerous joints and muscles. With two other models it cost over £1 million to construct. But even *E.T.* has ancestors, in film terms at least. Fritz Lang's *The Niebelungen* of 1924 boasted a spectacular mechanical dragon seventy feet long whose controls were operated by seventeen technicians (some inside the body, others in a trench underneath) which enabled the creature to breathe fire, drink water and bleed when wounded.

Few effects are completely new. We have mentioned motion-control photography which allows a camera (and if necessary the objects and artwork to be photographed) to be computer programmed to go through precisely the same moves over and over again while different elements of the final picture are added. Even this can be traced back at least to 1914 when an Edison cameraman devised a simple block-and-tackle rig to permit repeatable tracking-shots.

Nor do all effects have to be expensive or complicated. On *Flash Gordon*, a vapour trail from a rocket was made out of salt; cheap photographic cut-outs were used for as sophisticated a film as *2001*. When making *The Right Stuff*, shots of a rocket spinning out of control were achieved by throwing models out of a third-storey window. In *The Legend of Suram Fortress*, Sergei Paradjanov wanted to show the destruction of the fortress. Using simple photographic sleight of hand he shot the reflection of the building in a pool of water. When the surface was disturbed the castle began to shudder and disintegrate. The commercial failure of many large-budget fantasy films has demonstrated the lesson that audiences are not attracted to special effects *per se*; they must be located within and subservient to a story whose telling interests them.

CHAPTER SEVEN

THE FIFTH DIMENSION:
Sound

THE first six chapters have been devoted to analysing, in terms of sight alone, the film's artistic version of the four-dimensional space–time continuum re-created on the cinema screen. But, besides this, there is the world of sound, another dimension, another aspect of reality, the most significant thing about it perhaps being that it comes to us through a different sense organ which determines the nature of our experience of it.

Next to sight, hearing is the richest and most complex of our senses. Sound is the basis of one of the greatest of the arts, music. As speech it forms a medium for thought, and is the most important means of communication among human beings. As one can imagine, those who hoped the cinema would create a total illusion of reality were not likely to be satisfied with sight alone, and from the very beginning of the cinema every effort was made to incorporate sound. The history of sound in films is broadly similar to that of colour: early attempts and failures; the realization that the silent film was a valid art form and acceptable to audiences; technical progress in, and eventual perfection of, workable sound systems.

The mechanical reproduction of sound was invented as early as, or earlier than, the mechanical reproduction of moving pictures on a screen, and between 1892 and 1910 Edison, Pathé, Zecca, Henry Joly and Léon Gaumont tried out many different combinations of the phonograph and the film projector. But none of them was successful for public exhibition. It was the audion amplifier invented by Lee Forrest in 1906 but not perfected until the twenties which enabled sound to be amplified with enough volume and accuracy for theatre use. Despite successful demonstrations in the early twenties the studios were reluctant to adopt sound (the capital outlay was one factor) and only impending bankruptcy impelled Warners to gamble their future on *The Jazz Singer* which came out in 1927.[1] The movie, with Al Jolson singing, was an enormous hit and by the early thirties sound films (talkies) were being shown all over the world. Various methods of sound reproduction such as records synchronized with the projectors were used in the early days, but in the end a system of 'optical' sound became universal. In this system sound waves from a microphone are turned into optical variations on a 'sound-track' on the same strip of film as the images, and are turned back into sound by the same machine (sound projector) as throws the pictures on to the screen. Thus sound and picture are integrally one, a convenience from every point of view and ideal for synchronization.

For the first thirty years of its existence cinema had meant the silent film, a form that attained a high degree of sophistication and achievement. Films like *Intolerance*, *Greed*, *Battleship Potemkin*, *Earth*, *The Last Laugh*, *City Lights*, *Wings*, *The Crowd* and *Napoléon* demonstrated the range and authority of the silent film. The director was forced to describe, to depict, to narrate in pictures and nothing but pictures, enabling the silent film to develop a purely ideographic, powerful visual magic. Not that films were ever completely silent – the musical accompaniment whether by full orchestra or lone piano was always an important component of the film's presentation.

Even today, sight is the predominant partner in the combination of sight and sound. While visuals without sound are still perfectly valid, we cannot imagine sound without visuals being able to make a film. This illustrates an important difference between the film and the theatre, for almost any play can be adapted to the radio, and given in sound only, without too serious a loss. On the other hand, radio programmes on the cinema can only reproduce songs, excerpts from the dialogue, comment and interviews. Again, for an actor to talk in a play without intending to be heard would be as unreasonable as silent music or pictures painted to be looked at in

1. Plate 46.

the dark. But this often happens in a film – we see people talking behind glass, or in a crowd; it is the 'look' of them talking that interests the film-maker, and this can be better conveyed if words are not present to interfere with and disturb the image. In other cases, a film gives us the sound of speech, not the actual words – or not enough of the words to have any meaning: the buzz of conversation at a party, the menacing shouts of a crowd, the bustle of a market, the gabble of the loudspeakers on the railway station at the beginning of *Monsieur Hulot's Holiday*, the music of a strange dialect or a snatch of conversation in a foreign language. The examples have a different significance: in *Monsieur Hulot*, the meaninglessness is a joke which is funny because railway loud-speakers frequently are incomprehensible; in the case of the crowd, a menacing meaningless sound can be more frightening than actual words; and in the other cases the music and rhythm and the sensuous feel of the conversation can be better conveyed without the interference of meaning. Meaningless speech is also used with comic effect in Altman's *M.A.S.H.*, when a V.I.P. arrives by helicopter and the ceremony of his arrival becomes ridiculous both because we cannot hear the no doubt important speeches and because people have to crouch in absurd positions to avoid the whirling blades. In Buñuel's *The Discreet Charm of the Bourgeoisie*, dialogue in a police station is drowned first by passing planes and then by a clattering typewriter until the subordinate, afraid to ask again, goes off and does the wrong thing. In Godard's *Made in USA*, key narrative information is frequently rendered inaudible by extraneous noises making the plot unclear and concentrating attention on other elements of the film. Kubrick's *2001* is largely silent. If there is conversation it is dull and unimportant. The crucial dialogue is not heard at all – we share the view of HAL, the computer, as it lip-reads the mouths of the astronauts planning to disconnect it. Jean-Jacques Annaud's *Quest for Fire* contained only the primitive language of the pre-historic tribes (especially created by Anthony Burgess), a device that would hardly be possible in a stage play.

Even when we do hear words, and their meaning is important, the sound and intonation and the appearance of the characters as they say them may be of as much or more significance. It is probably true to say that, despite the great advances in sound recording technology, dialogue has never been less clear on the screen than it is today. Partly this is a reflection of current conventions of realism that allow actors to mumble or to speak only so that their fellow performers (but not necessarily the audience) can hear. If Bazin drew attention to the ambiguity of the image in realist cinema, we can certainly see a growing ambiguity of aural communication. Just as the picture has to be scanned for information, the sound-track often offers several alternative cues. The Altman film *M.A.S.H.*, already mentioned, was important in this respect for taking this feature to new extremes so that several characters would be talking at once to the accompaniment of a cacophony of other sounds, announcements and so on.

THE COMING OF SOUND

The sound era marked the end of the 'international language' of the cinema. The talkies dramatically reduced the immediate potential audience for any film to those who shared the language in which it had been made. This change failed to destroy the dominance that Hollywood had established during the First World War, but it splintered the already weak European industries. No satisfactory answer has been found to the problem of translation. Dubbing destroys the organic relationship between the appearance of the performer and the sound and rhythm of the words.[1] Subtitles preserve the original sound-visual combination but at the cost of interfering with the image on the screen. The Italian solution is never to record live dialogue (direct sound) at all but to add the voices at a later stage – hence the comic scene in Truffaut's *Day for Night* in which actress Valentina Cortese asks why she cannot just reel off a list of numbers instead of the lines she can never remember – 'as I do for Federico'. The result is that Italian films are often full of actors from different countries all talking in their own language. Italian conventions do not demand that lips and

1. Done with care, dubbing can be less noticeable than is usually the case. Producer Robert Evans insisted that Louis Malle supervise the French version of *The Godfather*. He selected all the actors and directed the dubbing meticulously at a cost to Paramount of $100,000 but the money was well spent.

voices remain 'in synch', though the results can look alarmingly haphazard to those accustomed to other practices.

A less permanent hurdle facing the infant sound film was the problem of deciding how dialogue should be used. Just as, in its beginnings, the cinema had copied the scenery and static viewpoint of the theatre, so, when it was able to combine speech with its pictures, it copied the continuous dialogue of the theatre. As for the silent film, so for the sound film, development meant escaping from theatrical influence.

In the theatre, dialogue is continuous and may serve the functions of creating an atmosphere, describing events offstage, revealing a character, and so on. All these things the cinema can do visually, and if they are also conveyed verbally there will be audiovisual pleonasm, as bad as or worse than the pleonasm and repetition of poor writing. Again, dialogue on the stage is generally not ordinary language. It is often poetry or poetic prose and, even if it aims at a realistic effect, even it if uses slang or peasant idiom, it is still far from common speech. Film scripts also often use an enriched dialogue, and poetic prose or poetry (as in the British documentary *Night Mail*, directed by Harry Watt and Basil Wright, or in the many films of Shakespeare plays) are perfectly suitable for use in a film in certain cases.

But it soon became clear that the different conditions of film and theatre demand different dialogue – both in quantity and quality. The early talkies simply talked and talked and talked. Because actors now had voices it was assumed that they had to be used as often as possible. As early sound equipment was relatively crude they also had to talk very clearly, enunciate every syllable and ensure they were articulating in the direction of the microphone. What they were saying was, as often as not, simply lines from stage plays thinly adapted for the screen. Long speeches were the norm and, all too often, information that could have been conveyed in pictures (and had been in silent films) was laboriously conveyed through dialogue.

Not only were early sound films full of chatter, they were also static. The noisy cameras (and their unfortunate operators) had to disappear into vast sound-proofed structures. Camera movement became almost impossible resulting in long fixed shots. At first every sound had to be recorded live at the moment of shooting –

music, background sounds, speech – all had to be captured, whether on disc or film, simultaneously. As directors were eager to impress audiences with the range of sound, a deafening and intrusive mixture of creaking hinges, chinking glasses, rustling dresses (sounding more like a forest fire) and whatever else seemed appropriate, was the result.

Quite quickly, however, sound recording and editing became more sophisticated; quieter, mobile cameras appeared, and directors and their crews learned how to handle what was essentially a new medium. The script grew shorter and consisted less of speeches than of conversation structured to be supportive of the action. In the theatre of course, the dialogue *is* the play: it exists as a valid independent literary form in its own right, and forms the basis of an indefinite number of performances and interpretations. In the cinema, on the contrary, there is only one original, authentic film, and the shooting script is a technical blueprint for putting together bits of sight and bits of sound (of which speech is only one element among several) to form a celluloid mosaic. For some films the script can be published in a modified form for reading, but, much more than a published play, this is a reproduction of the film mosaic in another medium. Any script will be as different from the actual film as a book of architect's plans and drawings is different from an actual building. Also, visualizing a film from a script may be as much of a technical accomplishment as reading a musical score.

Plays do continue to be adapted successfully for the cinema, but they rarely maintain their theatrical form. Olivier's Shakespeare films, Lumet's *Long Day's Journey into Night*, Clive Donner's *The Caretaker*, Peter Yates's *The Dresser* and many others have kept much of the original dialogue while still being turned into films. The 'filmed play' has now virtually disappeared (except occasionally on television), various degrees of 'opening out' being utilized to make the drama cinematic or, more successfully, the theme and characters are retained as the basis for what is essentially a new work. Performances photographed from the stalls are now confined to recordings of rock concerts (Scorsese's *The Last Waltz*, Jonathan Demme's *Stop Making Sense*). Even operas are now commonly taken out of the theatre and reconstructed in the surroundings in which their action is set – Losey's *Don Giovanni*, Rosi's *Carmen* –

or on elaborate sets – Zeffirelli's *La Traviata* and *Otello*. Again, television seems the more suitable medium for the unadorned recording of original stage productions: on the small screen the visual limitations of such an approach are less obvious.

Film Music

It hardly needs pointing out that music has always been closely associated with film. Early silent pictures had some sort of (often random) accompaniment. Griffith introduced an orchestral score composed of popular themes to add a new dimension to *Birth of a Nation*. Excerpts from Grieg, Wagner, Tchaikovsky, Rossini, Beethoven and others were interwoven with traditional airs like 'Dixie' and 'The Star Spangled Banner' and original music by composer Joseph Briel and the whole score was circulated with the film, the conductor having 226 cues to guide synchronization of music and image. Earlier, Saint-Saëns had written the music for a film of *The Assassination of the Duke of Guise* and original scores remained more common in Europe than in the USA. The collaboration between Eisenstein and Prokofiev was especially fruitful with the latter's theories and practice as influential in the area of film music as Eisenstein's were in the area of the image. *Alexander Nevsky* represents the apogee of their association.

With *The Jazz Singer* and the coming of sound, the role of music changed. On the one hand it was under much greater control by the film-maker, on the other it was reduced to only one level of a multi-layered soundtrack. Even so, the American cinema in particular retained the tradition of full symphonic scores for many years. Composers like Max Steiner, Erich Wolfgang Korngold, Dmitri Tiomkin and Alfred Newman produced music of real virtuosity, though its overwhelming presence could over-emphasize what the screen was already showing.

As early as 1930 directors like René Clair (*Sous les Toits de Paris*), G. W. Pabst (*The Threepenny Opera*) and Jean Cocteau (*The Song of a Poet*) had shown what could be achieved with less pervasive accompaniment and how brevity and lighter instrumentation could be virtues. Carol Reed's simple zither motif in *The Third Man* (1949) was highly influential, and *2001* reintroduced the use of classics, suitably selected and adapted. Composer John Williams has refined the specially composed score and, using all the qualities of new stereophonic systems, has provided a continuous and dynamic backdrop to the films of Spielberg and Lucas which helps their adventure stories to achieve speed and impact – and moulds the viewer's reactions. Films set in exotic or little known parts of the world (*Aguirre, Wrath of God* and the many subsequent South American movies for example) can benefit from using the instruments and rhythms native to the area. Electronic and other forms of 'difficult' music can also be used in film even though audiences would not normally listen to such music in its own right.

Pop and rock music are now the commonest forms of accompaniment in Western-made films, with theme songs important commercially in enabling films and records to publicize each other. The pervasive nature of such music in modern life means that films can include almost constant music, all of it justified in the narrative. In Renoir's *La Grande Illusion*, there are only two occasions when music occurs which is not attributable to a source within the film. George Lucas's *American Graffiti* has a story that switched constantly from one character to another as his restless teenagers indulge in their mysterious rites during one critical night in their lives. The whole tapestry is held together by the rock music that spills out of juke boxes and record-players or from car radios tuned in to the ubiquitous offerings of disc jockey, Wolfman Jack. Made in 1973 but set eleven years earlier, *American Graffiti* pioneered the vogue for establishing a film's era through its music. Since then films like Hal Ashby's *Coming Home*, Lawrence Kasdan's *The Big Chill* and innumerable teenage dramas have made music integral to the structure of the film.

The Jazz Singer was only the first of a continuing series of pictures which have included musical performers as central characters, thus giving music a crucial and justifiable role in the film – *New York, New York, Coalminer's Daughter, The Buddy Holly Story, Diva, Amadeus, Round Midnight,* and *Sid and Nancy* are recent examples. Other films set their action in an environment that guarantees continuous musical background, such as a night-club or radio station. More experimental are films like Lindsay Anderson's *O Lucky Man!* with its musical commentary by Alan Price, the films of The Who's rock-operas *Tommy* and *Quadrophenia* and David Byrne's enigmatic exploration of small-town America in *True Stories*.

Some of these could be described as modern musicals though they differ markedly from the style of the classic musicals of the thirties, forties and fifties. Films like Bob Fosse's *All That Jazz* and Attenborough's *A Chorus Line* are more in the traditional pattern. Perhaps the real inheritor of the traditional form has been the Indian cinema, whose films almost invariably include musical numbers derived from old Hollywood blueprints. Musical conventions, however, are very different in the Asian countries from those with which we are familiar. In the silent days, specialist narrators were employed in cinemas to tell the story, add noises and generally become part of the entertainment – a development of the use of narrators in traditional shadow and puppet theatre performances. The separation of sound and image continues in the use of 'playback' singers in Indian films. The actors mime to the songs and the voices are supplied by a tiny number of well-known singers whose voices may bear little resemblance to the speaking voices of the actors.[1] In the relatively crude Punjabi pictures, music is often continuous with the volume merely lowered during dialogue scenes.

The coming of the sound film also enabled the artist to use silence in a film with a positive dramatic effect. Silence cannot have a positive value for instance in a radio play, because this consists of words only, nor in a silent film, because this contains no words. On the stage the effect of silence cannot be drawn out or made to last as it can in the cinema. In a film the effect of silence can be extremely vivid and varied and a silent glance can speak volumes. Two examples from *La Grande Illusion* illustrate the point. In one scene a group of men are gathered round, opening a case which has been sent into their German prison and which they expect to contain food delicacies; there is bustle, chattering, excitement, expectation. Then the lid bursts open and shows the case full of books. Suddenly there is complete silence – more effective than any comment. It is a silence which each spectator will interpret differently to suit himself, and which should no doubt be interpreted differently for each prisoner. Another example occurs earlier

1. There is a parallel here with the practice, now generally abandoned, of casting stars in operas with their voices supplied by others (e.g. Sophia Loren in *Aida*, Gina Lollobrigida in *Pagliacci*).

in the film, when the prisoners are dressing up for a concert, turning over piles of costumes; there is the same bustle, a buzz of conversation, a coarse laugh at some women's corsets. Suddenly one of the prisoners appears dressed as a girl – he is a pretty young man and the impersonation is well nigh perfect: he looks like a young, appealing girl. Gradually (this time) the noise stops; conversations die away; the men turn to look at him – each busy with his own precious thoughts.

The twenty-minute robbery sequence in *Rififi* is a celebrated example of absolute silence over an extended period and with an obvious narrative justification. Mel Brooks's attempt in *Silent Movie* to make a comedy without words fails because there is no obvious reason why nobody speaks and we do not any longer accept this convention, while the actors did not know at what level to pitch their performances when deprived of speech. A more significant example is Ingmar Bergman's *The Silence*, a story of two sisters and a little boy marooned in a hotel in a strange country whose language they do not understand. Most of the time their sole contact is an old waiter with whom they can communicate only in sign language. The film is silent for most of the time, but this silence conveys a wide variety of meanings. In different situations it expresses boredom, lust, drunken stupor, agonized unhappiness, the wonder of childhood, the resignation of old age. Long periods of silence are also used effectively in Pasolini's *The Gospel According to St Matthew* and in Ermanno Olmi's *The Tree of Wooden Clogs*, where they denote the verbal impoverishment of the peasants and signify their acceptance of fate and the rule of the landlords.

SOUND AND REALITY

The various distinctions we have drawn between film and reality in relation to space and time can be fruitfully applied to sound also. In the first place, isolation of a sound and its reproduction in a film has an effect similar to the isolation and framing of the image – it makes possible an artistic selection. Thus, since the introduction of sound, it has been a function of the cinema not only to make people see but 'to make people hear'. The sound cinema has given us more sensitive hearing, taught us to appreciate the quality of natural sounds – the wind in the leaves, tyres screaming on the asphalt, the deep breathing of a sleeping man. There is the panting of the fugitives in the submerged forest in King Vidor's *Hallelujah*, the noise of trains during the fight in *Sous les Toits de Paris*, the wild howling of the storm in *Man of Aran*, the ticking of the police commissioner's watch in *The Informer*, the whistle of the express in *Brief Encounter*, the whirring of the helicopters overhead in *Apocalypse Now*.

As with the image, so with sound. It can be used in ways which are either more, or less, true to life. It can be almost entirely functional, providing information and reflecting exactly the aural dimension of what we see. Alternatively it can be expressive of emotions, moods, atmosphere, or it can represent a wholly new idea, symbolic of something not seen at all. Whichever way sound is used it is rarely, in fact, realistic. In the outside world our ears are assaulted by many different aural cues, most of which we learn to ignore, selecting only those which we perceive as relevant or interesting. We hear what we attend to. In the cinema the opposite happens – we attend to what we hear, what the film-maker draws to our attention. To quote Tarkovsky once more, 'The sounds of the world reproduced naturalistically in cinema are impossible to imagine: there would be a cacophony. Everything that appeared on the screen would have to be heard on the soundtrack . . . If there is no selection then the film is tantamount to silent . . . accurately recorded sound adds nothing to the image.'[1]

Sound engineering is a process of selection, amplification, distortion and mixing as much as simple recording. The effect of perfectly natural sound may be very different in a film from its impact in real life. In Hitchcock's *Torn Curtain*, in a scene already quoted in which a Russian agent is gassed, there is a point when the only sound heard is the soft hissing of the gas – yet this soft sound rivets our attention. In *Henry V* at the battle of Agincourt the 'swish' of a volley of arrows comes at us with a deadly menace. In Victor Saville's *I Was a Spy*, based on Edith Cavell's work for the Belgian resistance, German soldiers come into a café to arrest the heroine (Madeleine Carroll). Realizing that her daughter will probably be shot, the mother behind the bar lets a glass fall from

---

1. *Sculpting in Time*, pp.159–62.

her hand. In a scene already tense, the sudden noise is almost like an electric shock. In Bergman's *Winter Light* there is a scene in which a suicide's body is found on a bank. Throughout the sequence, which is filmed in long and medium shots, we hear nothing but the rippling of the water in the stream. No dialogue, footsteps or other sounds are allowed to intrude on the regular incessant flow of the brook. A life has ended, but life goes on – a message that sounds crude in words but is made acceptable when expressed at this almost subliminal level.

More obviously stylized is the use of sound in Polanski's *Repulsion* in which the girl's increasing madness is accompanied by both ordinary noises given overtones of hysteria through amplification (the sound of the doorbell, footsteps), and hallucinatory images of cracking walls and pavements supported by equally emphatic rending noises.

In Renoir's *La Bête Humaine* an adulterous couple leave a dance-hall and return to the woman's flat where they plan to murder her husband but where the man (Jean Gabin) in a fit of sadistic madness strangles her. But for a few words and her screams, the scene is silent. After a cut to the dance-hall where a tenor is singing, we are returned to the flat where Gabin realizes what he has done. This time the flat is not silent but filled with the song from the dance-hall. We realize that the music must have been audible all the time, but that the couple had been so absorbed by passion, violence and fear that they did not hear it.

If sound can be taken away, it can also be added – as in the familiar scene in films with a sporting theme in which the hero/ heroine visits the venue of a forthcoming event and, in the silence and emptiness, imagines the roar of the crowd that will shortly assemble.

In Joseph Losey's *The Servant* there is a complex interaction of sounds, actions and visual images which builds an atmosphere of sexual tension. Tony (James Fox) is attracted to the maid but is trying to resist his feelings. Standing at the sink, apparently alone in the house, he hears a girl's laugh and the sound of a car outside. His attention is attracted by the dripping of a tap. He looks at it, then turns to see the maid behind him. Losey cuts quickly between the two and the tap whose dripping we still hear. As they move towards each other the dripping grows faster and louder, and Losey changes to close-ups. Finally Tony turns back, tightens the tap and the tension is broken by the sound of the telephone.

Music can of course play the part taken here by the dripping tap, commenting on the action through its rhythm and orchestration. Alternatively it may be used as a refrain, referring the audience back to a scene in which the same music was used previously and so drawing the two scenes together in the mind. In a thriller the reappearance of a tune may indicate that some action is to be repeated. Another convention is to associate a character with a particular theme so that its performance will immediately recall that character to mind, whether or not they appear on the screen. 'Lara's Theme' from *Dr Zhivago* is an obvious example.

Pudovkin wrote of his film *The Deserter*, an early sound film of 1931, that, 'For the dock sequences I used only natural sounds: heavy hammers, pneumatic drills at different distances, the noise of riveting, sirens, falling chains. All these noises I recorded on location then mixed them, altering their duration and intensity like notes of music. As a finale I showed the ship nearing completion, while the sound in a complex orchestration mounts to a peak. It was real musical composition: I had to feel the length of each sound-shot as a musician feels each note.' Modern sound production is an even more sophisticated process with multi-track recording techniques, Dolby Signal Enhancement, synthesizers, stereophonic reproduction and all the other advances carried over from the record industry. An infinite range of both natural and created sounds is now available to the film-maker.

SOUND MONTAGE

The independent recording of sound allows montage effects within the soundtrack itself, and also between the sound and the images. Though we use the same word, 'montage', for sound combinations and for visual combinations, there is a fundamental difference between the two. The essence of visual montage is that we see one image after the other and mentally combine or contrast them. There may be montage in this sense in the case of a sound: a high-pitched voice may alternate with a deep voice, orchestral music may be followed by ethnic African rhythms, the noise of battle replaced by raindrops falling on a leaf. Kubrick's bone/spaceship match-cut can be equated with Nicolas Roeg's sound cut, in *Don't Look Now*, from the mother's scream at the discovery of her daughter's death to the equally jarring roar of pneumatic drills at work on a Venice street. In Wolfgang Peterson's *The Boat*, the noisy, claustrophobic buzz of life in the beleaguered German U-boat is regularly contrasted with shots from the outside of the vessel as it slides through the water to the sound only of the quiet hum of its engines. The contrast of the visuals is strongly reinforced by the dramatic contrast of sounds. In Cimino's *The Deerhunter*, our first arrival in Vietnam is met by an astonishing barrage of noise and shouting which emphasizes the chaos of war in comparison to the previous scenes in America.

But this sort of combination is not (as it is with visuals) the only combination or even the most important. There is a wide variety of relationships between sound and vision to be considered, and sounds are more flexible than images in their capacity to overlap or be happening simultaneously. It is rare for an audience to see more than one picture at a time but it may well listen to a whole range of sounds at the same time – though normally only one layer of dialogue and one of music are included.

Siegfried Kracauer in *The Nature of Film* gives a complex and exhaustive analysis of the different combinations of sound and image and distinguishes three different contrasts of image–sound in combination: *(a)* synchronism – asynchronism; *(b)* parallelism – counterpoint; *(c)* actual and commentative sound. *Synchronism* is the same combination of sound and image as we would experience in real life (we look at a person and hear him talking). *Asynchronism* is a combination of sound and image we would not experience in real life (we look at an empty nursery and hear the voices of the children who have just been playing there). *Parallelism* is a combination in which sound and image repeat one another and one of the two is redundant – parallelism implies audio-visual pleonasm. Parallelism can be either synchronous or asynchronous. If a character in the film mentions London and the visuals show 'Big Ben' this might be an example of asynchronous parallelism. René Clair gives an example of synchronous parallelism: 'It is not important to *hear* the sound of applause if one *sees* the hands which applaud.' *Counterpoint*, on the other hand, is a combination in which both sound and image make an essential contribution to the total effect and can also be synchronous or asynchronous. In Rossellini's *Paisa* we hear the cry of a forlorn child wandering among the bodies of those killed by Nazis, both before (asynchronous) and after (synchronous) the infant appears on the screen. In both cases the wailing sound adds to the effect of the visuals. The third contrast is between sounds which belong naturally to the world shown on the screen (*actual*) and those which do not (*commentative*). Most dialogue is, of course, actual (and synchronized) but a voice-over is commentative. Very often the unseen narrator also figures in the story so the same voice will be both actual and commentative at various times. *Citizen Kane*, which was as innovative in its use of sound as in its handling of images, consists largely of six flashbacks, each told by a different narrator, all of whom figure also in some of the other flashbacks.

All these distinctions are clearer in theory than in practice and analysing even a simple scene in terms of Kracauer's oppositions soon becomes very complicated. A straightforward dialogue between two people will switch back and forth between synchronized (when the speaker is in shot) and asynchronized (when we see the listener). Kracauer was by no means the first to reflect on the question of synchronism. As early as 1930 the Russians had been considering the matter, and Eisenstein, Pudovkin and Alexandrov drew up a manifesto which contained this passage:

> ... only the method of using sound in counterpoint with the visuals offers new possibilities for developing and perfecting the art of montage. Experiment with sound should be concentrated on using asynchronism between sound and visuals. This approach will lead in time to the creation of a new orchestral counterpoint of visual and sound images.

This passage indicates that the Russians recognized at once that non-natural asynchronism was likely to be more interesting artistically than the more natural synchronism. It has been pointed out by Anthony Asquith that in practice it is not always possible to use natural synchronism. He explains in *The Cinema 1950*[1] that an audience can grasp the meaning of visuals more quickly than that of sounds. So in any sequence in which there is quick cutting from one shot to another, it is not possible to accompany each shot with

---

1. Ed. Roger Manvell, Penguin Books, 1950.

the sound appropriate to the visuals. If sound changed every second or so it would become unintelligible. 'Further, there is no underlying unity in the sounds as . . . in the movement of the images.' Thus the practice is to use one sound, often music, to accompany a variety of rapid images.

Kracauer reaches two interesting general conclusions. First, he is persuaded that image–dialogue combinations are more likely to give rich and varied artistic results when the images predominate over the dialogue than when the dialogue predominates over the visuals. Secondly, he points out that constant visual illustration of dialogue (one of the characters mentions Paris and the film cuts to a shot of the Eiffel Tower, etc., etc.) can be extremely redundant and boring, even although it is asynchronism of sound and image. Thus, in this analysis, counterpoint is by definition better than parallelism, but asynchronism may or may not be better than synchronism.

The first example of sound moving from synchronism to asynchronism comes from the *The Jazz Singer*. During some of Al Jolson's songs, the camera leaves the singer to wander among the places he sings about. Richer, more subtle examples are to be found in the films of the British documentary school of the thirties, many of which have extremely complex sound-tracks. In Basil Wright's *Song of Ceylon* the visuals show us romantically beautiful tropical scenes, while the sound-track prosaically quotes from business letters, enumerates the contents of old bills of lading or gives the prices of copper, tea, rubber, and other commodities. This both provides an effective contrast and also relates the seemingly remote forests to our own everyday existence.

In John Ford's *The Long Voyage Home*, the story of a cargo-boat carrying dynamite across the Atlantic during the war, there is a sequence of an air-attack treated entirely in counterpoint. The camera remains on the bridge of the ship and shows the panic of the crew. We see nothing of the planes except their shadows sweeping across the deck, but we hear the roaring of their engines, the whistling of their dive-bombing, the crackle of machine-guns, the crump of bombs. The effect is terrific and the danger seems worse because it is not seen. Also, as the camera never looks up, the treatment suggests a person so terrified he dare not raise his head.

An amusing combination of sound and image can be found in Bergman's comedy *Smiles of a Summer Night*. Inside a garden pavilion we *see* two enemies playing Russian roulette, twisting the revolver chambers and firing. It is the older man's turn. We cut to outside the pavilion and *hear* a shot. We think the man is killed, especially as his opponent appears in the doorway laughing wildly. Then he says to the women who have come up, 'It was only a blank. Think I'd use a real bullet on *him*!' Then (stressing the anti-climax) we cut to inside the pavilion and *see* the 'hero' black-faced and disconsolate.

Here sound and image are related in a way that misleads the audience. In a similar way the relationship may be an ironic one with each offering quite different messages. *Citizen Kane* is full of such moments. When Kane's second wife, Susan Alexander, has her disastrous operatic debut, we first see the actual scene, hear the thin voice failing miserably on the high notes, listen to the meagre applause. While the sound-track continues to carry her pathetic warbling, we are shown the notices in Kane's own newspapers, praising her performance, celebrating an imaginary triumph, a deception that is all too apparent to our ears. Later, Susan abuses her husband for giving his old friend, Jed Leland, a large cheque as compensation for being sacked for his bad review of Susan's efforts. As her tirade continues we see Kane opening an envelope from Jed and pouring out the torn-up pieces of the cheque.

Welles was also adept at using overlapping sound at moments of transition. The first of many examples in the film occurs after the young Kane has been taken away from home to receive the education appropriate to his new wealth. We see his efficient but impersonal guardian wishing the boy an unconvincing 'Merry Christmas, Charles'. Charles, under his Christmas tree, looks far from merry. When we cut back to the guardian again he is adding 'And a Happy New Year' – but it is now nearly twenty years later and he is seen to be dictating a letter to Kane. The device comments on the distant nature of their relationship while also gluing together the two scenes. In Tarkovsky's *Nostalghia* the director links past, memory and dream (all shot in sepia) and present (in colour) through sounds which are always those of the present – the circular saw, running water. The mysterious sepia world is penetrated by the continuing present through its sounds. The whole film is a careful visual and aural composition (though with little music), designed to overlap and link past and present, reality and vision.

There is a charming example of audio-visual montage in an Indian film, *Wedding Day*, director Mrinal Sen. The hero earns a living by peddling his wares to daily commuters on a railway train. His stock-in-trade includes a red dye for women's feet, an Indian equivalent for lipstick. In one sequence, he wakes in the night and sits lovingly contemplating his beautiful young bride. Into the stillness on the sound-track there breaks the noise of the train and his voice in an interior monologue saying, 'When you cannot sleep at night and sit awake looking at the one you love, think how much a little present of red dye for her feet would please her.' Before he has finished speaking, the visuals catch up with the words and we cut to the train with him now actually speaking the words. It is a brilliant example of economy and forms a neat link between two main aspects of the story – the hero's happy marriage and his gradual ruin in business.

A good many modern movies feature sound on records, loud-speakers or tapes, and there is always the possibility of interplay between an actual and a recorded voice. In Boulting's *Brighton Rock* the vicious gang-leader Pinkie makes a record for his adoring young girlfriend in which he says: 'You want me to say I love you. But I hate you. I hate your stupid loyalty and trust . . .' After he is killed, when she comes to play it for the first time to comfort her grief, we expect, knowing what is on the record, that she will be bitterly hurt. But it has been scratched and when she plays it the message goes 'You want me to say I love you – I love you – I love you – ' In *M.A.S.H.* the camera concentrates on the ugly camp loud-speaker to make of it a malignant personality. Sometimes the announcements are harsh commands, sometimes garbled nonsense, and on one occasion when the microphone has been put under the camp commander's bed, it broadcasts a tender love scene between him and one of the nurses, scandalously amplified. At the end of the movie it broadcasts a parody announcement: 'Next week's picture will be *M.A.S.H.*, dealing with the heroic deeds of those dare-devil doctors in the Army Medical Corps . . .' In Terrence Malick's *Badlands* the hero makes a recording as evidence that he and his girl are going to commit suicide. There is a good example in Alan Pakula's *The Parallax View*. The hero, Warren Beatty, penetrates a dangerous murder organization and in one scene the agent he has contacted is talking to him confidentially. Then the camera cuts to his friend's office and we hear the agent's words repeated. Only when we trace them to a tape recorder do we realize that the hero has taped the conversation and sent it to his friend.

Coppola's *The Conversation* takes the analysis of recorded sound as its subject and becomes a visual and aural essay on looking and listening. Its hero, Harry, is a surveillance man, an eavesdropper, 'the best bugger on the West Coast'. The plot hinges on a tape-recording that we see Harry (Gene Hackman) making in the first scene of the movie. A continuous zoom from high over Union Square brings us slowly down to a young couple involved in a very nervous conversation. We hear them long before we see them but a crucial part of what they discuss is obliterated by extraneous sounds. In a long central scene we watch Harry apply all his skill and science to the task of reconstructing the conversation in the Square from all the various recordings, some made from a few feet away by a confederate, others from hundreds of yards away by directional microphone. The irony of the film is that, for all his expertise, Harry misses the truth until too late. He deciphers the exact words spoken but misinterprets their emphasis and thus the whole meaning, imagining that the couple are intended victims rather than conniving killers.

In *Blow Out*, Brian de Palma also touched on the complex and ambiguous nature of sound. His hero is a film sound recordist whose job is to supply the aural accompaniment (recorded in the real world) to the visual images created in the studio. The plot involves his discovery that night-time sounds he has recorded include the crack of a gunshot that proves an accident to have been murder. Sad and disillusioned, at the end of the film we see him cynically use the screams of a real victim (his own girl-friend) to supply the mock-terror for a lurid horror movie.

It will be seen from the complexity and variety of these examples that audio-visual combination and alternation is more complicated than visual montage alone, since there can be interplay not only between the visuals and noise effects, music or words, but between each of these three elements as well. Directors like Godard,

Fassbinder, Altman and others have begun to show how sound can be used with as much imagination and effect as the visual image. Yet many film-makers neglect this aspect and it is still the practice that while the camera's needs are invariably considered, the microphone's are too often neglected. It is a sad irony that, despite technical progress, the sound-tracks of many films are less audible today than in the past.

METAPHORIC AND SUBJECTIVE USE OF SOUND

Audio-visual montage enables sound to be used independently of the visuals both symbolically and subjectively. In cartoons the sound frequently represents a simple metaphor or a symbol: Pluto's tail vibrates like a tuning fork, Donald Duck turns corners with a scream of tyres, Terry Gilliam's Monty Python cartoons are accompanied by a wide variety of squeals, burps and other odd noises.

Boris Barnet's first sound film *Okraina (Suburbs*, 1933) includes a scene of an official send-off for a body of troops at a railway station. A Tsarist spokesman harangues the crowd, which cheers repeatedly, but in the film the cheers cannot be heard for they are drowned by the whistling of the train. The sound expresses symbolically how the grim reality of departure for the war predominates over the spurious patriotic enthusiasm aroused by the orator. Music can also be used symbolically as a leitmotif. In Jean-Pierre Melville's film *Léon Morin, Prêtre*, a sequence of harsh chords is used to typify the German occupation forces. When, after liberation, the heroine and her little girl, accompanied along the road by two American soldiers, pass a wrecked German tank, the harsh chords come back on the sound-track, irresistibly recalling the earlier background of the film. In the same film a quite different dancing bugle motif is used for the Italian troops. Organ music is used for scenes showing the heroine with the priest in church, but piano music for scenes in his flat. Hurdy-gurdy music is used to typify two gossiping old spinsters. In a scene where the priest (Jean-Paul Belmondo) has brought the heroine a book on theology and is reading it to her, louder and louder electronic music is used to express the heroine's stronger and stronger obsessive sexual feeling for the priest, until she reaches out to take his hand.

The extraordinary sounds of David Lynch's films have already been referred to – the hissing, clanking subterranean underworld that always seems about to engulf the cosy existences of those above. In *Blue Velvet* he includes a very different sound – that of a radio station whose aural motif is the sound of a falling tree, symbolizing the name (and business) of the town – Lumberton. But on another level the banality of this refrain suggests the smugness and self-satisfaction of a Middle America which the film's story shows to be full of superficial virtues.

Like images, sound can be used subjectively to express the impressions or state of mind of a character. Needless to say, the Russians experimented with subjective sound at an early stage. Pudovkin set out to make a film to be called *Life is Very Good*. At one point a mother mourns the loss of her grown-up son, but instead of hearing her sobs we hear a baby crying. This was intended to suggest that the woman still thought of her son as a young baby. In another part of the film a woman is having a brief moment's farewell conversation with her husband whose departure for the war is imminent. The poor woman is distracted and every minute keeps hearing (in her mind) the noise of the departing train, before it actually moves. Unfortunately audiences failed to understand this use of sound: they simply thought that a baby was crying in another room and a train leaving from another platform. Conventions can be challenged but they cannot be disregarded entirely. As we have noted before, it is important to establish the credibility of a scene before commenting upon it. Pudovkin had to scrap his entire sound-track and was left with a silent film that he called, perhaps with irony, *A Simple Case*.

Hitchcock fared better with his first experience of sound when making *Blackmail* which contains the famous scene in which the heroine, having accidentally killed a man with a knife, has breakfast with her family. The unsolved case is under discussion but in the girl's mind the conversation soon becomes a confusion of vague noises. All she can hear is the word 'knife' repeated over and over again in her frightened mind – until she is returned to reality by her father's voice asking her to pass the bread-knife.

Allied to the subjective use of sound is the use of the interior monologue, an offspring of the commentary. The commentary was at first confined to documentary films and, as in the example already given from *Song of Ceylon*, is a special case of audio-visual montage. Its first use in a feature was in Sacha Guitry's *Le Roman d'un Tricheur*, in which the verbal element is a thread to tie the visual episodes together. The interior monologue seems first to have been used in R. Z. Leonard's film *Strange Interlude* (1932), based on Eugene O'Neill's play, in which the characters' thoughts as well as their conversation are heard. The idea was more successful in the cinema than on the stage, as on the screen the actors did not have to move their lips to make their thoughts audible. The use of interior monologue was proposed by Eisenstein much earlier in 1930, for a film to be based on Dreiser's book *An American Tragedy*, and he wrote at the time: 'It is clear that the correct thing for sound films is the interior monologue.' It is a great pity that Eisenstein's plans for the film came to grief.

Others have argued that, on the contrary, the interior monologue is a sign of structural weakness, that the images themselves should be able to carry the thoughts without the need of verbal expression. Yet it is a convention that audiences readily understand and accept, and it can be used to powerful effect, especially when thought and action are not at one. For every *Blade Runner*, where the voice-over was clearly added to smooth over gaps in plot and character, there are many films which build the device into the structure of the work. It can be effective in both serious and comic situations.

In Irving Rapper's *Now Voyager* we see Bette Davis playing the part of a shy, repressed woman, going quietly about the house, but on the sound-track we hear her introspective thoughts of guilt and remorse. In Oliver Stone's *Platoon*, the young hero, newly arrived in Vietnam, is only able to express certain feelings in his letters home to his grandmother which we hear him writing in his head. Indeed it is not clear that he ever does write or even has a grandmother. It could be his way of allowing himself to collect his hidden thoughts.

Rather different is the case of Bob Hope in Norman McLeod's *The Paleface*, in which the comedian is able to have an amusing argument with his conscience, a disembodied voice, as if it were another self. Woody Allen plays with the convention in a scene in his film *Annie Hall* in which, early in their screen relationship, he and Diane Keaton are seen trying to impress each other with sophisticated dialogue, while a series of subtitles show what they are really thinking and the miserable impression both are sure they are giving.

Allen used a less original but equally striking 'voiced thought' in the opening of *Manhattan*. Here it has a narrative justification in that the words we hear are those of Isaac, a writer, trying to start a book. The device therefore becomes a comment on artistic creation itself – and its pretensions. As we gaze at a sequence of black and white shots of the city, the voice of Isaac agonizing over his typewriter is heard: '"Chapter One. He adored New York City. To him, it was a metaphor for the decay of contemporary culture. The same lack of individual integrity to cause so many people to take the easy way out . . . was rapidly turning the town of his dreams . . ." No, it's gonna be too preachy. I mean, you know, let's face it, I wanna sell some books here. "Chapter One. He adored New York City, although to him it was a metaphor for the decay of contemporary culture. How hard it was to exist in a society desensitized by drugs, loud music, television, crime, garbage." Too angry, I don't wanna be angry . . .' As an economical and witty introduction to various facets of the metropolis and Isaac's relationship to it, it is hard to imagine this approach being equalled.

In *Terminus*, John Schlesinger's film about Waterloo Station, pop songs are used as a kind of commentary. When the boat train from South Africa comes in and there are reunions after long parting, we hear the song 'I wouldn't Have Known You'. A train full of West Indians brings the song 'Jamaica Boy', while rich, sophisticated American tourists leave for the Continent to the tune of 'Paris, Rome, Madrid'. In this case the songs merely support and comment lightly on the visuals, in a way now familiar from the numerous films that incorporate songs. But a commentary can provide a strong ironic contrast. In a devastating sequence in Resnais's *Muriel* we see a young man, Bernard, showing his girl-friend a film of his soldier companions in their camp in Algeria. The film in bright colour shows cheerful shots of troops relaxing, laughing and enjoying themselves. To accompany it, the sound-track carries Bernard's sombre voice describing how he and his friends tortured and killed an Algerian girl.

Both Terrence Malick's films to date have included narration by a young girl, giving her partial and inadequate view of proceedings.

In *Badlands*, Holly is a love-struck, naïve accomplice to a teenage boy with psychotic tendencies. In the stilted vocabulary of a dime-store novelette she describes their progress across country, using flat, unemotional tones that contrast starkly with the pictures of the boy's senseless violence and slaughter. Child-like, she tells us little that we would want to know, describing in detail what they ate but saying nothing of their relationship.

In *Days of Heaven*, the voice really does belong to a child, Linda, who is none the less a good deal more worldly-wise than Holly. She is attached to her elder sister who is on the run with her lover, and their adventures are detailed in an elliptical and digressive manner, full of silences and lacunae. Linda's comments form an often very funny account of their situation, both 'knowing' and innocent, matter-of-fact and full of wonder. Essentially a minor character, her role distances us from the doomed couple, her remarks giving us little in the way of inside information. Both we and Linda are left to guess at what is really going on. We see a lot but are told little. A similar approach binds together Peter Weir's *The Mosquito Coast* in which we are set apart from the central character, the increasingly unstable *paterfamilias* played by the potentially sympathetic Harrison Ford, through the comments of the eldest son whose ambivalent attitudes colour our own.

Noises too may carry metaphoric or subjective associations and significance. In the fantasy sequence that open Buñuel's *Belle de Jour*, the heroine, Severine, imagines herself in a horse-drawn carriage, accompanied by her husband. Suddenly she is taken from the carriage and brutally whipped and raped. During the assault we hear the horse bells continuing to ring, and the association of bells with her masochistic desire for degradation is established. The sound of a coach and other bells figure frequently thereafter to signify her sexual perversity.

In Bresson's *Un Condamné à Mort S'est Échappé*, the sounds of trains, trams, bicycles and cars are all that the imprisoned man can hear of the outside world – they stand in for the idea of freedom. Bresson has always laid great emphasis on the importance of sound, arguing that while sound and image must be related and balanced within the frame, one must always dominate. They must not simply support each other – 'if equal, they damage or kill each other, as we say of colours.' Instead he conceives of sound and image as 'working as in a relay, first one and then the other.'

Whether or not we go as far as to agree with Bresson that 'the eye leads always to the exterior, the ear leads more to the interior', it is clear that sound plays a more vital role than the humble status accorded to the sound recordist in the industry hierarchy might indicate, and that it is governed by broadly similar principles to those which apply to the image. One suspects that the full artistic possibilities of sound have by no means been exploited.

CHAPTER EIGHT

THE OTHER SENSES:
Taste, Touch and Smell

WE have now discussed the cinema as it affects two of our senses – sight and sound. In fact this completes the review of the cinema as it exists and the film up to the present directly affects these two senses only, apart from the innate sense of time. But since we are making a comparison between film and reality we ought to take into consideration our whole experience of reality and this includes other senses besides sight and sound – smell, taste, touch, and the kinaesthetic sensations of our own bodily movement. Ought the cinema to include these senses? Is it possible? Is it desirable? Does their omission qualify, limit, or impoverish the film spectacle? These are questions we should briefly consider.

As might be expected, advocates of *cinéma total* would be glad to incorporate these senses also in the entertainment they offer and if it becomes technically possible to expand show-business in this way, it will very likely be done. Their use is mentioned, half in satire, in Aldous Huxley's *Brave New World*. Some film performances have already been supplemented by spreading different smells around the auditorium or by distributing 'scratch-and-sniff' cards.

For entertainment of a sensational kind, the more that can be added the better, and we must look forward to the 'sensation cinemas' of the future. One day it may be possible to shut oneself up in a room in London and be transported on a trip to Japan, with all the sights, sounds, and scents artistically contrived: the taste of Japanese food, the feel of a breeze in our hair, a spray of cherry-blossom brushing our cheek, its fragrance in our nostrils, the hand of a friendly guide on our shoulder. This sort of thing has existed for years in the fun-fair's 'chamber of horrors', and many modern theatres have devised 'experiences' of various kinds. If these include a film element which plays an important part, perhaps predominates, they can be regarded as media allied to cinema. In practice as the number of elements increases, artistic control will become harder, and they may find it difficult to rise above the fairground level. It is interesting to note an unusual movie (*Westworld*) about an elaborate 'experience' entertainment in which tourists indulge their fantasies in a community of robots. Also relevant is Mark Robson's *Earthquake* which uses a device called 'sensurround'. This gives the audience the impression that the cinema itself is shaking, but as it depends on the transmission of shock waves in the air, it should strictly be classed as a special sound effect. Apart from the complexity of 'sensation cinema' there are other difficulties about incorporating taste, touch and smell.

In the first place taste and touch and smell are senses less suited to communicating artistic experience. Physiology teaches us that, although they are far more delicate and complex than was once supposed, they are more limited than sight or hearing. They are certainly responsible for many sensuous pleasures, but pleasures which belong rather to the realm of our active experience, than to the more reflective kind of artistic experience. Much of the pleasure of sport and games is in the *doing* and we can hardly have kinaesthetic sensations for instance except by ourselves acting and achieving. We cannot enjoy the pleasures of taste without actively eating and drinking. This very activity will interfere with the detachment that is necessary if the spectator is to participate as fully with his eyes and his ears as he does in an artistic experience. Wordsworth, for instance, defined the essence of poetry as 'emotion recollected in tranquillity'. Smell is more passive and it is perhaps significant that this is the sense which has been experimentally exploited.

Mostly, these senses are also dependent for their full enjoyment on the contribution of sight and hearing. Every good cook knows how important it is for his dish to look attractive, and the best dinner is one at which there is good conversation. The perfumer is careful to make his flacons elegant in appearance. We hesitate to touch a harmless snake because it looks as though the skin will be slimy and cold, even if we have been assured that it is actually warm and dry.

It is in their disagreeable aspects that these senses take a dominant role – it is when we are racked with pain that we cannot escape from the tyranny of our sense of touch, and no visual magic will disguise the smell of decay or the taste of unpleasant medicine. This introduces a second reason why it is not necessarily desirable that the cinema be all-inclusive. There is some advantage to be gained in abstraction from reality. If it is done in the right spirit, it is proper for art to show us unpleasant things. Paintings show us the agonies of martyred saints, bloody battles, old age, suffering, ugliness, and death. Dickens's novels dwelt on poverty, slums, cruelty to children, and other evils of his time. But these experiences are transmuted by art into something very different from actuality; they become *artistic experiences*. We may be deeply conscious of the suffering and misery involved, indeed we may be more conscious of it than if we were actually implicated in the reality – but our involvement is intellectual and sympathetic. Because the senses are less involved and the imagination has free play, art can touch us to pity, shame, revulsion, and can send us away reflective and conscious of an abuse that needs redress. If the audience are involved in too strong and crude a sense experience, the effect could be to deaden this power of sympathy. The impact of films is very strong as it is – over-stimulated patrons regularly vomited during performances of *The Exorcist*, responding to the green bile regurgitated on screen. Shocking in a different way is Andrzej Wajda's *Kanal*,[1] which has the grim setting of the sewers of Warsaw during the destruction of the city by the Nazis. To carry on the war, to survive and fight back at the Germans, the men had to live and die in excrement. It is the ultimate debunking of war; war reduced to its (literally) filthy reality, at the other end of the scale from the romantic heroes of the many battle epics. Pasolini's last work *Salo* also strove to show, in appalling detail, the horrors of human cruelty by setting de Sade's *120 Days of Sodom* in a part of northern Italy held by the Fascists. Four intellectual torturers (a banker, a duke, a bishop and a judge) assemble a group of forty young people whom they subject to every form of perversion before

1. Plate 47.

a final ritual of violation, torture and death. The film's subject is the depravity of power which reduces human victims to objects. Most audiences find it almost unbearable, an alienating and degrading experience. Nobody could accuse Pasolini of being titillating or exploitative, but the explicitness of his treatment works against his intention. The implicit contract between audience and film-maker has been broken, the conventions too rudely shattered. The cinema today may be more daring than in the past and almost any subject can now be dealt with, but we still continue to find value in restraint. It is interesting that Wajda's *Kanal*, the most artistically successful of the three films, was shot in black and white. Hector Babenco showed his awareness of the problems when he made *Kiss of the Spider Woman*, about two men suffering in a South American prison. The torturing of one of the men is central to the situation but the actual incidents are never shown. As the director has said, 'I show his back in the first three scenes of the film – it's bleeding and that's it. That is ten times more mysterious and effective in a cinematic way.'

Here we touch on the eternal problem of art, taste and censorship. No society is without its taboos – religious, political, sexual, social, even artistic. No audience is without its prejudices. Art has always been subject to censorship, because it is so closely bound up with society. Not only can it provide release, a vicarious outlet, for feeling and impulses which do not find expression in everyday life, but it can also act as a field for social experiment, can promote and reflect changes in the mores of a society, can advocate reforms, attack abuses. It can undermine authority, as witness many examples from *The Barber of Seville* to *The Gulag Archipelago*. At the same time censorship imposed by authority is by its nature approximate, often ineffective, and may be dangerous if the society thereby becomes incapable of change. Some official censorship can be justified on legal, moral and 'prevailing standards' grounds: few would nowadays argue against the censoring of scenes of exploitative sexual violence, for example. But the most important censorship is that exercised by the artist himself as part of the discipline of his art. It is rarely the sincere artist who falls foul of official censorship – more often the exploiter seeking to provide crude sensation. Both artist and exploiter (and it has to be admitted that history may change the category into which any film-maker is assigned) are constrained by the conventions of the time and by the laws of the market-place. Film is an expensive medium and the pressures to play safe, not to attack the prejudices of the audience (or the financier) are clearly powerful. Yet the breaking down of the consensus society with an agreed code of practice into a more splintered pattern with differing standards, a trend that reached its height during the controversial liberalizations of the sixties, has left the position confused. What is beyond debate is that the cinema has changed its role in recent years. Since the War, the mass audience has deserted it for television and other forms of entertainment and leisure. One response has been that many films now concentrate on material that is unsuited to broadcast television. In terms of commercial movies this means stories aimed at adolescents (the main cinema-going audience and an age-group that has always been poorly served by television) and those deemed too 'adult' for the small screen. The result is the inclusion in films of material that would have been unacceptable in the past.

Conventions have been broken and new ones accepted in their place – but this should not be confused with an impetus towards greater realism. What could be less real than the slow-motion deaths with which we are now so familiar, the close-ups of bullets exploding in flesh, or the vast intertwining limbs of sexual acts? This is not how we experience such moments in real life, merely the way in which we currently accept them on screen. How different this approach is from the older conventions (particularly after the imposition of censorship in America in the early thirties) in which suggestion was all. Without revealing much to public gaze, filmmakers still contrived to create scenes of great power.

Fritz Lang's *M* is about a child murderer, and the director has spoken of his presentation of the crime:

> If I could show what is most horrible for *me*, it may not be horrible for somebody else. *Everybody* in the audience – even the one who doesn't *dare* allow himself to understand what really happened to that poor child – has a horrible feeling that runs cold over his back. But everybody has a *different* feeling, because everybody *imagines* the most horrible thing that could happen to her. And that is something I could not have achieved by showing only one possibility – say, that he tears open the child, cuts her open. Now, in this way, I force the audience to become a collaborator of mine; by *suggesting* something I achieve a greater impression, a greater involvement than by showing it.

There is a famous sequence at the end of Lewis Milestone's *All Quiet on the Western Front* in which the hero, Paul, a German soldier, is shot by a French sniper. The sniper is shown carefully aiming his rifle but all we see of Paul is his hand stretching out to try and touch a butterfly that has come to rest. We recognize it as Paul's hand because we already know he is a butterfly collector, and, because of the sniper, watch it stretching farther and farther in anxious suspense. Then there is a shot, the hand jerks, slowly drops, and lies still. Paul's death is as vivid as if we had seen a full picture of him dying. The same technique of suggestion, of letting the spectator use his imagination, appears in an incident in Satyajit Ray's gentle film, *Mahanagar*. An old man has gone out visiting and he is shown labouring up a steep flight of stairs with the help of a stick. As he reaches the top, Ray cuts to a shot of someone coming to greet him, and we watch the expression on this strange face change to alarm. Then follows simply a shot of the old man's stick clattering down the stairs. We never see the old man collapse but for that very reason his accident impresses us all the more. Again in Buñuel's strong film, *Diary of a Chambermaid*, when the man-servant, Joseph, proceeds to kill a goose with sadistic relish, the camera turns away at the crucial moment. Partly because of the context this deliberate averting of the eyes strengthens the impact of the slaughter. A different but, in its own context, equally effective treatment occurs in *The Tree of Wooden Clogs* when the peasants cut the throat of their pig. Because their attitude is unemotional and the scene is shot in a simple, unexploitative manner, we see it as just one more part of a hard and unsentimental way of life.

Changes in attitude now give the film-maker a freer choice between showing or not showing. He can turn away or he can gaze, and the two approaches imply a different attitude, convey different meanings. Earlier we saw how new techniques continue to broaden the spectrum from which the film-maker can select. Here we see that in the area of content also his choice has become wider. No director is compelled to 'show all' any more than he is forced to use every technical and stylistic device at his disposal. Many will continue to believe that it is more effective to appeal to the mind and the emotions rather than directly to the senses. 'Heard melodies are sweet, but those unheard are sweeter.' The worst fears are those which exist in our imagination. The best meals are those we remember from our youth. We live in a mental world and the mind interprets the messages it receives from the senses sometimes incorrectly, always partially. This is a point to be returned to in discussing the nature of film reality. Suggestion may also be far more effective than full statement because it is more stimulating. In attacking a person, innuendo will penetrate deeper and have a more devastating effect on any intelligent listener than straightforward abuse. Suggestion demands a contribution from the listener, flatters him by demanding it, and involves him much more than if he is merely a passive recipient. The artist can say too much and become boring. Secondly, in supplying mentally the images that are omitted, each viewer will imagine something different, something to suit his own case. There is a story of a successful blackmailer who threatened strangers by accusing them of some unnamed crime, merely saying 'I know all about you, everything is discovered.' If his success is truly reported, it is no doubt because the threat was couched in such vague terms that the details of their crimes were supplied by the victims themselves. The same applies to character-reading, fortune-telling and the horoscopes printed in papers, which are in such general terms that they apply to almost any case. In skilful hands each client can be made to tell his own fortune. The same was undoubtedly true of horror movies until quite recent times. The most terrible monsters were those we hardly saw, the worst tortures those whose details were withheld – supplied instead by our own worst fears and imaginings.

The cinema nowadays has greater ability to convey on screen apparitions of evil that match those created in the recesses of our own minds. But if special effects can now enable film-makers quite legitimately to frighten and horrify us as never before, they have also made it all too easy to overstep the mark and present images that merely encourage the viewer to take pleasure in the giving of pain, to identify with the unmotivated aggressor and to enjoy the humiliation of the powerless. If the debate over video nasties owed less to considered appraisal than to moral panic, there is still little doubt that the charge of depravity was not always misplaced.

Violence is also now too often used to add a morally dubious level of excitement to films that may be lacking in other qualities.

Director Don Siegel has noted how the wider 'freedom of expression' with 'censorship playing a less and less important role' gives the film-maker 'full responsibility and enough rope to hang himself'. While he has described his own *Dirty Harry* as a 'wall-to-wall carpet of violence', he has also explained how he deliberately avoided explicit violence in his earlier film *The Killers*, preferring not to show repeated scenes of his villains inflicting damage. Instead, he made clear 'right from the pre-credit sequence that they were capable of everything: from the first shots, one sees them brutally beating a blind woman, then savagely battering down the hero point blank. The thing is so shocking that from then on I didn't need to make them do any more.'

Nor is it only explicit horror and violence that are now at the film-maker's command. Nudity and sex are no longer the prerogative of the pornographer. With the replacement of the old rigid censorship codes by age-related classification systems, combined with the cinema's search for audiences not satisfied by the family-oriented broadcast media, almost any subject can now be approached and treated in a direct fashion. Louis Malle has filmed stories of child prostitution and mother–son incest (*Pretty Baby* and *Le Souffle au Coeur*), admittedly in a rather glossy style. Homosexuality has been widely dealt with in films like Frank Ripploh's *Taxi Zum Klo*, Bernard Blier's *Tenue de Soirée*, Stephen Frears's *My Beautiful Laundrette* and *Prick Up Your Ears*, Friedkin's *Cruisin'*. Homosexual prostitution and child drug addiction were the subject matter of Ulrich Edel's *Christiane F*, while Lynch's *Blue Velvet* had at its core a sordid sado-masochistic relationship. Barbet Schroeder's *Maîtresse* looked at bondage and domination, while Oshima's *Ai No Corrida* (*Empire of the Senses*) straddled the gap between art and pornography, using images usually confined to the latter in a gruelling story of sexual obsession and violent passion.

In contrast, we may consider the case of Claude Lanzmann's *Shoah*, a nine and a half hour documentary consisting entirely of interviews with Poles and Czechs who recall their war-time experiences as both victims and collaborators. Their memories of Treblinka, Auschwitz and the Lodz ghetto are so intense and harrowing that no visuals are needed. Their words and faces, together with sights of the camps as they are today, are more than enough to convey the smell of death and the taste of humiliation and genocide.

In short, the visual and sound resources of the cinema can, if they are sufficiently vivid, suggest other sense impressions by an association of sense memory similar to association of ideas. The cinema can suggest impressions of touch and taste without there being any actual sensory experience. Although our physical perceptions are independent of each other, the feelings they arouse in us are an interrelated whole. Baudelaire says in his poem *Correspondances*:

> Just as the sounds of far-off echoes blend
> Into a shadowy, soul-felt symphony
> Vibrant as night and colourful as day
> So colours, scents and sounds all interact.

The whole Symbolist school of French poetry following Baudelaire made this one of their aesthetic principles.

In a famous sequence from Pudovkin's *Storm over Asia*, the hero, a Mongol trapper, rouses the envy of a Yankee trader by showing him a magnificent silver-fox skin he has come to town to sell. A close-up of the pelt lit perfectly, shows us the thick gleaming fur just as a slow ripple runs through it bringing out the closeness of the hairs and depth of the pile so vividly that the viewer can virtually *feel* the richness of its texture for himself. In *Une Partie de Campagne* there is a sensuous tracking-shot of a rainstorm on the river in which we can hear the rushing, sweeping sound of the rain and *feel* the sharp, clean, stinging coldness of the drops. One could give many other instances, from luxurious beds whose comfort we can feel at a glance, to sumptuous repasts we enjoy with our eyes. Sound can have similar associations. The end of Bresson's *Le Procès de Jeanne d'Arc* is dominated by the fearful noise of a huge conflagration, until we can almost smell the smoke and feel the heat of the flames.[1] In a sequence in Adrian Lyne's *Nine 1/2 Weeks*, the young man blindfolds his girl-friend and gives her a variety of things to eat. As she is deprived of her sight we also are somehow made to rely on our other senses to a greater degree than usual. Though we can see the fruit, the raw egg and so on, we also have a vivid impression of their texture and taste. We feel with the woman and share her sensuous impressions.

1. Plate 48.

If showmen of the future can bring us scents and flavours and Rupert Brooke's 'rough male kiss of blankets' in an artistic and enjoyable form, then so much the better. In the meantime we can enjoy the many-sided richness of the cinema as it exists, since it can evidently give a good account of itself through the senses of sight and sound alone.

CHAPTER NINE

REALITY AND ARTISTIC CREATION

IN the introduction we said that art touches on reality at three points at least: it arises from the artist's experience; it has to be expressed in a tangible medium; it has to be presented to a real audience. The preceding chapters have been concerned with the second of the three stages: the manner in which the artist's experience is expressed in the tangible medium of a film. In this last chapter we discuss the impression of reality which a film makes on its audience – or which an audience reads into a film. We noted in Chapter 5 how Bazin, in his earlier writing, referred to the camera's ability to record 'pure' reality, and how he argued, at one stage, that cinema was moving towards perfect mimesis, or copying, of objective reality. A version of Bazin's position was maintained by Tarkovsky, who wrote that 'In film, every time, the first essential in any plastic composition, its necessary and final criterion, is whether it is true to life, specific and factual; that is what makes it unique.' Dismissing symbols for their imposing of 'extraneous meaning', he argued that, '... the purity of cinema, its inherent strength, is revealed not in the symbolic aptness of images (however bold these may be) but in the capacity of these images to express a specific, unique, actual fact.'[1] His model is Bresson, whose guiding principle was the elimination of expressiveness, the desire to 'do away with the frontier between the image and actual life; that is, to render life itself graphic and expressive.'

In fact, neither Bresson nor Tarkovsky made films that were

1. Tarkovsky, *Sculpting in Time*, p. 95.

documentary or neo-realist in style. Both impose themselves on their material in the choice and ordering of their images and how they are presented. Bazin himself had been forced to recognize a 'reality achieved through artifice' and to admit to not one, but 'several realisms', with the cinema a form of language, a network of signs that refer to, but are separate from, reality.

FILM AND REALITY

Film is a stage away from reality and, although the audience in the cinema may react strongly to the images they see in a film, they do not treat them like real events. This is an obvious statement but it is worth looking at the reasons why this is so.

Firstly, when we go to the cinema, we go there to see a film, and this colours our subsequent behaviour. The persuasion of reality which the cinema exerts on our *senses* may be very strong: in a 3-D film when someone stabs at the audience with a sword, we may instinctively duck, or we may feel quite giddy during a sequence in Cinerama showing a bob-sled ride. But at once our mind rejects these instinctive reflex reactions and we feel silly, much as we would if we went up to a wax figure of an attendant in Madame Tussaud's and asked it the time.

This, of course, is *trompe-l'oeil* which occurs in many forms of art, and it may be enjoyable simply as a joke at the spectator's expense. It exists at one end of the scale in the plastic ink-blots, flies, spiders, and poached eggs of the practical joker. On a slightly higher level, in Roman Polanski's film *Mammals* the audience is fooled at the start of the film by being shown a blank screen which turns out to be a field of snow. In Bert Haanstra's *Fanfare* we see cows gliding mysteriously through the fields until the camera alters its angle to show us the barges which are carrying them. These are simple examples but there is an element of this sense illusion in more serious cinema. It depends on habit and our habitual way of looking at things and taking them for real – seeing is believing. As we saw in the example of the fairground 'Crazy Cottage', habitual reactions may be extremely strong, and there may be a situation in which we react despite ourselves – our mind knows it is an illusion, but our body is caught in a conditioned sensory reaction. We may very well enjoy the resulting surge of visceral feeling freed of the unpleasant concomitants of reality, and even deliberately cultivate it. This is the thrill of the scenic railway as well as the thrill of the adventure or horror film. People like to 'be scared to death' or to 'enjoy a good cry' provided it is in the cinema and not in real life.

Nevertheless it would be wrong, because there is an illusion, to say that the spectator is deceived by the artist. The spectator wants to be deceived and he himself contributes to the deception. The situation is more like a game with conventions which both parties accept before the game starts. If the artist observes the conventions the spectator will accept the reality (perhaps a better word would be 'validity') of what he sees.

The interesting thing is that, when the physical compulsion of *trompe-l'oeil* is at its strongest, our mind remains critical. In cases where the physical reality is less, our mental acceptance may be stronger, and such cases are the general rule in the cinema where physical reality is unattainable. It is clear that our sensory impression of a thing or an event, and our mental belief about it, are two different things although they occur together, interact and combine. A better description of our mental attitude in most cases is, not belief, but 'suspension of disbelief'; and this includes recognition in a film of a mental truth, validity, reality – call it what you will – as important or more important than the physical reality.

The second reason why an audience reacts differently to film and reality is because the events on the screen are not happening 'here-and-now'. This may seem to contradict what has already been said and what is said later about the immediacy of film. In Chapter Four, for instance, it was said that in a film of the sinking of the *Lusitania* the picture on the screen showed the audience people drowning before their eyes. It is true that some forms of art have a greater immediacy than others and that film is one of those which gives the spectator a powerful impression of 'being-present'. Nevertheless all art has a certain historicity and even with film we are still looking at a *picture* of the people drowning.

Kracauer in *The Nature of Film* credits the cinema with giving a very strong feeling of 'being-present', and says a film can give the spectator a sense that the events presented are, like life, not completed. He concludes that the construction natural to the cinema is an 'open-ended' one – meaning the kind of plot which is a slice of life, not the rounded, finished, inevitable ending of formally constructed tragedy or comedy. An artistic medium certainly has an influence on the type of construction which suits it best, but in fact Kracauer's analysis applies much more accurately, as we have already noted, to television. That medium provides the real 'here-and-now' image, whereas the formally planned, conclusive structure of the traditional narrative is ideally suited to the limited time-span of a night out at the pictures.

The historicity of art goes with its durability – *ars longa vita brevis*. It is a quality of art to last and many arts enable an experience to be perpetually renewed. As has been said earlier, one of the things which make people value and cultivate art is its everlasting quality. A novel or a film is capable of being re-read or re-seen *ad infinitum*. The events of real life, on the other hand, cannot be exactly repeated. History never repeats itself but art does, even if the viewer's perception of the film may change from viewing to viewing.

It is interesting from this point of view to compare a film with a *personal performance* by a great musician or actor. The play or the music as written is, like the film, fixed for all time, but the actual performance itself is, like life, transient and incapable of exact repetition. Consequently such a personal performance will give the audience the very strongest feeling of 'here-and-now', of 'being-present', stronger than a film. The hysteria and emotion that can greet a pop star, a diva, a film star when present in the flesh, is not accorded to their screen image.

Although the 'being-present' feeling given by a live performance may therefore seem stronger than that of a film, one can perhaps say that the two forms are different not so much in intensity as in kind. In the case of a personal appearance the 'here-and-now' feeling belongs to the performance, to its manner rather than to its content, whereas, in the case of a film, the 'here-and-now' feeling belongs to the things portrayed, with their strong connection with physical reality, not to the performance of the film itself.

There is a third reason why the spectators react differently to a film and to reality: because the events on the screen are happening to other people, not to them. This third reason for a difference in attitude will affect the film audience more or less strongly according to the type of treatment and the extent to which the spectator identifies himself with one or other of the characters. The novelist can take a detached attitude and write about his characters in the third person or he can write as if the hero or heroine were telling the story in the first person. It is the same with a film. The spectator will be least involved with the most indirect treatment in which the camera clinically observes the characters, maintaining a psychological (and perhaps also a literal) distance. He will be most involved when the cinema takes the part of one of the characters, draws us into their situation, so that we look with the heroine at the blade of the circular saw inching nearer, or when (in Hitchcock's *Rebecca*) we follow with Rebecca's own eyes her approach to Manderley and hear her thoughts voiced in our ears.

THE REALITY OF THE FILM IMAGE

Film reality may not be objective reality, but the cinema still gives a stronger feeling of real life than other arts. There are several reasons for this. First, there is the ability of the cinema to reproduce movement. There is a fascination about movement in itself without any added interest, which automatically attracts one's attention. The natural sights which hold our gaze most strongly are such things as running water, passing clouds, the dancing flames of a fire, the flight of birds. It is the same with art. Ballet depends almost entirely on movement, and the practised gestures of an actor or the precision of slapstick are part of the theatre's appeal. In the cinema, graphic composition in becoming mobile comes alive, and, both with cinema and television, movement affords the image greater impact, drawing the eye to certain parts and away from others – as it does in life.

Second there is the point, already mentioned, that the photographic image created by a mechanical process is superficially more objective than other artistic methods of reproduction and therefore apparently gives a scientific assurance of authenticity.

A third reason for film's strong impression of reality is the feeling it gives of 'being-present'. We mentioned this in Chapter Four, when writing of film being in the present tense, and in the previous section we compared it with the effect of a real actor's presence in the theatre. It is connected with, even part of, the factor just given

– the impeccable authenticity of the photographic image. It depends too on the mental attitude of the spectator rather than on the physical perfection of the reproduction, for it is strongest in the case of newsreels and documentaries regardless of the quality of the photography and hence regardless of actual likeness to the original. An old newsreel of the First World War with its grainy image, bad lighting, uncertain definition, and jerky movement – we believe in it implicitly, far more than we do in the theatrical studio settings of the thirties, glamorized by soft-focus and back-projection, although these may give a better imitation of the real thing. Nevertheless, we *do* believe in studio settings, in all the tricks of the cinema, and even in completely formalized décor; and this is very largely because they come to us through the medium of the same camera which gives us the newsreel. There is a transfer of belief from the documentary to the fiction film and our implicit, possibly misplaced faith in the one helps to make the other more real.[1]

How far we can trust documentary footage is a vexed question. The Direct Cinema exponents of the sixties (Don Pennebaker, the Maysles brothers, Richard Leacock) and the French *cinéma vérité* of Rouch and Marker, tried through unnarrated, unstructured footage to achieve a greater degree of objectivity, and their followers still pursue this aim on television with 'fly-on-the-wall' techniques. The results certainly *look* more objective (i.e. less fictional) but this hardly guarantees authenticity. An alternative approach is to assume that all filming is subjective, to lay one's cards on the table and make no pretence of seeking any essential truth. Emile de Antonio moved in this direction in films like *Point of Order* and *Milhouse*, neither of which earned him any gratitude from Senator McCarthy or Richard M. Nixon respectively. De Antonio's sometime collaborator Haskell Wexler has made a series of 'committed documentaries', and two features – *Medium Cool* (1969) and *Latino* (1986). The former, the more interesting, is a mixture of documentary and fiction with the story of a television news photographer gradually becoming aware of the implications of his job during the political events of 1968, climaxing at the Democratic Convention in Chicago and the demonstrations that

1. Plate 50.

accompanied it. Shot in the midst of the riots (at one point a technician warns the director 'Look out, Haskell – it's real!'), the film conveys a mood of conviction that spills over into its fictional plot. The film's climax is a comment on image, object and representation. In the chaos of the riots, the hero is killed in a car crash. Almost immediately we observe a TV crew busy filming the scene (the hero had been doing exactly this when we first saw him), with Haskell Wexler himself handling the camera. He pans from the bodies in the car and aims his camera straight at the audience. On the sound-track we hear the rioters' slogan, 'The whole world's watching.'

A more recent film that plays with the concept of documentary truth in a rather different way is Woody Allen's *Zelig*, the story of the 'chameleon man'. Zelig is a total nonentity whose lack of character is compensated for by his ability to merge with his surroundings by changing his features to conform with his company, whether it be Negro jazz musicians, Hassidic Jews, the overweight or whatever. By degrees, he becomes a celebrity and we see him admiring the baseball style of Babe Ruth, sharing a ten-gallon hat with Tom Mix and ruining one of Hitler's speeches at a Nazi rally. In all these and other similar scenes, we see Zelig in the same frame as the celebrities.[1] We know the shots are faked in the laboratory but to our eyes they appear completely authentic.

The best-known documentarist of recent years is Frederick Wiseman, a lawyer turned film-maker, whose lengthy examinations of American institutions and their role in preserving order appear to be entirely disinterested. But they are far from being straight recordings. Wiseman shoots up to thirty times the amount of film he eventually uses. The final film results from the choices made and structures imposed during editing, a stage which he has described as 'dreaming the film into coherence'.

Even so, a documentary style still carries 'authenticity'. Fellini's *And the Ship Sails On* starts like a Lumière film – silent, flickering sepia images of a turn-of-century port, figures rushing about at the behest of an overcranked camera. Gradually faint sounds are heard – harbour noises and then simple music. Finally, as a procession of cars arrives, colour seeps into the images and Lumière gives way to

1. Plate 51.

Méliès as the occupants of the vehicles start to sing Verdi at the tops of their voices as they climb aboard a manifestly fake liner. This five-minute history of the cinema also illustrates the way in which the recreation of historical settings can be effective on film.[1] The cinema can be more convincing in this respect than any stage setting, although the further back in time, the harder it is to appear authentic. This is especially so for periods before the invention of the camera. Not only do we know how people looked as a result of photography, but we are more familiar with images of the recent past. Previous centuries are both unfamiliar and unknown. To replace our knowledge of how people behaved and talked, various conventions have arisen. Some, like those of the Western, have become so pervasive that 'legend has taken over from truth'. Who would ever believe that only sixty-three train robberies were recorded in the whole of the USA and Canada between 1870 and 1933?

The amount of information in every frame of a film is a drawback here. Where the novelist or playwright can suggest period in a few words and leave the reader to supply the details as far as he wishes or is able, film shows all. In addition the writer is protected by a cushion of words. An anachronism like Shakespeare's 'The clock hath stricken three' in Julius Caesar would be far more shocking if we actually saw the offending clock upon a Roman mantelpiece.

The Concrete Nature of Film

This brings us to a fourth characteristic of film's relationship to reality: the fact that it is composed of concrete images. This sets it apart from the novel or play composed of abstract written or spoken words, and returns us directly to the debate over the relationship between the image and the object portrayed. Astruc coined the term 'caméra-stylo' to suggest that film is a kind of writing in pictures and we have already seen film referred to as a form of language, albeit one that has no element comparable to the single word – as the old adage 'a picture is worth a thousand words' testifies.

Here let us merely conclude that film is a form of communication

1. Plate 49.

whose meanings are allusive and open to interpretation. Words can change their meaning over time or in different contexts, and filmic images are also subject to cultural review. The propaganda films *Cocaine Fiends* and *Sex Madness*, made in 1939 as dire warnings against drugs and promiscuity, were re-released in the seventies as comedies. In the eighties they look a good deal less amusing.

If the language of film is always fluid, its images often ambiguous, it can none the less express several ideas simultaneously. What we see may be not only a simple concrete image in its own right, it may also represent something with which it is associated, and also be symbolic of something quite different.[1] The concrete image can convey abstract ideas through the conventions shared between film-maker and audience. Kon Ichikawa's film, *The Key*, is about an elderly man almost at the point of death, but relentlessly driven by sexual desire. On his knees he contemplates his wife's naked body and, as he gazes impotently at it, the golden skin dissolves into the curving sand-hills of a desert. This single dissolve says as much as a good many words, but in quite a different way. Buñuel's criticisms of conventional religion are frequently conveyed in concrete terms in *Viridiana*, notably when, at the height of a drunken orgy, he groups his rogues and vagabonds at a long table in a parody of da Vinci's picture of *The Last Supper*. It is only the recognition of this arrangement of figures that endows the image with this meaning.

In Anthony Harvey's *Eagle's Wing*, a white woman has been captured by Indians and is dragged along at the end of a rope. Falling to her knees she comes face to face with a scorpion, its tail raised to strike. Her grinning captor saves her by ramming a hollow crucifix, more booty from the stagecoach hold-up, down on top of it. Shortly after, we see the posse in pursuit reach the same spot. An eager cowboy reclaims the holy symbol, only to be stung by the scorpion still clinging to it. Religion can bring death as well as salvation.

In Michael Curtiz's *Casablanca* the French commander (Claude Rains), at the same time as he condones the shooting of a Nazi general, drops an empty bottle of Vichy water into a waste-paper basket. In Preminger's *Laura* an antique clock is shattered by the

1. Plates 52 and 53.

shot which kills the girl. Not only is the time significant but it
points symbolically to the criminal, the owner of the clock, a
collector who is prepared to destroy something beautiful rather
than part with it. The end of Carné's *Le Jour se Lève* is full of
meaningful images. All night the doomed hero (Jean Gabin) has
been besieged in his room by the police. Finally at dawn he shoots
himself. There is the irony of his ending his life as a new day
begins and the camera cuts to a fine shot of the rising sun. Then it
surveys the room in chaos, a symbol of a life ended in chaos and
tragedy. Then a smoke-bomb thrown by the police bursts and fills
the room – there is the relentless inevitability of the law and also
irony in the fact that it is no longer needed. Finally a cheerful alarm
clock rings – but there are only dead ears to hear it.

There have been many films in which we see the gangster or the
victim dying on waste-ground or a rubbish dump – Wajda's *Ashes
and Diamonds*, Fellini's *Il Bidone*, the little boy in *Los Olvidados*. At
the conclusion of *Once Upon a Time in America* the gangster-turned-
politician commits suicide by throwing himself into the jaws of a
municipal garbage lorry, one more piece of human rubbish.
Photographs themselves are frequently used to symbolize the past
– usually a more placid, untroubled time, well expressed by the
unblinking gaze of the still picture.

Film has a price to pay for its vividness. There is a universality
of denotation about the word which the film cannot equal. We
read:

> Oh western wind when wilt thou blow
> That the small rain down shall rain?
> Christ, that my love were in my arms . . .

In a film the words 'my love' have to be expressed as Garbo or
Monroe, Fonda or Streisand. The inability of even these goddesses
to match the simple words 'my love' illustrates the incomparable
force of imagination. It is its very facelessness which gives the word
such a power of evoking dreams, as these lines have had over the
centuries. One can give another example from the theatre which
uses both abstract words and concrete actions. One might think
that it would be more effective for a violent murder to be shown on
the stage, but in Greek plays it most often occurs off-stage and
then is reported in words. There are special reasons for this in the

ritual nature of Greek drama – the use of masks would make violent action unsuitable, and so on; nevertheless, the effect of this indirect presentation, of saying the abstract word instead of showing the concrete deed, can be tremendous.

The nearest that the cinema gets to the generalized expression of words is in films with a greater degree of abstraction. In *Last Year in Marienbad*, the characters have no history, no families, no professions, no names even, but letters instead; they wear a neutral uniform – evening dress; the place is remote, without associations, we are not quite sure where. The film approaches as near as possible to the universal reference of the words 'man', 'woman', 'fear', 'love'. In David Lynch's *Eraserhead* even these concepts become ambiguous as his unearthly characters move surreally through a mechanistic world of horrors and repulsion.

There is a saying of Walter Pater which is relevant to this point: 'All arts aspire to the condition of music.' Music goes farther in the way of abstraction, in dispensing with particular meaning, than any other art. Although it may successfully convey an incidental meaning, programme music even in the hands of Strauss, Tchaikovsky or Beethoven is of secondary importance. Also, although music combines so well with other artistic elements (e.g. in ballet, film, opera), it is generally (except in the case of the greatest opera in which the music overwhelmingly predominates) both lighter in weight and less deeply felt than when it is undiluted. Pure music is the freest of all arts and is able to communicate immediately and intimately with the listener.[1] It strikes through and beyond reason and emotion. It can stir us to the depth of our being without arousing specific thoughts or emotions and move us to a state of indefinable rapture.

There are areas of film-making that tend towards abstraction. In the sixties when Western culture as a whole was increasingly fragmented and permissive, many film-makers took advantage of the prevailing climate, which encouraged experimentation, to push film along lines already travelled by modern art. Underground and 'expanded' film-makers experimented with different ways of producing images (flicker films, scratch films, etc.) and made pictures

1. It is not surprising that in *Close Encounters of the Third Kind* Spielberg shows that it is through music that humans and aliens can communicate.

that were patterns of light and colour devoid of script, narrative or recognizable objects. Structuralist films looked at the very process of making a film, its raw materials and techniques; others questioned the accepted relationships between audience and artist and between film and other media. These experiments continue and they have had their effect on mainstream, narrative cinema, but not perhaps as extensively as their proponents of the sixties hoped. Film-makers like Stan Brakhage and Michael Snow, Ed Emswiller and Hollis Frampton are influential – but their successors are mostly working, not in film, but in video, a medium that seems better suited to their concerns, being cheaper, more manipulable, and offering a more direct relationship between author and audience.

Narrative cinema does not allow the same freedom; its images cry out for meaningful interpretation, though their removal from reality can, as has frequently been noted, afford them a quality closer to dreams than to life. Cinematographer Vilmos Zsigmund has proposed a relevant explanation for the failure of *Heaven's Gate*, whose structure and content, he felt, failed to conform to the conventions and expectations of its audience. Zsigmund saw the film as an essay in light and tone rather than as a study in character or a well-shaped narrative, and suggested that its reputation would rise as a result of moves towards this sort of cinema in the future. It seems unlikely that film's patterns of light will ever become as abstract as music's patterns of sound, but it is equally likely that current conventions will change. As society and culture evolve, so the role of the cinema and the meaning and importance of its images may take new forms.

THE ROLE OF THE ARTIST

It is clear from what has been said that the reality of a film exists at two levels at least – the physical and the mental. On both levels the film-maker will best convince his audience by creating an artistic whole in keeping with the nature and purpose of the particular film, and broadly within the convention the audience will accept. It may be as important for the artist to avoid destroying the illusion as to do anything positive to create it, and paradoxically this may involve him in avoiding a too specific use of realistic details.

The physical level will include such things as décor, props, costume, appearance, habits, manners, customs, speech. For instance, belief in a historical film may be killed stone dead by intrusion of modern speech idioms. And not only slang. In Joseph Mankiewicz's fourteen-million-pound epic, *Cleopatra*, there is the following exchange between Elizabeth Taylor (Cleopatra) and Rex Harrison (Caesar) – *Cleopatra*: 'I seem to have rubbed you up the wrong way.' *Caesar*: 'I'm not sure I want to be rubbed by you at all.' *Cleopatra*: 'I shall have to insist that you mind what you say.' Later she says to him: 'We've gotten off to a bad start, haven't we?'

What is the audience to think of this? Quite apart from colloquialisms, the phrases themselves, the attitudes they represent, the flavour they convey, the associations they evoke – all are modern and all combine to destroy the feeling of period achieved in some of the ceremonial and battle scenes. As one reviewer dryly remarked: 'If the purpose of this dialogue is to reduce these awe-inspiring figures to human proportions, the director has been more successful than I think he would have wished to be.' There is no need and it is not possible to copy historical reality exactly. The audience knows (vaguely) that the Romans spoke Latin but only Derek Jarman's *Sebastiane* has actually shown them speaking it, more as part of the film's 'camp' quality than for verisimilitude. It is sufficient for the dialogue to have an archaic flavour. Scott in his historical novels deliberately cultivated a style different from the idiom current at the time he wrote, a neutral style without period associations. This is a problem the silent film did not have to meet. Dreyer's *The Passion of Joan of Arc* has faults but it almost completely avoids modern associations. In Bresson's *Le Procès de Jeanne d'Arc* the Maid's beauty-parlour hair-style and, even more, the English voices with their cultivated, high-pitched accent, destroy the feeling of period. We do not really know how English was spoken in the time of Joan of Arc, but more neutral voices would have been more successful. Nor do we know how Joan did her hair, but the treatment in Dreyer's film was better: Falconetti's hair was simply hacked off, and avoided association with particular styles.

There are many cases in which the unique ability of the camera and microphone to reproduce a real location, real accents or the raciness of slang or dialect is a delight. Generally speaking, dubbing takes away from a film because an authentic native accent is replaced by something more remote: it is hard to believe that Bill Forsyth's Scottish comedies have the same subtle impact in the American dubbed versions. However, in cases where dubbing adds a touch of realism it can be successful: in French versions of their comedies Laurel and Hardy talk French with a strong American accent; in a French version of Richard Williams's cartoon *Love Me, Love Me, Love Me*, the commentary is spoken by an English man speaking broken French. Because difficulty in talking foreign languages is so real, it adds to the effect.

However, there are other circumstances in which it is important for the film-maker to escape from the limiting references of realism by formalizing, by abstracting, by simplifying, by leaving the spectator to fill in the detail with his own imagination. In the décor of a Fu Manchu thriller every detail may be obtrusively correct and yet the whole (more Chinese than China itself) fails to persuade us, whereas *The Cabinet of Dr Caligari*, using only abstract angles, creates an immediately convincing world of evil.[1] The advantage of suggestion over plain statement has already been discussed in Chapter Eight.

Also in a sense on the physical level, but different from the elements we have been discussing, are those which go to make the style of the film-maker: framing, camera-angle, lighting, cutting, use of music, and so on. These elements do not correspond to anything in the physical world, but are features of the medium in which the film-maker embodies his ideas. Thus there is no question, with these elements, of fidelity to reality; it is a matter of choice, arrangement, manipulation. We have considered each of these separately and come to the conclusion that rigidly applicable rules of universal validity cannot be formulated; but the most successful artists are those whose style is suited to the film and the audience. As E. H. Gombrich says in *Art and Illusion*:

> The form of a representation cannot be divorced from its purpose and the society in which the given visual language gains currency.

1. Plate 30.

Another point may be added: style will generally seem more natural when it is unobtrusive, when it is the art that conceals art. At the same time the extent to which the mechanics of creation are hidden from the spectator differs in different conventions, and it may not matter which is chosen provided the artist is clear about it and the audience accepts it. We are so used to credits in a film that we hardly regard them as non-realistic. As a kind of signature Hitchcock's appearance in minor roles has become well known. But taking this further in Agnès Varda's *Lion's Love* the actors persuade the director to come and join them and she walks over from behind the camera and takes part in the film. At the end of Lindsay Anderson's *O Lucky Man!* the hero is shown taking part in a film with Anderson directing. Fellini's *And the Ship Sails On*, whose opening we have already described, concludes by bringing its history of the cinema up to date through the introduction of the same device. The camera pulls back from its shot of lifeboats leaving the sinking liner to reveal the studio and the film crew at work and then zooms into the lens of another camera.

In the oriental theatre the scene-shifters have always come on in full view of the audience, a convention copied by the Western theatre to some extent. In Shinoda's movie *Double Suicide* it is transferred to the cinema, and the black-robed hooded figures who help the lovers on the scaffold actually add to the tragic effect. Harry Watt's *People Like Maria*, has the director in the studio explaining how the film was planned. The camera may be more or less obtrusive. McBride's *David Holzman's Diary* is a movie entirely based on a camera-crazy youngster who films everything about him – himself, his girl, his friends – until they turn on him or leave him. Finally he has to raise money on his camera and the film loses its visuals and comes to an end. There are many films about making a film, from silent comedies to Reisz's *The French Lieutenant's Woman* and Wenders's *The State of Things*. In Godard's *Contempt* (*Le Mépris*), the film director is played by Fritz Lang who at one point is interviewed about his own early films. At the end of Skolimowski's *Le Départ*, the young hero turns on the camera and we see part of the film being burnt. In Dennis Hopper's *The Last Movie*, the Peruvian peasants are so impressed with Sam Fuller's filming that they set about 'filming' themselves using bamboo cameras and planning the real violence which they assume is all part of the fun of film-making. In Woody Allen's *The Purple Rose of Cairo*, one of the characters steps off the screen during a matinée performance attended by the star-struck heroine, to general confusion. A number of recent films, including the Burt Reynolds *Cannonball Run* pictures and Jackie Chan's *Police Story* have adopted the stratagem of including, during the closing credits, a sequence of reject takes of fluffed dialogue, miscalculated stunts and other mishaps, which refer the audience to the process of film-making. Animation is a more artificial form which lends itself to this exposure of methods. Max Fleischer's Koko the Clown cartoons, made in the twenties, included arguments between the clown and Fleischer himself. The clown always got the better of things, much as the ventriloquist's dummy gets the better of his master.

The second level on which a film exists is mental. On this level reality is a reality of ideas, of emotions, of behaviour, of character, of fundamental, universal truths. The artist seeks to create an artistic whole which will convince by its emotional or ideological depth and verity – or he may choose not to. Many of Godard's films are intellectual exercises apparently without deep emotion in them in which everything is made to look faked or formally symbolic – the torture in *Le Petit Soldat*, the rape in *Les Carabiniers*, the suicide in *Pierrot Le Fou*, the cannibalism in *Weekend*, the prostitution in *Vivre Sa Vie*, the sexual perversions of *Slow Motion*. Many films have explored these subjects in a less detached way. And yet Godard's films do reflect the director's moral sensibility, his passion almost, not in the content or the way it is presented, but in the sheer poetry of Godard's film-making; a passion that derives from the composition of his images and the construction of his sequences, from the elements of film-making themselves.

On an erotic level, sex movies are often ultimately trivial, unconvincing and even unarousing because they lack any sincere feeling or belief. But Buñuel in *Tristana*, Sternberg in *The Blue Angel*, Roeg in *Bad Timing*, Beineix in *Betty Blue*, Visconti in *Ossessione* can convey the strength and destructiveness of passion and lust, because they bring emotional conviction to their work and their beliefs become our beliefs. Again there are movies like Wellman's *Oxbow Incident*, Capra's *Mr Deeds Goes to Town*, Lumet's

Twelve Angry Men. The sentiments are impeccable and they carry us along with their pace and style – but a doubt remains. Somehow they are too neat, too pat, too clever. Films like *Greed, La Grande Illusion, Pather Panchali, Los Olvidados, Tokyo Story,* or *La Terra Trema*; all these are possibly less polished, less smooth (if more original) in construction and style than the other films just mentioned. But they leave us in no doubt about the film-maker's passionate sincerity and depth of feeling and they convince us more fully of their deep truth. False nobility, sentimentality, cheap sex, as opposed to real nobility, sincere feeling, true passion – all these may arise from the artist's failure to feel deeply enough, or from his inspiration becoming diluted and lost in the process of realization. Even so, the artist is a creature of his time. Passing years and changes in society, culture and the audience may reveal truths in hitherto unsuspected corners, while reducing last year's artistic triumph to this year's pretentious failure.

In art the mental level, which we may call also the level of imagination, is the more important. E. H. Gombrich writes in discussing Constable:

> What a painter inquires into is not the nature of the world but the nature of our reaction to it . . . his is a psychological problem.

If this is true of painting, the artist's account of the physical world, it will be even truer of film, dealing as it does more fully and explicitly with feelings and ideas. Even in his ordinary life, an artist, like any human being, will be as much affected by his mental as by his physical environment. 'Nothing is either good or bad but thinking makes it so.' In his art, free from the immediate pressure of the physical world, the balance will tilt on the side of the mental.

There is another reason from the side of the viewer why the mental level or the level of imagination is particularly important in art. In ordinary life, for much of the time, all our senses and our body itself are very fully occupied in doing and reacting – our imagination, if it is active at all, is busy with utilitarian reasoning, anticipating, serving the needs of the situation. In the cinema, on the other hand, our body is quiescent and only two of our senses are actively engaged. But our imagination is at full stretch: directed and stimulated by the film-maker's emotionally charged, expressly-selected material and by his technique of presenting it. Thus it may be that a film will succeed in taking hold of the spectator's mind in a stronger, deeper, possibly more lasting way than reality itself.

In practice, in the artist's work the two levels, physical and mental, will occur together, interpenetrate and interact and both are important. For the finest art, perfection of form must be combined with greatness of conception, and the combination must offer the audience emotions, ideas and experiences that relate to them. The film-maker must know what he has to say as well as how to say it. Failure of execution may spoil a film but even worse is the brilliantly executed work without content. Flashy technique and glittering style are never enough.

THE ROLE OF THE SPECTATOR

It is the artist or, in the case of film, artists who create the work of art: but it is the spectator who completes the picture at the moment of viewing. At one time it was thought that those who sat and listened or watched were quite passive. Education was a process 'of pouring knowledge into empty heads' and cinema-going was criticized because the audience were 'doing nothing'. In fact watching a film involves fairly intense sensory and intellectual activity, and in all arts the spectator must make some contribution for the communication of the artist's experience to be complete. Like the work of the artist the contribution which the spectator makes will also be on two levels, the physical and the mental.

It is scientifically well-established that physical sense perception consists not merely of taking an impression of an external stimulus but is a positive activity. As Thouless in *General and Social Psychology* writes: 'perception is an activity of the mind itself of which sensory stimulation is generally a determining cause, but not a necessary condition . . . a perception is not something produced by a stimulus, but by the activity of the organism itself.'[1] When we see a film, a

1. In the phrase 'but not a necessary condition' Thouless refers to that part of an area of perception which is void of sensory stimulation but filled in by the mind following a pattern of expectation. For example, show a spectator an incomplete letter (R) and he will fill in the top part of the upright of the 'R' following a pattern of expectation although this area is void of sensory stimulation. Many optical illusions also show that our eyes follow preconceived patterns.

lifetime of habitual visual experience operates to validate the illusion on the screen, and the viewer unconsciously corrects imperfections or omissions in the image, and will see it as perfectly real even when the likeness is no more than approximate. Our senses both of sight and sound also have a high tolerance for poor quality of reproduction, and automatic sense adjustments operate, without our being aware, to ensure a constant level of good vision or good hearing. Thus, up to a certain point, poor print quality or a bad sound-track will not disturb a cinema audience, particularly if they are absorbed in the film.

Because perception is an activity of the organism it is to some extent the organism not the stimulus which determines what the perception will be. It is like an activity being triggered off rather than an impression being taken. Our sense of cold, for instance, depends on special nerve endings which feel cold and nothing else, and they will still register cold if they are touched with something warm. At a higher level a film image brings into play a complex of analogies and similarities determined by conditioned reflexes which outweigh any optical alterations from reality.[1] It follows that absolute fidelity of the film image to its original (if it were possible) is superfluous, and that individual perceptions of a film will vary from person to person. Such variations, slight at the perceptual level, will be much greater when it comes to intellectual and emotional responses.

The circumstances in which a film is seen in the cinema (the darkness, the size of the screen with its larger-than-life figures, the audience – alone but sharing the reactions of others) give it a unique emotional impact. In the narrative cinema, this impact is usually conveyed through the characters with whom spectators are encouraged to feel some sort of identification. This identification reached its peak in the star system that has flourished from

1. Reality is in the eye of the beholder. Barry Levinson's *The Natural* is realist in all senses – but cameraman Caleb Deschanel has described the lighting he used as 'preposterous in lots of ways ... the choices are made for dramatic reasons more than any other' – an example of Bazin's artificial reality. Nestor Almendros has spoken of how he would move pictures on a wall from one position to another so that the frame in Truffaut's films would be balanced: audiences never notice that the paintings have moved from shot to shot; perceptual reality is not infringed.

Hollywood to Bombay (significantly television produces personalities rather than creating stars). We can trace the roots of the star system back into remote prehistory. In the earliest times, kings and princes were deified, gods and goddesses humanized, given earthly habitation in temples, offered food and drink and their intervention sought in human affairs. Some of these beliefs carried over into the church and popular religion in the Middle Ages retained magical elements – the worship of saints, miracles and wonders – an element even of the fairground. Though modern religion has been intellectualized and refined and science has fostered disbelief, such elements survive in popular form today and, despite differences in attitudes and motives, film stars, along with sporting heroes and pop culture personalities, can be regarded as descendants of the saints of popular legend.

The role of the star; the relationship between actor and part (and the viewer may be aware of both simultaneously); and the relationship between the stars and the narratives which they often threaten to overwhelm – these are all issues that have been widely debated. The position of the star, in the industry and in society, has changed to reflect social change and differing attitudes towards the image. From the glamorous semi-deity created and almost literally owned by the studio, it has evolved into the less glossy, more idiosyncratic, though not necessarily more human and realistic (cf. Stallone, Schwarzenegger) figure of today. Stars are not likely nowadays (as James Stewart once did) to turn down a part because it does not reflect their accepted image. Even so, a known face immediately gives the viewer a certain perspective on what he sees – the actor's own personality and image is one set of signs and signals through which the drama is interpreted. The viewer builds up a relationship between the actor and his part which reflects the viewer's own character, needs and desires. Whether the film works or not will depend to a high degree on how this relationship is established.

SUBJECTIVITY OF VALUES IN ART

The foregoing analysis of the artist's and the viewer's contribution to the film illusion enables us to attempt an answer to the questions: 'How are we to judge a work of art? What is good? What is bad? How are we to tell?' We have said that, because every spectator himself contributes to the total artistic impression, the same film may be viewed differently by different people. The world of art is different from that of mathematics and science in which, once the basic postulates are accepted, the conclusions follow by an impersonal logic, demonstrably and universally the same for everybody. The scientist can prove everything. The artist on the contrary can prove nothing; he can only offer his experience which the individual viewer may or may not recognize and accept, as corresponding to something he esteems. Nor can the critic prove anything. For the value of a work of art can be assessed only by reference to a subjective judgement.

Scientific rules or laws are far more particular, exact, rigid and universal than those of art. Unless they are based on fallacious reasoning or faulty observation, they are permanently valid although they may be 'absorbed' into a wider concept as Newtonian physics have been absorbed into Einsteinian physics. In art we have stressed the provisional nature of rules. This applies whether we are considering the artist's technique (rules of procedure) or what the finished product should be like (critical dictates). It is perhaps better to regard rules in art as a matter of style and having the same sanction as style. Within a style certain conventions must be accepted though even here there is room for development and personal variation. But in a different style the conventions may be completely different.

At the same time the artist needs to have rules in the sense of procedures. E. H. Gombrich shows clearly that a graphic artist cannot paint or draw without following a formula (a *schema*) and even the greatest artists have 'played the sedulous ape' by imitating previous artists. At any one time, in any one culture, a set of general guidelines will exist the ignoring of which constitutes a very positive statement. These guidelines will of course be internalized by the film-maker so that he unconsciously conforms to the currently accepted norms governing the complex combinations of sound and images. The film-maker has not got the graphic artist's problem of imitating reality – but he has instead the task of choosing between different filmic realities and applying the necessary technical skills to achieve on film what is in his mind. Such skills must of course be learnt, either through education in film school, through observation on the studio floor, or through trial and error.

The particular difficulty of film lies in the mobility, the number and complexity of the elements which compose it, and the consequent variety of interpretations and evaluations which the same work may generate.[1] Whereas some general agreement may in theory be possible over the way meaning is conveyed, the empirical operation of the medium and how it works, the aesthetic evaluation is bound to be more controversial. If a work is only finally completed, its meanings established, at the moment of viewing, when author, text and audience meet at a particular moment of social, cultural and personal history, there can never be a final verdict on any work. Films mean different things to different people and to the same people in different circumstances and at different times. The reputation of any author will inevitably be unstable and subject to revision.

Even so, at any one period there is likely to be a consensus of popular opinion derived from the existing conventions, tastes, social and historical circumstances and other factors. The role of the critic is to interpret and evaluate within this framework. It can be argued that the judgement of posterity will carry the greatest weight because it consists of layer upon layer of both popular and informed individual judgements and this must be recognized as our best criterion of quality in a work of art. Even in this case, to set against the gain in determinacy there are disadvantages; for as works of art recede they become part of a social tradition and valued unquestioningly for other than artistic reasons. They become sacrosanct and, by growing beyond criticism, grow more remote and formidable. Secondly, the canon by which they were created becomes archaic so that it is impossible for any but an antiquary to enter fully into the spirit of their creation. Contemporary appreciation, although it may be more debatable, can be both more spontaneous and more complete.

It may be a sign of richness in a work of art both that it attracts a conflict of critical judgements and also that it appeals strongly from

1. Umberto Eco identified a whole series of codes to which the film image is subject: codes of recognition, transmission and tonality which transform the object into the image; iconic codes which enable one to understand the transformation; connotative codes, of taste and style, which relate the image to the world. Each code gives rise to conventions and rules which enable communication between film-maker and audience.

several different aspects. To take the first point, many of the artists and works of art which are ultimately most highly valued have difficulty in gaining acceptance in the first place. This is perhaps because most important artists have an originality which in one way or another fails to accord with current artistic fashions; they break 'the rules' and it may take them a lifetime or longer to convince anybody that their method of expression is equally valid. *Greed* is one film masterpiece that reached the screen only as a shadow of its original conception, reduced to well under a quarter of its length, and many films have suffered similar (if less extreme) fates. It is hard now to remember, or understand, the fierce controversy which surrounded *Last Year at Marienbad*, while Michael Powell's *Peeping Tom*, reviled on first release, is now acclaimed.

As for the second point, different aspects (or levels) do exist in most art, but only the occasional work has the resources and balance to appeal with equal force from them all. In Shakespeare's plays we have the beauty of the poetry, the excitement of the plot, the interest of the characters, the morality of their actions, the intellectual impact of their conversation. A film like *The Killing Fields* exists as an exciting story of courage and endurance, as a powerful indictment of American imperialism and as a superb example of documentary-style camerawork. Renoir's *La Règle du Jeu* is in one aspect a knock-about bedroom farce, in another a study of tragic personal relationships, in yet another a serious criticism of the society of the period. *Jour de Fête* is, on the surface, merely a gay comedy full of Tati's inimitable slapstick. But, underneath, it is a criticism of the senseless pace of modern life and of modern bureaucracy, and from this aspect it has as much depth as many more pretentious works. Towards the end of the film, the postman's cap is donned by a little boy who delivers the letters while the postman takes off his coat and gets on with a useful job – harvesting. Different aspects may be appreciated by different audiences and they may be given different values. Thus the same film may be several different things to different people and, for the audience concerned, one aspect or level is just as real and important as another.

NATURE OF FILM: CONCLUSION

Because the film gives such a feeling of reality this does not mean that it can only be used, or ought only to be used, naturalistically.

Like any form of art the cinema is capable of an infinite range of styles and can take in its stride fantasy, formalism, symbolism, surrealism, and abstract compositions. The very realistic quality of photography can be used to give a special force to fantastic elements.[1] In Samuel Fuller's *Shock Corridor*, the story of a man who gets himself shut in a mental asylum to solve a murder, there is the terrifying image of a raging thunderstorm with howling wind and torrents of rain which occurs *in* the corridor *inside* the building. It is a subjective image of mental disturbance and the impact is very powerful. In Polanski's *Chinatown* there is the surrealistic image of a flock of sheep driven into a council chamber during a public meeting. It is explained realistically as a protest, but at the same time it represents the unexpected, typical of later twists and turns in the story. It is significant that the most effective ghosts in the cinema are the most realistic.[2] In Oshima's *The Empire of Passion*, the murdered husband returns to haunt his wife and her lover but retains his humble status, at one point offering the woman a lift in the rickshaw through which he had earned his living. In Pasolini's *The Gospel According to St Matthew*, both the angel who announces the birth of Christ and the devil who tempts Jesus during his forty days of fasting are treated like any other character in the film and in both cases are wholly convincing. These scenes are far more effective than they would have been with double-exposure or misty soft-focus. The force of the effect arises from the contrast between the absolute realism of the image and the knowledge that it is after all a ghost. The same is true also of Tarkovsky's *Solaris* in which the hero, Kelvin, is sent to a space station and discovers that the few men left there are being hounded towards madness by apparently live duplicates of dead friends. The cold-blooded Sartorius survives by dismissing his visions as purely scientific phenomena, but Kelvin is drawn helplessly into a relationship with his dead wife. Even when he destroys her, she reappears as alive, alluring and touching as before, a materialized figment of his dreams and fears. Similar again is the black-cloaked figure of death who engages the crusading knight in a game of chess in

1. Plate 54.

2. Plate 55.

Bergman's *The Seventh Seal*. His very physical presence brings a chill, even in moments of comedy, as when he chops down a tree in which a victim has taken refuge.

We have continually emphasized the illusory nature of screen reality. The old saying, 'The camera cannot lie', is only true up to the point that human intervention takes place. As soon as the camera is put to use it becomes a tool through which the film-maker achieves his purpose. The most neutral documentary footage can be put to any number of purposes, to the annoyance of those who still expect the camera to be an agent of truth. There have been numerous debates over the morality of using footage from one battle to represent another, and the whole issue of 'faction' in which real historical events are taken as the basis for fictional, and probably unhistorical, stories. There are those who argue that the images should not be simply true to the film itself, but also, somehow, true to the original event. There is an ironic tale told by Balazs of an attempt to subvert *Battleship Potemkin*, itself to some extent a propaganda exercise, by simply changing the position of one sequence so that the story of oppressed slaves revolting against wicked officers becomes a tale of unjustified revolt against authority.

In fact the viewer does not necessarily subscribe to the saying that 'seeing is believing'. The audience seeks to believe not what it sees but what it conceives, and it is not the fidelity of the image to an assumed reality which counts, but the ease with which it can be accepted as reality in its own right. It is not a question of reproducing real objects on the screen, but of creating filmic objects which belong to an autonomous category of reality that borrows only its appearance from that of nature. The transformation from the one to the other is guided by the accepted conventions of cinematic technique and art.

To move us a work of art must possess both authenticity and credibility; but the authenticity and credibility which we demand of a work of art are not those which we require of natural objects. In our eyes the two worlds are different and we do not adopt the same physical reactions or attitude of mind towards them. The real world appeals to our senses more than our imagination, while the world of art is designed to work the other way round.

The world of the imagination has its own premises, laws, and conventions, but they are not the same as those of the physical world. The artist knows them, the physicist does not. At the same time the world of imagination is just as real and important as the world of the senses. There is nothing unreasonable or perverse about it except in the case of fanatics and eccentrics. When it is creative, as with the thinker, the philosopher, the artist, or the inventor, it functions in just as 'real' terms as the physical world. In fact, it is the mind that we know directly (*cogito ergo sum*) while the physical world comes to us at second hand through the partial and distorted report of the senses. Certainly in art the imagination is the final arbiter of the real.

We all live in the world as we imagine it: every day we create it for ourselves. The world of the cinema screen is also our creation. The film-maker uses his experience, his skills, his technique and his imagination to express an artistic truth. John Boorman, writing of his time in Brazil making *The Emerald Forest*, noted that 'The Indians, with their music, dance and ritual, are constantly striving to escape from their material lives into the spirit world. In making a movie we take the material elements of our society and transmute them into a stream of light flowing on to a wall, hoping that it will contain something of *our* spirit.'

INDEX OF FILMS AND DIRECTORS

THIS index includes only directors whose films are mentioned in the text. The listings are not intended to be complete, including only their best known or most characteristic works. Page references to film titles can found in the general index. (s) indicates a short film.

ANSTEY, EDGAR (UK): *Granton Trawler*, 1934 (s); *Housing Problems*, 1935; *Enough to Eat*, 1936.

ANTONIONI, MICHELANGELO (It): *Le Amiche*, 1955; *Il Grido*, 1958; *L'Avventura*, 1960; *La Notte*, 1961; *L'Eclisse*, 1962; *The Red Desert*, 1964; *Blow-up*, 1966; *Zabriskie Point*, 1969; *The Passenger*, 1974; *Identification of a Woman*, 1982.

APTED, MICHAEL (UK): *The Triple Echo*, 1972; *Stardust*, 1974; *Coalminer's Daughter*, 1979; *Gorky Park*, 1984; *Gorillas in the Mist*, 1988.

ARNOLD, JACK (USA): *It Came from Outer Space*, 1953; *The Creature from the Black Lagoon*, 1954; *The Incredible Shrinking Man*, 1957.

ASHBY, HAL (USA): *Harold and Maude*, 1971; *The Last Detail*, 1973; *Shampoo*, 1975; *Bound For Glory*, 1976; *Coming Home*, 1978; *Being There*, 1979.

ASQUITH, ANTHONY (UK): *Pygmalion*, 1938; *The Way to the Stars*, 1945; *The Browning Version*, 1951; *The Importance of Being Earnest*, 1952; *Orders to Kill*, 1958.

ASTRUC, ALEXANDRE (Fr): *The Crimson Curtain*, 1953 (s); *La Longue Marche*, 1966; *Flammes sur l'Adriatique*, 1968.

ATTENBOROUGH, RICHARD (UK): *Oh! What a Lovely War*, 1969; *Gandhi*, 1982; *A Chorus Line*, 1985; *Cry Freedom*, 1987.

BABENCO, HECTOR (Brazil): *Pixote*, 1981; *Kiss of the Spider Woman*, 1985; *Ironweed*, 1988.

BADHAM, JOHN (USA): *Saturday Night Fever*, 1977; *Dracula*, 1979; *Whose Life is it Anyway?*, 1981; *War Games*, 1983; *Short Circuit*, 1986.

BARNET, BORIS (USSR): *The Girl with the Hat Box*, 1927; *Okraina (Suburbs)*, 1933; *A Wonderful Summer*, 1950.

BEINEIX, JEAN-JACQUES (Fr): *Diva*, 1981; *The Moon in the Gutter*, 1983; *Betty Blue*, 1986.

BENEDEK, LASLO (USA): *Death of a Salesman*, 1952; *The Wild One*, 1954.

BENTON, ROBERT (USA): *Bad Company*, 1972; *Kramer v. Kramer*, 1979; *Still of the Night*, 1982; *Places in the Heart*, 1984; *Nadine*, 1987.

BERESFORD, BRUCE (Aust): *Don's Party*, 1976; *The Getting of Wisdom*, 1977; *Breaker Morant*, 1980; *Tender Mercies*, 1982; *Crimes of the Heart*, 1986.

BERGMAN, INGMAR (Swe): *Summer Interlude*, 1950; *Sawdust and Tinsel*, 1953; *Smiles of a Summer Night*, 1955; *The Seventh Seal*, 1956; *Wild Strawberries*, 1957; *So Close to Life*, 1958; *The Face*, 1958; *The Virgin Spring*, 1960; *Through a Glass Darkly*, 1962; *Winter Light*, 1963; *The Silence*, 1964; *Now About These Women*, 1964; *Persona*, 1965; *Hour of the Wolf*, 1966; *The Shame*, 1968; *A Passion*, 1969; *Cries and Whispers*, 1973; *Scenes from a Marriage*, 1974; *Autumn Sonata*, 1978; *From the Life of the Marionettes*, 1980; *Fanny and Alexander*, 1982.

BERTOLUCCI, BERNARDO (It): *La Commare Secca*, 1962; *Before the Revolution*, 1964; *Partner*, 1968; *The Spider's Stratagem*, 1970; *The Conformist*, 1971; *Last Tango in Paris*, 1973; *1900*, 1976; *La Luna*, 1979; *The Last Emperor*, 1987.

BLIER, BERTRAND (Fr): *Les Valseuses*, 1974; *Get out your Handkerchiefs*, 1977; *Buffet Froid*, 1979; *Notre Histoire*, 1984; *Tenue de Soirée*, 1986.

BOGDANOVICH, PETER (USA): *Targets*, 1968; *The Last Picture Show*, 1972; *Paper Moon*, 1973; *Nickelodeon*, 1976.

BOORMAN, JOHN (UK): *Point Blank*, 1967; *Hell in the Pacific*, 1968; *Deliverance*, 1973; *Zardoz*, 1974; *Excalibur*, 1981; *The Emerald Forest*, 1986; *Hope and Glory*, 1987.

BOROWCZYK, WALERIAN (Pol): *Dom, Once Upon a Time*, 1957 (s) (both with JAN LENICA); *Renaissance*, 1963 (s); *Jeux des Anges*, 1964 (s); *The Theatre of Mr and Mrs Kabal*, 1967; *Goto, Isle of Love*, 1968; *Blanche*, 1971; *Immoral Tales*, 1974.

BOULTING, JOHN AND ROY (UK): *Brighton Rock*, 1947; *Lucky Jim*, 1957; *I'm All Right, Jack*, 1959.

BRAKHAGE, STAN (USA): *Dog Star Man*, 1963; *The Art of Vision*, 1964; *Scenes from under Childhood*, 1968.

BRESSON, ROBERT (Fr): *Les Dames du Bois de Boulogne*, 1945; *Diary of a Country Priest*, 1950; *Un Condamné à Mort S'est Échappé*, 1956; *Pickpocket*, 1959; *Le Procès de Jeanne d'Arc*, 1962; *Au Hasard Balthazar*, 1965; *Mouchette*, 1967; *Four Nights of a Dreamer*, 1971; *The Devil, Probably*, 1972; *Lancelot du Lac*, 1974; *L'Argent*, 1985.

BROOK, PETER (UK): *Moderato Cantabile*, 1960; *Lord of the Flies*, 1963; *Marat/Sade*, 1966; *King Lear*, 1970; *Carmen*, 1984.

BROOKS, MEL (USA): *The Producers*, 1967; *Blazing Saddles*, 1974; *Young Frankenstein*, 1974; *Silent Movie*, 1976; *High Anxiety*, 1977.

BROOKS, RICHARD (USA): *The Blackboard Jungle*, 1955; *Cat on a Hot Tin Roof*, 1958; *Elmer Gantry*, 1960; *Lord Jim*, 1964; *In Cold Blood*, 1967; *Looking for Mr Goodbar*, 1977.

BUÑUEL, LUIS (Sp): *Un Chien Andalou*, 1928 (s); *L'Âge d'Or*, 1930; *Los Olvidados*, 1950; *El*, 1950; *Nazarin*, 1958; *Viridiana*, 1962; *The Exterminating Angel*, 1962; *Diary of a Chambermaid*, 1963; *Simon of the Desert*, 1965 (s); *Belle de Jour*, 1966; *Tristana*, 1970; *The Discreet Charm of the Bourgeoisie*, 1972; *The Phantom of Liberty*, 1974; *That Obscure Object of Desire*, 1977.

BYRNE, DAVID (USA): *True Stories*, 1985.

CAMUS, MARCEL (Fr): *Black Orpheus*, 1958; *Bird of Paradise*, 1962.

CAPRA, FRANK (USA): *Long Pants*, 1927; *Platinum Blonde*, 1932; *The Bitter Tea of General Yen*, 1933; *It Happened One Night*, 1934; *Mr Deeds Goes to Town*, 1936; *Mr Smith Goes to Washington*, 1939; *Why We Fight*, 1945; *It's a Wonderful Life*, 1946.

CARNÉ, MARCEL (Fr): *Drôle de Drame*, 1937; *Quai des Brumes*, 1938; *Hôtel du Nord*, 1938; *Le Jour se Lève*, 1939; *Les Visiteurs du Soir*, 1942; *Les Enfants du Paradis*, 1945; *Les Portes de la Nuit*, 1946; *Thérèse Raquin*, 1953.

CARPENTER, JOHN (USA): *Dark Star*, 1974; *Assault on Precinct 13*, 1976; *Halloween*, 1978; *Starman*, 1984.

CASSAVETES, JOHN (USA): *Shadows*, 1959; *A Child is Waiting*, 1963; *Faces*, 1967; *Husbands*, 1970; *A Woman under the Influence*, 1974; *Opening Night*, 1977; *Gloria*, 1980; *Love Streams*, 1983.

CHAFFEY, DON (USA): *The Girl in the Picture*, 1956; *The Prince and the Pauper*, 1962; *Jason and the Argonauts*, 1963; *One Million Years BC*, 1966; *Pete's Dragon*, 1977.

CHAN, JACKIE (HK): *Police Story*, 1986.

CHAPLIN, CHARLES (USA): Numerous shorts and *The Kid*, 1922; *A Woman of Paris*, 1923; *The Gold Rush*, 1925; *The Circus*, 1928; *City Lights*, 1931; *Modern Times*, 1936; *The Great Dictator*, 1940; *Monsieur Verdoux*, 1947; *Limelight*, 1952; *A King in New York*, 1957.

CIMINO, MICHAEL (USA): *Thunderbolt and Lightfoot*, 1974; *The Deerhunter*, 1978; *Heaven's Gate*, 1980; *Year of the Dragon*, 1986; *The Sicilian*, 1987.

DANTE, JOE (USA): *The Howling*, 1980; *Gremlins*, 1984; *Explorers*, 1985; *Innerspace*, 1987.

DASSIN, JULES (USA): *Brute Force*, 1947; *Naked City*, 1948; *Rififi*, 1954; *Never on Sunday*, 1960; *Phèdre*, 1961; *Topkapi*, 1964.

DE ANTONIO, EMILE (USA): *Point of Order*, 1963; *Rush to Judgement*, 1967; *In the Year of the Pig*, 1968; *Milhouse*, 1971; *Painters Painting*, 1972; *Underground*, 1976.

DELANNOY, JEAN (Fr): *The Pastoral Symphony*, 1946; *Les Jeux sont Faits*, 1947; *Aux Yeux du Souvenir*, 1948.

DEMME, JONATHAN (USA): *The Last Embrace*, 1979; *Melvin and Howard*, 1980; *Stop Making Sense*, 1984; *Something Wild*, 1986.

DEMY, JACQUES (Fr): *Lola*, 1961; *La Baie des Anges*, 1962; *Les Parapluies de Cherbourg*, 1963; *Les Demoiselles de Rochefort*, 1966; *Peau d'Ane*, 1971.

DE PALMA, BRIAN (USA): *Sisters*, 1973; *Phantom of the Paradise*, 1974; *Obsession*, 1976; *Carrie*, 1976; *Dressed to Kill*, 1980; *Blow Out*, 1981; *The Untouchables*, 1987.

DE SICA, VITTORIO (It): *Shoe Shine*, 1946; *Bicycle Thieves*, 1948; *Miracle in Milan*, 1951; *Umberto D*, 1952; *Two Women*, 1961; *The Garden of the Finzi-Continis*, 1971.

DISNEY, WALT (USA): *Snow White and the Seven Dwarfs*, 1938; *Pinocchio*, 1940; *Dumbo*, 1941; *Fantasia*, 1941; *Bambi*, 1942.

DONEN, STANLEY (USA): *On the Town*, 1949; *Singin' in the Rain*, 1952; *Seven Brides for Seven Brothers*, 1954; *Charade*, 1963; *Movie Movie*, 1978.

DONNER, CLIVE (UK): *The Caretaker*, 1963; *Nothing but the Best*, 1964.

DONNER, RICHARD (USA): *The Omen*, 1976; *Superman*, 1978; *Lethal Weapon*, 1987.

DOVZHENKO, ALEXANDER (USSR): *Zvenigora*, 1928; *Arsenal*, 1929; *Earth*, 1930; *Ivan*, 1932; *Aerograd*, 1935; *Shchors*, 1939.

DREYER, CARL (Den): *Master of the House*, 1925; *The Passion of Joan of Arc*, 1928; *Vampyr*, 1930; *Day of Wrath*, 1940; *Ordet*, 1955; *Gertrud*, 1964.

DUPONT, EWALD (Ger): *Variety*, 1925; *Piccadilly*, 1929.

EAMES, RAY AND CHARLES (USA): *Parade*, 1952 (s); *House*, 1955 (s); *Toccata for Toy Trains*, 1957 (s).

FLAHERTY, ROBERT (USA): *Nanook of the North*, 1922; *Moana*, 1926; *Man of Aran*, 1934; *Louisiana Story*, 1948.

FLEISCHER, MAX (USA): Numerous shorts including *Koko the Clown*, *Betty Boop* and *Popeye*. *Gulliver's Travels*, 1939; *Hoppity Goes to Town*, 1941.

FLEMING, VICTOR (USA): *The Wizard of Oz*, 1939; *Gone with the Wind*, 1939; *Dr Jekyll and Mr Hyde*, 1941.

FORD, JOHN (USA): *The Iron Horse*, 1924; *The Lost Patrol*, 1934; *The Informer*, 1935; *Drums Along the Mohawk*, 1939; *Stagecoach*, 1939; *Young Mr Lincoln*, 1939; *The Grapes of Wrath*, 1940; *The Long Voyage Home*, 1940; *My Darling Clementine*, 1946; *Fort Apache*, 1948; *She Wore a Yellow Ribbon*, 1949; *The Searchers*, 1956; *The Man Who Shot Liberty Valance*, 1962; *Cheyenne Autumn*, 1964; *Seven Women*, 1966.

FORMAN, MILOS (Czech): *Peter and Pavla*, 1964; *A Blonde in Love*, 1965; *The Fireman's Ball*, 1967; *Taking Off*, 1971; *One Flew Over the Cuckoo's Nest*, 1975; *Ragtime*, 1981; *Amadeus*, 1985.

FORSYTH, BILL (UK): *That Sinking Feeling*, 1979; *Gregory's Girl*, 1980; *Local Hero*, 1982; *Comfort and Joy*, 1984; *Housekeeping*, 1987.

FOSSE, BOB (USA): *Sweet Charity*, 1968; *Cabaret*, 1972; *Lenny*, 1974; *All That Jazz*, 1980; *Star 80*, 1983.

FRAMPTON, HOLLIS (USA): *Artificial Light*, 1969; *Zorns Lemma*, 1970.

FRANJU, GEORGES (Fr): *Le Sang des Bêtes*, 1949 (s); *Hôtel des Invalides*, 1951 (s); *Le Grand Méliès*, 1952 (s); *La Tête contre les Murs*, 1958; *Les Yeux sans Visage*, 1959; *Judex*, 1963; *Thérèse Desqueyroux*, 1964; *Thomas L'Imposteur*, 1964; *La Faute de l'Abbé Mouret*, 1970.

FRANKENHEIMER, JOHN (USA): *The Manchurian Candidate*, 1962; *The Birdman of Alcatraz*, 1962; *The Train*, 1964; *Seconds*, 1966; *Grand Prix*, 1967; *The French Connection II*, 1975; *Black Sunday*, 1977.

FREARS, STEPHEN (UK): *Gumshoe*, 1973; *Bloody Kids*, 1980; *The Hit*, 1984; *My Beautiful Laundrette*, 1985; *Prick Up Your Ears*, 1986; *Sammy and Rosie Get Laid*, 1987.

FRIEDKIN, WILLIAM (USA): *The Birthday Party*, 1968; *The Boys in the Band*, 1970; *The French Connection*, 1970; *The Exorcist*, 1973; *Cruising*, 1980; *To Live and Die in L.A.*, 1986.

FUGARD, ATHOL (S. Africa): *Boesman and Lena*, 1973.

HERZOG, WERNER (Ger): *Even Dwarfs Started Small*, 1970; *Fata Morgana*, 1971; *Aguirre, Wrath of God*, 1973; *The Enigma of Kaspar Hauser*, 1975; *Heart of Glass*, 1976; *Nosferatu*, 1978; *Fitzcarraldo*, 1980; *Cobra Verde*, 1987.

HILL, GEORGE ROY (USA): *Thoroughly Modern Millie*, 1967; *Butch Cassidy and the Sundance Kid*, 1969; *Slaughterhouse Five*, 1972; *The Sting*, 1974; *The World According to Garp*, 1982.

HILL, WALTER (USA): *The Driver*, 1978; *The Warriors*, 1979; *The Long Riders*, 1980; *Southern Comfort*, 1981; *Streets of Fire*, 1984.

HITCHCOCK, ALFRED (UK/USA): *Blackmail*, 1929; *The Thirty-Nine Steps*, 1935; *The Secret Agent*, 1937; *The Lady Vanishes*, 1938; *Rebecca*, 1939; *Spellbound*, 1945; *Notorious*, 1946; *Rope*, 1948; *Strangers on a Train*, 1951; *Rear Window*, 1953; *The Man Who Knew Too Much*, 1956; *Vertigo*, 1958; *North By Northwest*, 1959; *Psycho*, 1960; *The Birds*, 1963; *Marnie*, 1964; *Torn Curtain*, 1966; *Topaz*, 1969; *Frenzy*, 1972; *Family Plot*, 1976.

HODGES, MIKE (UK): *Get Carter*, 1971; *Pulp*, 1972; *Flash Gordon*, 1980; *A Prayer for the Dying*, 1987.

HONDA, INOSHIRO (Jap): *King Kong Meets Godzilla*, 1967.

HOOPER, TOBE (USA): *The Texas Chainsaw Massacre*, 1974; *Poltergeist*, 1982; *The Texas Chainsaw Massacre II*, 1986.

HOPPER, DENNIS (USA): *Easy Rider*, 1969; *The Last Movie*, 1971; *Out of the Blue*, 1980; *Colors*, 1988.

HU, KING (HK): *A Touch of Zen*, 1969; *Raining in the Mountain*, 1979.

HUDSON, HUGH (UK): *Chariots of Fire*, 1980; *Greystoke*, 1983; *Revolution*, 1986.

HUGHES, HOWARD (USA): *Hell's Angels*, 1930; *The Outlaw*, 1944.

HUSTON, JOHN (USA): *The Maltese Falcon*, 1941; *Across the Pacific*, 1943; *The Treasure of the Sierra Madre*, 1947; *The Asphalt Jungle*, 1950; *The Red Badge of Courage*, 1951; *The African Queen*, 1951; *Moulin Rouge*, 1952; *Moby Dick*, 1955; *The Misfits*, 1960; *The Night of the Iguana*, 1964; *Reflections in a Golden Eye*, 1967; *Fat City*, 1972; *The Life and Times of Judge Roy Bean*, 1973; *The Man Who Would Be King*, 1975; *Wise Blood*, 1979; *Under the Volcano*, 1983; *Prizzi's Honor*, 1985; *The Dead*, 1987.

ICHIKAWA, KON (Jap): *The Burmese Harp*, 1955; *The Key*, 1959; *Fires on the Plain*, 1960; *Alone on the Pacific*, 1963; *An Actor's Revenge*, 1963; *Tokyo Olympiad*, 1965.

KUROSAWA, AKIRA (Jap): *Rashomon*, 1950; *Living*, 1952; *Seven Samurai*, 1954; *The Lower Depths*, 1957; *Throne of Blood*, 1957; *The Hidden Fortress*, 1958; *Red Beard*, 1964; *Dodeska Den*, 1970; *Dersu Uzala*, 1975; *Kagemusha*, 1980; *Ran*, 1985.

KURYS, DIANE (Fr): *Diabolo Menthe*, 1978; *Coup de Foudre*, 1983; *A Man in Love*, 1987.

LAMORISSE, ALBERT (Fr): *The Red Balloon*, 1955 (s); *Le Voyage en Ballon*, 1960.

LANDIS, JOHN (USA): *National Lampoon's Animal House*, 1978; *An American Werewolf in London*, 1981; *Into the Night*, 1985.

LANG, FRITZ (Ger/USA): *Der Müde Tod*, 1921; *Dr Mabuse the Gambler*, 1922; *The Niebelungen*, 1924; *Metropolis*, 1926; *M*, 1931; *The Testament of Dr Mabuse*, 1933; *Fury*, 1936; *You Only Live Once*, 1937; *Ministry of Fear*, 1944; *Rancho Notorious*, 1952; *The Big Heat*, 1953; *The 1000 Eyes of Dr Mabuse*, 1960.

LANZMANN, CLAUDE (Fr): *Shoah*, 1985.

LEACOCK, RICHARD (USA): *Primary*, 1960; *Football*, 1961; *The Chair*, 1963.

LEAN, DAVID (UK): *In Which We Serve*, 1942; *Brief Encounter*, 1945; *Great Expectations*, 1946; *Oliver Twist*, 1947; *The Bridge on the River Kwai*, 1957; *Lawrence of Arabia*, 1962; *Dr Zhivago*, 1965; *Ryan's Daughter*, 1970; *A Passage to India*, 1985.

LEONARD, ROBERT (USA): *Strange Interlude*, 1932; *The Great Ziegfeld*, 1936; *Pride and Prejudice*, 1940.

LEONE, SERGIO (It): *A Fistful of Dollars*, 1964; *The Good, the Bad and the Ugly*, 1967; *Once Upon a Time in the West*, 1968; *Duck, You Sucker*, 1971; *Once Upon a Time in America*, 1984.

LESTER, RICHARD (UK): *A Hard Day's Night*, 1964; *The Knack*, 1965; *Help!*, 1965; *Petulia*, 1968; *The Three Musketeers*, 1974; *Cuba*, 1979; *Superman 2*, 1980.

LEVINSON, BARRY (USA): *Diner*, 1982; *The Natural*, 1984; *Tin Men*, 1987; *Rain Man*, 1988.

LINDER, MAX (Fr): Numerous shorts, some included in the anthology *Laugh With Max Linder*, 1963.

LOACH, KEN (UK): *Cathy Come Home*, 1966 (TV); *Kes*, 1969; *Family Life*, 1972; *Looks and Smiles*, 1981; *Fatherland*, 1986.

LOGAN, JOSHUA (USA): *Bus Stop*, 1956; *South Pacific*, 1958; *Camelot*, 1967; *Paint Your Wagon*, 1969.

LOSEY, JOSEPH (USA/UK): *The Boy with Green Hair*, 1948; *M*, 1950; *Blind Date*, 1959; *The Criminal*, 1960; *The Damned*, 1961; *Eva*, 1962; *The Servant*, 1963; *King and Country*, 1964; *Accident*, 1966; *The Go-Between*, 1971; *A Doll's House*, 1974; *The Romantic Englishwoman*, 1975; *M Klein*, 1976; *Don Giovanni*, 1979; *Steaming*, 1984.

LUCAS, GEORGE (USA): *THX 1138*, 1971; *American Graffiti*, 1973; *Star Wars*, 1977.

LUMET, SIDNEY (USA): *Twelve Angry Men*, 1957; *Long Day's Journey into Night*, 1962; *The Pawnbroker*, 1963; *Fail Safe*, 1964; *The Hill*, 1965; *The Anderson Tapes*, 1971; *The Offence*, 1973; *Serpico*, 1974; *Dog Day Afternoon*, 1975; *Network*, 1976; *Equus*, 1977; *The Verdict*, 1982; *Daniel*, 1983; *Power*, 1985; *The Morning After*, 1986.

LUMIÈRE, LOUIS (Fr): Numerous shorts including *Workers Coming out of a Factory; Train Coming into a Station; The Waterer Watered*, 1895–8.

LYNCH, DAVID (USA): *Eraserhead*, 1976; *The Elephant Man*, 1980; *Blue Velvet*, 1986.

LYNE, ADRIAN (USA): *Foxes*, 1980; *Flashdance*, 1983; *Nine½ Weeks*, 1986; *Fatal Attraction*, 1987.

MCBRIDE, JIM (USA): *David Holzman's Diary*, 1967; *Breathless*, 1983; *The Big Easy*, 1987.

MCLEOD, NORMAN Z. (USA): *Monkey Business*, 1931; *The Paleface*, 1948; *The Secret Life of Walter Mitty*, 1948.

MAKAVEYEV, DUSAN (Yug): *The Switchboard Operator*, 1966; *WR – Mysteries of the Organism*, 1971; *Montenegro*, 1981; *The Coca Cola Kid*, 1984.

MALICK, TERRENCE (USA): *Badlands*, 1974; *Days of Heaven*, 1978.

MALLE, LOUIS (Fr/USA): *Lift to the Scaffold*, 1957; *Les Amants*, 1958; *Zazie dans le Métro*, 1960; *Le Feu Follet*, 1963; *Viva Maria*, 1965; *Le Souffle au Coeur*, 1971; *Lacombe Lucien*, 1974; *Pretty Baby*, 1978; *Atlantic City*, 1980; *My Dinner with André*, 1981; *Au Revoir Les Enfants*, 1987.

MAMOULIAN, ROUBEN (USA): *Dr Jekyll and Mr Hyde*, 1932; *Love Me Tonight*, 1932; *Queen Christina*, 1933; *Becky Sharp*, 1935; *The Mark of Zorro*, 1940; *Blood and Sand*, 1941; *Silk Stockings*, 1957.

MANKIEWICZ, JOSEPH L. (USA): *A Letter to Three Wives*, 1948; *All about Eve*, 1950; *Julius Caesar*, 1953; *Guys and Dolls*, 1955; *The Quiet American*, 1958; *Suddenly Last Summer*, 1959; *Cleopatra*, 1963; *Sleuth*, 1972.

MARKER, CHRIS (Fr): *Cuba Si!*, 1961; *La Jetée*, 1963 (s); *Le Joli Mai*, 1963; *Sunless*, 1983.

MARQUAND, RICHARD (USA): *Eye of the Needle*, 1981; *The Return of the Jedi*, 1983; *Jagged Edge*, 1985.

MAY, ELAINE (USA): *A New Leaf*, 1970; *The Heartbreak Kid*, 1972; *Mikey and Nicky*, 1978.

MAYSLES, ALBERT AND DAVID (USA): *Showman*, 1963; *Salesman*, 1969; *Gimme Shelter*, 1970; *Grey Gardens*, 1975.

MAZURSKI, PAUL (USA): *Bob and Carol and Ted and Alice*, 1969; *Blume in Love*, 1973; *An Unmarried Woman*, 1978; *Down and Out in Beverly Hills*, 1985.

MEDAK, PETER (UK): *Negatives*, 1969; *A Day in the Death of Joe Egg*, 1970; *The Ruling Class*, 1971.

MÉLIÈS, GEORGES (Fr): Numerous shorts including *The Indiarubber Head*, 1901; *Trip to the Moon*, 1902; *The Coronation of Edward VII*, 1902; *Conquest of the Pole*, 1912.

MELVILLE, JEAN-PIERRE (Fr): *Les Enfants Terribles*, 1949; *Bob, le Flambeur*, 1956; *Léon Morin, Prêtre*, 1961; *Le Deuxième Souffle*, 1966; *Le Samourai*, 1968; *Le Cercle Rouge*, 1970.

MILESTONE, LEWIS (USA): *All Quiet on the Western Front*, 1930; *The Front Page*, 1931; *Of Mice and Men*, 1940; *A Walk in the Sun*, 1945; *Mutiny on the Bounty*, 1962.

MILLAR, GAVIN (UK): *Dreamchild*, 1985.

MINNELLI, VINCENTE (USA): *Cabin in the Sky*, 1942; *Meet Me in St Louis*, 1944; *The Pirate*, 1948; *An American in Paris*, 1950; *The Band Wagon*, 1953; *The Bad and the Beautiful*, 1953; *Lust for Life*, 1956; *Gigi*, 1958; *Two Weeks in Another Town*, 1962.

MURNAU, FRIEDRICH W. (Ger): *Nosferatu*, 1922; *The Last Laugh*, 1924; *Tartuffe*, 1925; *Faust*, 1926; *Sunrise*, 1927; *Tabu*, 1931.

NEEDHAM, HAL (USA): *Hooper*, 1978; *The Cannonball Run*, 1980.

PASTRONE, GIOVANNI (It): *Giulio Cesare*, 1909; *The Fall of Troy*, 1910; *Cabiria*, 1914.

PECKINPAH, SAM (USA): *Guns in the Afternoon/Ride the High Country*, 1962; *Major Dundee*, 1965; *The Wild Bunch*, 1969; *The Ballad of Cable Hogue*, 1970; *Straw Dogs*, 1971; *The Getaway*, 1972; *Pat Garrett and Billy the Kid*, 1973; *Bring Me the Head of Alfredo Garcia*, 1975; *Convoy*, 1978.

PENN, ARTHUR (USA): *The Miracle Worker*, 1962; *Micky One*, 1965; *The Chase*, 1966; *Bonnie and Clyde*, 1967; *Little Big Man*, 1971; *Alice's Restaurant*, 1973; *Night Moves*, 1975; *The Missouri Breaks*, 1976.

PENNEBAKER, DON (USA): *Don't Look Back*, 1966; *Monterey Pop*, 1968.

PETERSEN, WOLFGANG (Ger): *The Boat*, 1981; *The Never-Ending Story*, 1984; *Enemy Mine*, 1986.

PICK, LUPU (Ger): *Shattered*, 1921; *New Year's Eve*, 1923.

POLANSKI, ROMAN (Pol/UK/USA): *Two Men and a Wardrobe*, 1958 (s); *Knife in the Water*, 1962; *Repulsion*, 1964; *Cul-de-sac*, 1966; *Dance of the Vampires*, 1966; *Rosemary's Baby*, 1968; *Macbeth*, 1971; *Chinatown*, 1974; *The Tenant*, 1976; *Tess*, 1979; *Frantic*, 1988.

POLLACK, SYDNEY (USA): *They Shoot Horses, Don't They?*, 1969; *Jeremiah Johnson*, 1972; *The Way We Were*, 1973; *Three Days of the Condor*, 1975; *Absence of Malice*, 1981; *Tootsie*, 1982; *Out of Africa*, 1985.

POMMERAND, GABRIEL (Fr): *Légende Cruelle*, 1951 (s).

PORTER, EDWIN (USA): *The Life of an American Fireman*, 1902; *The Great Train Robbery*, 1903; *Rescued from an Eagle's Nest*, 1907 – all shorts.

POWELL, MICHAEL (UK): *The Spy in Black*, 1939; *49th Parallel*, 1941; *The Thief of Baghdad*, 1941; *The Life and Death of Colonel Blimp*, 1943; *A Canterbury Tale*, 1944; *I Know Where I'm Going*, 1945; *A Matter of Life and Death*, 1946; *Black Narcissus*, 1947; *The Red Shoes*, 1948; *Battle of the River Plate*, 1956 – all with EMERIC PRESSBURGER. *Peeping Tom*, 1960.

PREMINGER, OTTO (USA): *Laura*, 1944; *Carmen Jones*, 1955; *Porgy and Bess*, 1958; *Anatomy of a Murder*, 1959; *Exodus*, 1960; *Advise and Consent*, 1961; *In Harm's Way*, 1964.

PUDOVKIN, VSEVOLOD (USSR): *Mother*, 1926; *The End of St Petersburg*, 1927; *Storm over Asia*, 1928; *A Simple Case*, 1932; *The Deserter*, 1933.

RAIMI, SAM (USA): *The Evil Dead*, 1980; *The Evil Dead II*, 1987.

RIVETTE, JACQUES (Fr): *Paris Nous Appartient*, 1960; *La Religieuse*, 1967; *L'Amour Fou*, 1967; *Out 1/Spectre*, 1971; *Celine and Julie Go Boating*, 1974; *Duelle*, 1976.

ROBSON, MARK (USA): *Isle of the Dead*, 1945; *The Harder They Fall*, 1956; *Peyton Place*, 1958; *The Prize*, 1964; *Von Ryan's Express*, 1965; *Earthquake*, 1974.

RODDAM, FRANC (UK): *Quadrophenia*, 1979; *The Lords of Discipline*, 1982.

ROEG, NICOLAS (UK): *Performance*, 1970; *Walkabout*, 1971; *Don't Look Now*, 1973; *The Man Who Fell to Earth*, 1976; *Bad Timing*, 1980; *Eureka*, 1983; *Insignificance*, 1985; *Castaway*, 1986; *Track 29*, 1987.

ROHMER, ERIC (Fr): *La Collectioneuse*, 1967; *Ma Nuit chez Maude*, 1969; *Clair's Knee*, 1971; *Love in the Afternoon*, 1972; *The Marquise of O*, 1976; *The Aviator's Wife*, 1981; *Pauline at the Beach*, 1982; *Full Moon in Paris*, 1984; *The Green Ray*, 1986.

ROMERO, GEORGE (USA): *Night of the Living Dead*, 1968; *Martin*, 1978; *Dawn of the Dead*, 1979; *Day of the Dead*, 1985.

ROSI, FRANCESCO (It): *Salvatore Giuliano*, 1962; *Hands over the City*, 1963; *The Mattei Affair*, 1972; *Lucky Luciano*, 1973; *Illustrious Corpses*, 1976; *Christ Stopped at Eboli*, 1979; *Three Brothers*, 1981; *Carmen*, 1984; *Chronicle of a Death Foretold*, 1987.

ROSSELLINI, ROBERTO (It): *Rome, Open City*, 1945; *Paisà*, 1946; *Germany, Year Zero*, 1947; *Stromboli*, 1950; *Europa 51*, 1952; *Voyage in Italy*, 1953; *The Rise to Power of Louis XIV*, 1966; *Socrates*, 1970; *Blaise Pascal*, 1972; *The Age of Cosimo de' Medici*, 1973.

ROUCH, JEAN (Fr): *I, a Negro*, 1958; *The Human Pyramid*, 1961; *Chronicle of a Summer*, 1961; *La Chasse au Lion*, 1965.

RUDOLPH, ALAN (USA): *Welcome to L.A.*, 1977; *Remember My Name*, 1978; *Choose Me*, 1985; *Trouble in Mind*, 1986.

RUSSELL, KEN (UK): *Women in Love*, 1969; *The Devils*, 1971; *The Boy Friend*, 1972; *Mahler*, 1973; *Tommy*, 1975; *Valentino*, 1977; *Altered States*, 1979; *Crimes of Passion*, 1985; *Gothic*, 1986.

SAVILLE, VICTOR (UK): *I Was a Spy*, 1933; *The Good Companions*, 1933; *South Riding*, 1938.

SNOW, MICHAEL (Can): *Wavelength*, 1966–71; *The Central Region*, 1971.

SOLANAS, FERNANDO (Arg): *The Hour of the Furnaces*, 1968.

SPIELBERG, STEVEN (USA): *Duel*, 1971; *The Sugarland Express*, 1974; *Jaws*, 1975; *Close Encounters of the Third Kind*, 1977; *1941*, 1979; *Raiders of the Lost Ark*, 1981; *E.T., the Extraterrestrial*, 1982; *The Color Purple*, 1985; *Empire of the Sun*, 1987; *Indiana Jones and the Last Crusade*, 1989.

STONE, OLIVER (USA): *Salvador*, 1985; *Platoon*, 1986; *Wall Street*, 1987; *Talk Radio*, 1988.

STORCK, HENRI (Belg): *Borinage*, 1933 (s); *The World of Paul Delvaux*, 1947 (s); *Rubens*, 1948 (s).

TARKOVSKY, ANDREY (USSR): *Ivan's Childhood*, 1962; *Andrei Rublev*, 1966; *Solaris*, 1972; *The Mirror*, 1975; *Stalker*, 1979; *Nostalghia*, 1983; *The Sacrifice*, 1986.

TATI, JACQUES (Fr): *Jour de Fête*, 1947; *Monsieur Hulot's Holiday*, 1953; *Mon Oncle*, 1958; *Playtime*, 1968; *Traffic*, 1971; *Parade*, 1974.

TAVERNIER, BERTRAND (Fr): *The Watchmaker of St Paul*, 1975; *Que la Fête Commence . . .* , 1975; *Deathwatch*, 1979; *Une Semaine de Vacances*, 1980; *Coup de Torchon*, 1982; *Sunday in the Country*, 1984; *Round Midnight*, 1986.

TEMPLE, JULIEN (UK): *The Great Rock 'n' Roll Swindle*, 1980; *Absolute Beginners*, 1986.

TESHIGAHARA, HIROSHI (Jap): *Woman of the Dunes*, 1963; *The Face of Another*, 1966; *Summer Soldiers*, 1972.

TRUFFAUT, FRANÇOIS (Fr): *Les Mistons*, 1958 (s); *Les Quatre Cents Coups*, 1959; *Shoot the Pianist*, 1960; *Jules and Jim*, 1962; *La Peau Douce*, 1964; *Fahrenheit 451*, 1966; *The Bride Wore Black*, 1967; *Stolen Kisses*, 1968; *L'Enfant Sauvage*, 1970; *Anne and Muriel/Les Deux Anglaises et le Continent*, 1971; *The Man Who Loved Women*, 1973; *Day for Night*, 1974; *The Story of Adèle H*, 1975; *The Green Room*, 1977; *Love on the Run*, 1978; *The Last Metro*, 1980; *Finally Sunday*, 1983.

USTINOV, PETER (UK): *Romanoff and Juliet*, 1961; *Billy Budd*, 1962.

WELLES, ORSON (USA): *Citizen Kane*, 1940; *The Magnificent Ambersons*, 1942; *The Lady from Shanghai*, 1947; *Macbeth*, 1947; *Othello*, 1952; *Touch of Evil*, 1957; *The Trial*, 1962; *Chimes at Midnight*, 1965; *The Immortal Story*, 1968 (s); *F for Fake*, 1973.

WELLMAN, WILLIAM (USA): *Wings*, 1927; *Public Enemy*, 1931; *A Star is Born*, 1937; *Oxbow Incident*, 1943.

WENDERS, WIM (Ger): *The Goalkeeper's Fear of the Penalty*, 1972; *Alice in the Cities*, 1974; *Kings of the Road*, 1976; *The American Friend*, 1977; *The State of Things*, 1982; *Paris, Texas*, 1984; *Wings of Desire*, 1987.

WEXLER, HASKELL (USA): *Medium Cool*, 1969; *Latino*, 1985.

WHALE, JAMES (USA): *Frankenstein*, 1931; *The Old Dark House*, 1932; *Bride of Frankenstein*, 1935; *Show Boat*, 1936; *The Man in the Iron Mask*, 1939.

WIDERBERG, BO (Swe): *Raven's End*, 1964; *Elvira Madigan*, 1967; *Adalen '31*, 1969; *The Ballad of Joe Hill*, 1971.

WIENE, ROBERT (Ger): *The Cabinet of Dr Caligari*, 1919; *The Hands of Orlac*, 1925.

WILDER, BILLY (USA): *Double Indemnity*, 1944; *The Lost Weekend*, 1945; *Sunset Boulevard*, 1950; *Ace in the Hole*, 1951; *The Seven Year Itch*, 1955; *Some Like It Hot*, 1959; *The Apartment*, 1960; *Kiss Me, Stupid*, 1964; *Meet Whiplash Willie/The Fortune Cookie*, 1966; *The Private Life of Sherlock Holmes*, 1970; *Avanti*, 1972; *The Front Page*, 1974; *Fedora*, 1978.

WILLIAMS, RICHARD (UK): *The Little Island*, 1958 (s); *Love Me, Love Me, Love Me*, 1963 (s); *A Christmas Carol*, 1972 (s).

WISE, ROBERT (USA): *The Set-Up*, 1949; *Executive Suite*, 1954; *West Side Story*, 1961 – with JEROME ROBINS; *The Haunting*, 1963; *The Sound of Music*, 1964; *Star*, 1968; *The Andromeda Strain*, 1971; *The Hindenburg*, 1975.

WISEMAN, FREDERICK (USA): *High School*, 1968; *Hospital*, 1970; *Basic Training*, 1971; *Welfare*, 1975; *Canal Zone*, 1977.

WRIGHT, BASIL (UK): *Night Mail*, 1935 (s) – with HARRY WATT; *Song of Ceylon*, 1935.

WYLER, WILLIAM (USA): *Jezebel*, 1938; *Wuthering Heights*, 1939; *The Little Foxes*, 1941; *The Best Years of Our Lives*, 1946; *The Heiress*, 1949; *Roman Holiday*, 1953; *The Big Country*, 1958; *Ben Hur*, 1959; *The Collector*, 1964; *Funny Girl*, 1968.

GENERAL INDEX